COLORADO BOULDERING

Phillip Benningfield & Matt Samet

Sharp End Publishing
Authentic Guides From Core Climbers

Colorado Bouldering: Front Range, BY PHILLIP BENNINGFIELD & MATT SAMET

©2012 Sharp End Publishing, LLC

Published and distributed by
Sharp End Publishing, LLC
PO Box 1613
Boulder, CO 80306
t. 303.444.2698
www.sharpendbooks.com

ISBN: 978-1-892540-61-4
Library of Congress Control Number: 2012938808

Cover photo credit
Paul Robinson on The Altruist V13. Photo by Andy Mann.

Opening page photo credit
TJ Birchfield sends the Eastern Priest V4. Photo by Andy Mann

Unlabeled photo credits
Phillip Benningfield, Matt Samet, or Andy Mann

Read This Before Using This Guide

Rock climbing, including bouldering, is extremely dangerous. A small and incomplete list of possible dangers include: loose rock, bad landings (eg. landing on uneven or rocky terrain, landing on a spotter.) Unlike roped climbing, every bouldering fall is a ground fall. As a result, the boulderer risks serious injury or death with every attempt. Falls are common while bouldering.

The symbols used in this guide describe boulders with almost certain injury potential. It is, however, highly probable that you could seriously injure yourself on a problem that doesn't receive a highball or bad landing designation.

It is your responsibility to take care of yourself while bouldering. Seek a professional instructor or guide if you are unsure of your ability to handle any circumstances that may arise. This guide is not intended as an instructional manual.

Acknowledgments:

We would like to take this opportunity to thank everyone who helped along the way. Without your direction, tidbits on history, guidance at new areas, and patience checking the topos, photos and text, we could not have finished the guide. Then there are people we must thank who are not climbers but certainly played an important role in giving us the support we needed to concentrate on the guide.

But more than anyone, we have to thank our regular bouldering partners. Your lame ass jokes, persistent teasing, irrelevant suppositions, mind boggling idiocies, pain-killing remedies, patience with our never-ending questions and excellent spots helped immensely.

A special thanks goes out to Adam Avery for his unyielding hospitality and delicious beers, Charlie Bentley, Cordless, Josh Deuto, Jay Droeger, John Gill, Chris Goplerud, Five Ten, Mike Freischlag, Justin Jaeger, Greg Johnson, Chris Jones, La Sportiva, Andy Mann, Metolius Mountain Products, Jim Michael, John Sherman, George Sowers, Pete Takeda, and Pete Zoller for their photos, philosophies, attentive eyes and in-depth knowledge of Colorado's boulders.

Other boulderers and friends we would like to thank are:

Jim Belcer
Tommy Caldwell
Mike Caldwell
John Conant
Bob Couchman
Cameron Cross
Patrick DeCicco
John Dunn
Ryan Fields
Herm Feissner
Charlie Fowler

Kurt Frye
Tom Gage
Mike Gash
Naomi Guy
Tyler Handy
Tom Hanson
Ned Harris
Dawn Heigele
Haven Iverson
Eric Johnson
Ken Kenney

Colin Lantz
Will and Jen Lemaire
Scott Leonard
Charles Lintott
Craig Luebben
Steve Mammen
Mark Milligan
Rob Mordock
Tony Nordi
Aaron Quinlisk
Chip Ruckgaber

Tim Ryan
Bennett Scott
Burton Stoner of OSMP
Bart Streghe
Trixie Tartasky
Matt Tiwonowski
Tim Toula
Dave Whaley
Pat Wilde
Mark Wilford

Contributors: Thank You.

 Herman Feissner 56

 Bennett Scott 100

 Peter Beal 168

 Paul Robinson 182

 John Sherman 202

 Scott Blunk 236

 Jamie Emerson 242

 Andy Mann 258

Sponsors: Thank You, Thank You.

We would not be able to print the slick publication you hold in your hand without our sponsors. The utter psych you feel when thumbing these pages can be attributed to their involvement. Support them as they exist for the climbing community.

Five.Ten Back Cover
Arc'Teryx 4
Metolius 11
Nicros 13
Organic 15
The Spot 19

Escape Rock Climbing Holds 67
Colorado Mountain School 82
Black Diamond 89
Neptune Mountaineering 115
Marmot 125
Boulder Rock Club 137

Sender Films: *First Ascent, The Complete Series* 181
Wilderness Exchange 189
Bent Gate 227
Movement Climbing & Fitness 247
Three Ball Climbing 252
La Sportiva 276

ARC'TERYX

TABLE OF CONTENTS

Paul Robinson sends Midnight Express V14 Photo: Andy Mann

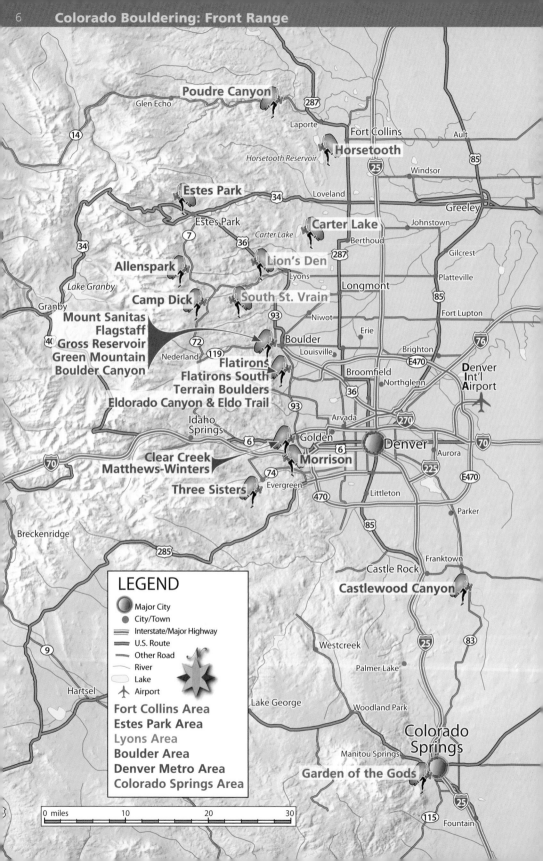

Poudre Canyon

Glen Echo

287

Laporte

Fort Collins

Ault

14

Horsetooth

Horsetooth Reservoir

25

Windsor

85

Estes Park

34

Loveland

Greeley

Estes Park

Carter Lake

Johnstown

7

36

Carter Lake

Berthoud

287

Gilcrest

Lion's Den

Allenspark

Lake Granby

Lyons

Longmont

Platteville

34

85

Camp Dick

South St. Vrain

Fort Lupton

Granby

93

Niwot

Erie

76

Mount Sanitas
Flagstaff
Gross Reservoir
Green Mountain
Boulder Canyon

40

72

Nederland

119

Boulder

Brighton

Denver
Int'l
Airport

Louisville

E470

Flatirons
Flatirons South
Terrain Boulders
Eldorado Canyon & Eldo Trail

Broomfield

Northglenn

36

93

Arvada

270

Idaho
Springs

6

Golden

Denver

70

Clear Creek
Matthews-Winters

70

6

Morrison

Aurora

225

E470

74

Three Sisters

Evergreen

470

Littleton

Parker

Breckenridge

85

285

Franktown

Castle Rock

Castlewood Canyon

9

Westcreek

25

83

Hartsel

Palmer Lake

**Colorado
Springs**

Lake George

Woodland Park

Manitou Springs

Garden of the Gods

115

Fountain

LEGEND

🔵 Major City
⚫ City/Town
Interstate/Major Highway
U.S. Route
Other Road
River
Lake
✈ Airport

Fort Collins Area
Estes Park Area
Lyons Area
Boulder Area
Denver Metro Area
Colorado Springs Area

0 miles   10   20   30

INTRODUCTION

Bouldering is the heart of climbing—be it traditional, sport or mixed alpine. Going bouldering is often a shared activity, but it always retains a highly personal feel—mentally and physically. Both feelings often occur at the exact moment when a spotter's encouragement is deafened by perfect concentration: the desire to grasp a distant minute edge, or trying to hold on to fleeting confidence as the feet cut loose way off the deck. These are the experiences—rarely shared and pure—for which this guidebook was written. There is an undeniably simple pleasure of having so much fun that the woods and canyons echo with unrestrained laughter.

Colorado's Front Range is inspiring in the sheer volume of beautiful problems and the immense effort put forth by the first ascentionists. The Front Range is graced with a plethora of boulders of every shape, size, and type of rock. From the pine-covered hillsides and maroon boulders in Eldorado Canyon to Castlewood Canyon's soft sandstone and desert environment to Fort Collin's vast selection of sandstone, the possibilities for problems are nearly endless. With all the areas covered in the guide, you will have to quit your demeaning job, grow another set of fingertips and devote yourself, like a monk, to the rock.

This guide highlights the best boulders that will bring the widest grins and greatest exclamations. Many obscure, chipped and low quality boulders will not be included (as the authors see fit). That is not to say that some boulders will not be to everyone's liking. Some areas with less than ideal stone have been included to get you and your crash pad away from The Simpsons or Oprah and to the boulders. It is important to remember that not every boulder will be as perfect as *The Eliminator* at Horsetooth Reservoir. Adventure, albeit limited, can be found on the low-traffic remote blocks that require gumption and the trust of fragile holds. Other areas have been included but have no in-depth descriptions due to bad rock, bad atmosphere (close to a major highway, piled with trash or smelling of waste), have very little development, or possible access problems (future slapstick homes being built by greedy developers). Whatever the area or situation you may find yourself in, simply turn the page of this guide and more good areas will be revealed.

Jim Garber on Poling Pebble V5, Flagstaff Mountain

Colorado Bouldering: Front Range is devoted specifically to bouldering. As bouldering relies on an individual's mental and physical tenacity—exclusive of all equipment but shoes and chalk—many problems that were originally done on toprope have been ignored. The safety of the rope inherently destroys the fear factor—an integral part of bouldering. An indistinguishable line exists between a solo and highball problem, therefore all ascents considered boulder problems have been left up to the author's judgment.

Enjoy!

HISTORY

Bouldering in Colorado—as we now think of technical bouldering— is five decades old. But the act of scrambling on boulders is certainly not limited to that meager time frame. When the technical side of rock scrambling began to be appreciated, climbers like Corwin Simmons and Bob Culp led the way. Not until 1967 did the "Master of Rock", John Gill come to Colorado and begin a seemingly systematic routine of ticking ultra-classic boulder problems.

Simmons and Culp began bouldering on Flagstaff Mountain in the late 1950s. During the early and late 60s more climbers discovered the easy accessibility and enjoyment of bouldering. Pat Ament, at the ripe old age of 14, bouldered on Flagstaff with Larry Dalke and eventually climbed such classic problems as *First Overhang*, *Red Wall Route*, *King Conquer Overhang* and *The Consideration*. These problems, even in today's staggering realm of difficulty, thwart many aspiring boulderers.

Colorado's most prolific boulderer has to be John Gill. In 1967 Gill moved to Fort Collins and promptly began turning the Dakota sandstone boulders lining Horsetooth Reservoir into one of the most famous bouldering areas in America. Rich Borgman helped Gill set standards that are still held in high regard. Gill did such difficult and treacherous problems as the *Pinch Route* on the Mental Block and the *Left Eliminator* on the Eliminator Boulder. Borgman's contributions were no less committing and are highlighted by *Borgman's Bulge* at the Torture Chamber and *Reach Overhang* at North Rotary Park.

As the 60s wore on more climbers took up this new avenue of climbing. Individuals like Paul Hagan climbed *Hagan's Wall* on Cloud Shadow at Flagstaff—one of the state's best problems. Bob Poling added *Poling Pebble* on Flagstaff, which still bouts today's boulderers, and Richard Smith, Eric Varney and Bob Williams all had a hand in creating the vast selection of classic problems on Flagstaff. As most climbers fade away Bob Williams has stuck with the ever-increasing difficulties, having climbed hard problems at Morrison throughout the 90s.

In the 70s a young kid from Boulder came to the forefront of bouldering. His name was Jim Holloway and his ability went unnoticed by some of his peers as they concentrated on their own endeavors. What has been written about him indicates that he was decades ahead of his time. Holloway's claim to fame is the Big Three: a collection of three problems —*Slapshot*, *Trice* and *Meathook*— which to this day are still unrepeated in their original sequences.

Another prolific boulderer and friend of Holloways was Jim Michael, who even to this day can be seen bouldering on Flagstaff. Holloway and Michael scoured the superb blocks at Horsetooth, Flagstaff and other areas leaving a legacy of great moves and classic problems.

As the 70s rolled along many excellent boulderers put up problems on Flagstaff. One of the most prolific was Rob Candelaria who climbed the classic *Hollow's Way* and the disintegrating *Butt Slammer* as well as many other committing problems. Neal Kaptain, Harrison Dekker and Dan Stone also put their strengths to work on the sharp sandstone of Flagstaff and Eldorado Canyon.

Further south on the Front Range at Ute Pass, Harvey Carter, Steve Cheyney and Stewart Green were picking plum lines on the incipient seams, slabs and sharp cracks. Also down south in areas like Eleven Mile Canyon, Bob Murray had a lasting affect putting up difficult lines on the spectacular granite lining the South Platte River.

In the 80s the Front Range got a fresh crop of boulderers with amazing strength and motivation. Christian Griffith repeated many of the classics. And through the years he has established stacks of variations to the existing problems on Flagstaff while repeating other testpieces like the *Moon Arête* at Horsetooth. Bob Horan was very prolific through the 80s and climbed many new problems on Flagstaff, Eldorado Canyon, and other areas across the state. Other noteworthy boulderers include John Sherman who added many problems in Eldorado Canyon as well as elsewhere throughout the state. Some of his problems easily rank as the best in the state, with *Germ Free Adolescence* in Eldorado and *The Ineditable* on Independence Pass vying for top honors. Chris Jones was an avid boulderer and repeated many hard problems (some without the need to use feet) at areas from Pueblo to Morrison. In the San Luis Valley many fine blocks were uncovered near Penitente Canyon and Del Norte by Bob Murray, Lew Hoffman and Bob D'Antonio.

One exceptional boulderer overshadowed by those hungry for fame was Skip Guerin. Guerin climbed *Over Yourself* on the Pebble Wall at Flagstaff, repeated only by Ben Moon. It stands as both a testament to his strength and his sense of humor. Other Guerin problems of significance are Flagstaff's *Mongolian Cosmonaut* and a number of micro-thin slab problems in Eldorado that seldom see repeats.

Fort Collins boulderers Steve Mammen and Mark Wilford had a vast influence on bouldering at Horsetooth as well as in Summit County, Carter Lake and Eldorado Canyon. Mammen's undeniable masterpeice, *Never Say Never* on the Milton Boulder, stands as a testament to his ability. Wilford also developed problems in Telluride and Naturita throughout the 80s and did first ascents like *Master of Disaster* at Horsetooth. These areas are but a fraction of the places visited and developed by these two gifted climbers. Surely there are hundreds of problems out in cow country that will unfortunately never see repeats by the less adventuresome.

Throughout the years that Gill, Ament, Murray, Mammen, Wilford, Sherman, Griffith and numerous other first ascentionists were lucky enough to create great classics, many women were repeating stacks of the established problems. Coral Bowman led the way in the late 70s followed by Carol Black, Beth Bennett, Bobbi Bensman, Hillary Harris and Annie Overlin. The most difficult ascents being Harris' repeat of *UCT* on Flagstaff and Overlin's repeat of *Doctor Slutpants* at The Ghetto.

As the 90s came rolling along more and more gifted boulderers came on the scene. At areas like Morrison, Flagstaff and Fort Collins the diehard boulderers visited the long thought to be climbed out boulders in search of elusive first ascents. Rufus Miller, Jim Karn, Chris Hill, Wallace Stasick, Dave Twinam, Jim Surrette and Calvin Fiddler pushed standards to a new level by giving problems direct starts, off-routing holds or in the case of Karn's double dyno *White Men Can't Jump* at Morrison's Lobby area, bypassing every intermediate. Other difficult problems done by this group were a direct start to *Just Right* at Flagstaff, *Lascivious* at Morrison's Lobby and *Power's Boring* in Morrison's Black Hole.

With bouldering gaining popularity by the day, the 90s was a time of blossoming energy and boldness. Jim Belcer, Dean Potter, Jim Hurst and Tommy Caldwell redefined the boulders at Lumpy Ridge in Estes Park as a top bouldering destination. The high-end problems at Lumpy—like *Right Angry Man*, *Sap and Podophile*—easily stretch the definition of sandbag. At Carter Lake and Castlewood Canyon, Matt Samet, Pete Zoller and Charlie Bentley climbed many difficult highballs and desperate power problems. Bentley's contributions stretch up and down the Front Range from repeats of many problems at today's standards. He has also done first ascents at Morrison that vie in difficulty with the estimated grades for the Big Three. In the Colorado Springs area Ian Spencer-Green pushed standards at the Garden of the Gods' Blowouts Area and at Ute Pass.

As the century turned, the number of climbers regularly getting out skyrocketed. Not only has this brought a huge increase in the amount of bouldering in the Front Range, but also in the standards. Climbers like Daniel Woods, Bennett Scott, Will Lemaire, Jay Droeger, Paul Robinson, Jamie Emerson, Justin Jaeger, Mike Freischlag, Dave Graham, Cameron Cross, Peter Beal, Ryan Olson, Chuck Fryberger, Austin Geiman, Chris Schulte and Nick Anderson have spearheaded this resurgence. Beautiful and impressive lines like Ty Landman's *Midnight Express*, Dave Graham's *Suspension of Disbelief*, and Ian Dory's *Doxology* are all products of the new generation. These problems are some of the best in the Front Range, and they are found in areas that have been bouldered at for years and years. In 2010 this culminated with Daniel's ascent of *The Game V15* in Boulder Canyon, and demonstrated that it only takes a second look, even in the most traveled of areas, to discover and interpret things anew.

The future of Colorado bouldering should grow by leaps and bounds as more areas are discovered or rediscovered. The climbing masses are once again realizing the beauty of a single edge or sloper. Even more so, the peace and fun of standing below virgin stone and eagerly awaiting a try, has grabbed the hearts of devoted boulderers and left them hungry for more.

Matt Wilder on PB Boulders Project   Photo: Andy Mann

Access

Access is more and more a touchy subject in the climbing community. As our numbers swell, impact becomes more readily visible. Some areas were omitted from this guide because locals politely asked us not to include them, or because climbing was already an endangered activity.

No private property bouldering areas are included in this guide with the exception of Morrison (the property owners tolerate boulderers, so respect them at all times). As much as we would all love to check out the *Ripper Traverse* in Pueblo or Sunshine Boulder or *Flute* at Horsetooth Reservoir, we should not. Trespassing endangers everyone's access to climbing areas. Other areas with access issues fall under the guise of environmental closures (The Ghetto, Green Mountain, etc.). Never go to an area during the time of a closure!

Certain areas in this guide are on National Forest or Bureau of Land Management land but have private access on dirt roads or trails. I have avoided directions to boulders that pass on private land and have chosen alternative directions that may have a longer, inconvenient approach. Please follow the directions given at all times to keep uptight people from threatening our access to the boulders. It may be a little bothersome, but live with it. In cases like the Poudre Canyon, certain areas are not included due to boulderers reoccurring disrespect for private property (ie: Kingpin Boulder at the Poudre's 420s).

Private areas or delicate access spots are not included: Pueblo, Beulah, Ute Pass (Colorado Springs), Split Boulders, The Sunshine and Flute Boulders (Horsetooth Reservoir), Arthur's Rock (Horsetooth Reservoir), Hagermeister and Nicky's Boulders (Estes Park), and many areas up the Poudre Canyon. There are many more too obscure to list, like Big Elk and Big Landia.

There are two immediate ways you can help with access issues: Don't trespass and Do join the Access Fund, (www. accessfund.org. Remember, while out bouldering do your best to reduce impact on the land and other people's psyches.

Problem Names

Boulder problems have existed so long in Colorado that the names have been changed for a multitude of reasons: a hold broke a decade ago which made a new name easy to swallow, the name was lost to obscurity as an area lost its popularity, the first ascentionist was a liar, or the name was so bad no one in his right mind could announce it in a public place. One of the most common reasons a name may sound wrong is the first ascentionist forgot what he called a problem along with his friends that were present. Whenever a name does not sound right or exactly match what has been used for the last few years keep in mind that memories get washed away by booze, boredom, work, or mental neglect. Probably that atrociously loose or lichen-covered face that you are sure is called *Ridiculous and Shallow* was ascended by some guy in tennis shoes well before you were wearing a diaper. Any vulgar or displeasing name (and there are quite a few) has not been censured to protect the easily offended. If the first ascentionist has a thing for genitalia then the name sticks since he/she put the problem up. Many areas and problems will have more than one name to assist in finding a problem. This only goes to show how one name fades away and a new one gains popularity.

Area / Boulder Names

We have taken the liberty of naming areas and boulders in places where no information was to be found. The reason we have done this is to help the reader find boulders and problems. Hence the boring, although useful names like Boulder 1, Orange Face and South Boulders. If individuals had given the correct names that we asked for at the boulders, in local climbing shops or through correspondence with local climbers via phone or mail, we would have certainly used the information. Consider the names only in helping locate problems and feel free to inform us of correct names for future editions. We would rather have the name given by a first ascentionist than some silly name I had to come up with on the spot.

STAR RATINGS:

No stars   Dirty or not especially interesting.
★   A pretty good boulder problem. Better than average.
★★   Puts a smile on your face if you send it but upsets you if you don't.
★★★   An exceptional boulder problem, well worth the effort. Two scoops please!
★★★★   One of Colorado's best, an "irrefutable classic."

SYMBOLS AND ABBREVIATIONS:

Bad Landing, Highball, Sit Down Start: Bad landings are indicated by a broken ankle emblem. We have used this icon for problems on uneven talus, logs or a sloping hillside. Also if the fall can be unbalanced due to the body's movement during a dyno, heel hook or slippage. For a highball problem an ambulance symbol is used. This designation is used for problems 15 feet or higher—although a few problems may only be a mere 14 feet two inches. Sit down start is sds in problem descriptions.

 Highball: You might need alternative transportation from the crag if you crater.

 Bad Landing: Roots, rocks, uneven terrain, or other factors create a dangerous landing.

 Both: Fogettaboutit. Don't bother falling.

COMPASS DIRECTIONS:

Problems are described using every compass direction. If a problem indicates the southwest arête that means the arête somewhere within the area of the south and west faces. If unsure read the problem description and check the photo or topo to narrow down the correct problem. Carrying a compass is highly recommended in remote or newly developed areas.

ORIENTATION:

For problems using left and right descriptions, the orientation is always as one faces the boulder or cliff. The orientation can be difficult to ascertain in gaps and chasms so look carefully at the photo, topo and other problem descriptions on the same boulder.

MEASUREMENTS:

Distances and height are given in either yards or feet. When exact distance is given, it has been measured with a tape measure. We have gone to great lengths to be as specific as possible when describing problems that are obscure or need extra information (variations, problems starting close to others, etc.). Nonetheless, use your best judgement if something seems awry.

APPROXIMATIONS:

Approximate means exactly that! The distance indicated in finding boulders and areas is a careful, oftentimes exacting process and is roughly accurate (a few yards shorter or longer) than the approximated distance. Be sure and keep in mind that the distance is approximate when using the directions (it was our experience that 50, 75 and 100 yards does not appear the same to two boulderers).

PHOTO / TOPO NUMBERS:

Problem numbers and lines on photos and topos are not always directly in front of a problem due to trees, bushes, or other boulders blocking a clear view or placement of the line or number. In this instance use the photo or topo to find the boulder, then use the problem's description to locate the correct problem. When a photo or topo is not used for a boulder, use the closest photographed or topoed boulder—orient oneself then read the boulders description to locate it and the problems.

TOPO DIAGRAMS:

Topos are obviously not to scale. All topos are drawn from a bird's eye view. The boulders are drawn as precisely as possible (many from standing on top of the boulder). Keep in mind a boulder may not appear as the shape drawn while standing next to it. If it does not look right stand on top—if possible—and locate the problems.

PRECAUTIONS

Bouldering can be extremely dangerous! Flakes break, feet skid off jugs, fingers melt from holds before their time, spotters are too stoned, drunk, or self-absorbed to pay attention. Bruises, large bloody flappers, broken ankles, twisted knees, scraped elbows, lacerated hands, torn tendons and sprained wrists are commonplace. Death is possible.

• Always use a crash pad—borrow, buy, or make your own.

• Learn how to spot correctly. Protect your skull; ask for multiple spotters, if needed.

• Try and use a spotter or two or three anytime you are unsure of a bad fall. The use of a spotter can not be overemphasized. A one-foot drop on uneven talus can easily tear ligaments or rip flesh.

• By using crash pads and attentive spotters regularly, a bouldering session can be far more challenging and rewarding than you ever thought.

GRADES

The grading scale used for problems is the Vermin Scale (V Scale). A comparison chart is included within the Introductory pages to better assist those boulderers who are stuck in the obsolete B Scale or in love with the Fountainebleau Scale. More climbers than we can remember, in more areas than we can remember, have compiled grades. Use the grade as a reference; if it does not seem appropriate (after ascending the problem, which is the only time you will have a clue to the correct grade) then go with your assessment. More than likely the grade will only differ by one insignificant number. Some problems are not given grades but question marks. This was necessary for problems that have not been repeated and were graded in an old scale, problems that have changed significantly and have not seen a recent known ascent, problems that no one does anymore, or problems that probably had toprope ascents but were given an obsolete bouldering grade. These problems are few and far between.

As is the nature of grades, when a problem has two conflicting grades we have ALWAYS chosen the lower grade. There are no slash grades (V6/7) or plus and minus grades (V4+). This keeps grades solid. It is not done to sandbag! Also it keeps the novice, whom so often wants to place a higher grade on a problem to verify his or her training has not been in vain, and whose prowess has not reached an all time low, in check. On the other hand the expert wants to place a higher grade on a problem to boost his or her fragile ego; or even more self-serving, place a lower grade on a problem to downplay the ascent and burst the bubble of an aspiring boulderer. In all these circumstances the grade is manipulated and toyed with for a ridiculous ego boost. This guide has not changed a single grade for such paltry reasons. As for the plus and minus grades non-inclusion, it helps to lend an entertaining, albeit limited sense of adventure.

GRADE COLOR-CODING

The grades in this guide have been color-coded to help one quickly glance through the book and determine if an area has suitable problems. Thanks to Dave Pegg at Wolverine Publishing for allowing us to use the same scale as Wolverine's Hueco and Bishop books. This can only help climbers who are familiar with Wolverine's fine products.

BOULDERING GRADE CHART:

VERMIN	GILL	FONTAINEBLEAU
V0	B1-	
V1	B1	5c
V2	B1	
V3	B1	6a
V4	B1+	6b
V5	B1+	6c/6c+
V6	B2-	7a
V7	B2	7a+/7b
V8	B2	7b+
V9	B2+	7c
V10	B2+	7c+
V11	B2+	8a
V12	B2+	8a+
V13	B2+	8b
V14	B2+	8b+
V15	B2+	8c

a. payne, rmnp, r. olson photo

ETHICS

Stand up for the ones you have! Otherwise they are not worth having in the first place.

When it comes to bouldering, the rock is your friend. Would you poke, hit and prod at your friend with a sharp, metal object? The idea behind bouldering is to enjoy the rock on its own terms, appreciating its natural state. If you're fortunate enough to find a pristine boulder, take a moment to consider what the process of putting up new problems involves.

WHAT TO DO / WHAT NOT TO DO

• Chiseling/Chipping: Don't! Don't even think about it! Enough has already taken place. The bottom line is to leave the rock alone. Leave it for someone with far superior technique, power and genetic make-up. Any problem that would go with a little work is certainly best left in its natural state.

• Cleaning: You have to be able to see and feel the holds. Don't go crazy and clean until you enlarge the hold. Brush the lichen, moss, spider webs and dirt off the problem…not the surrounding swath of rock or entire face. The most important considerations are to respect both the rock and other boulderers who are far more gifted and motivated.

• Be discreet with chalk, avoid using tick marks and don't project an overbearing verbal presence in areas with other users. In other words, use common sense. If you don't have any common sense then bring a friend who is more in touch with their humanity to help you out.

• Do not cut trees, limbs, or shrubs to gain access to one measly problem!

• Avoid placing crash pads or gear on vegetation.

• Stay on signed designated trails; use only designated areas where impact has already occurred. Never build your own trails, stairs or platforms.

• Be considerate of wildlife and other users. Respect all wildlife closures. Know and abide by all regulations!

• Pack out all litter.

• Leave dogs at home.

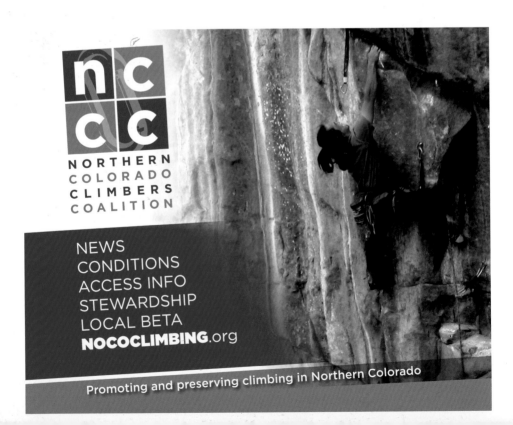

Jen LeMaire attempting Can Opener V11 Photo: Jim Thornburg

POUDRE CANYON

The Poudre Canyon is a beautiful corridor that stretches over 60 miles. Large granite outcrops line the road, an excellent fly-fishing river flows down canyon and temperatures fluctuate dramatically depending on how far one ventures up canyon. The 420s, a relatively small boulderfield nestled in ponderosa pines and quaking aspens, offer a quality sub-alpine excursion with problems ranging the scale from V0 to V13. The Gandalf Area provides a high fun factor.

*DO NOT boulder on private property as it damages already fragile relationships between climbers and negatively affects access issues. Many exceptional problems are close to or on private land so don't go looking for specific lines (i.e. Kingpin, The Bog, etc.) in the descriptions below. If information is inconclusive as to the land ownership we have left the problems out.

Directions

Hatchery Rocks: *Take State Route 14 west from US Route 287 up through the Poudre Canyon to Rustic. From the intersection of Hwy. 14 and Road 69 drive seven miles farther west on State Route 14. The boulders are on the right side of the road, 38.3 miles from the junction of CO 14 and Hwy 287. One of the blocks sits just off the road with the largest one behind. A large pull-out is directly before the boulders.*

420s: *From north of Fort Collins follow US 287 to Colorado 14. Head west (left) at the Conoco station. Follow the Cache La Poudre River for a long, long time. The pullout and parking for the 420's is 41.5 miles up the canyon. (1.0 mile past the Roaring Creek Trailhead—found on the road's right side). Parking is available on both sides of the road. Set your odometer when you turn onto CO 14 from Hwy 287.*

Walk by the brown metal gate in an opening next to the barbed wire fence. Follow the main old road through ponderosa pines and aspen groves for five minutes. You will walk right into Hank's Boulder, sitting in a small meadow surrounded by aspens. A small block sits next to Hank's with LW + RW. To reach the other boulders follow a distinct trail headed towards the cliffs and entering the woods. Cross a seasonal stream on rickity logs and the boulders appear immediately.

Merlin: *Located 1.7 miles past the 420s on the right side of the highway. Easily seen through the woods as the block rests 30 yards from the road.*

Gandalf: *Located 4.7 miles past the 420s at the Tunnel Campground on the left side of the highway. Enter the dirt pullout and drive down to the parking. The boulders sit on the opposite side of the river slightly downstream from the restrooms. The crossing is quite shallow in the fall but may prove impossible during high-water periods. A rockhop can be found about 100 yds down stream from the parking lot, when the river is up, but not raging.*

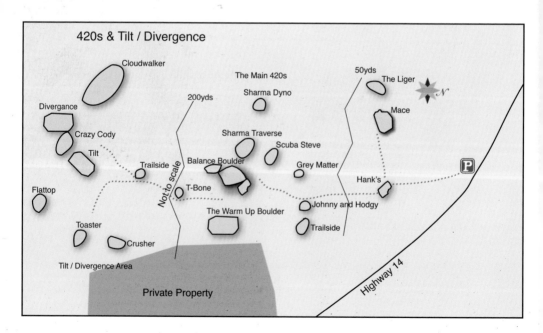

HATCHERY ROCKS

This small boulderfield consists of one outstanding granite block and a couple of decent cohorts. Located next to a peaceful highway that hugs the Cache la Poudre River, the area remains surprisingly congenial. The Hatchery Rocks are the first set of very good boulders in the Poudre Canyon.

HATCHERY ROCK

The largest boulder that has a small tree and block sitting in front of the east face. The surrounding boulders in the talus slope have potential for a few decent problems.

☐ 1. **V3** ★★★
Climb the southeast arête staying on the east face.

☐ 2. **V5** ★★★ 🌑
Climb the middle of the east face through a white crystal dike. An outstanding problem.

☐ 3. **V1** ★★ 🌑
The right side of the east face.

☐ 4. **V3** ★
The northeast arête up bomber jugs. The top-out to the left is much easier.

☐ 5. **V3** ★★★
A classic problem on the north face that climbs through bomber edges to a difficult, straight up top-out.

☐ 6. **V4** ★★
Just right of #5 is a problem that climbs the sloping edges left of the right-facing dihedral.

☐ 7. **V0**
The west face has a fun problem that climbs big, sloping edges.

The boulder closest the highway has numerous V0's that are great to warm up on. The short boulder just north of the roadside block has a sds V2 on the southwest arête.

CRITICAL MASS

Just down the road, across from the Big Bend Campground on the left, turn right on a dirt road. Hang a left and follow the double-track to the base of the cliff and some boulders.

☐ 1. **King Fin V4** ★★★
Climb the right arête on good holds.

☐ 2. **Critical Mass V12**
Start sitting on jugs in the back of the cave and climb the low roof. Faces the road. Good rock and movement, but very close to the ground.

Hatchery Rock

Critical Mass-King Fin

Critical Mass

420s

The best developed boulderfield in the Poudre that isn't private property and is loaded with problems for everyone. Problems cover the gamut from super easy beginner slabs to superb moderates to unbelievably hard creations. Weekends are a madhouse here so plan accordingly and come mid-week.

HANK'S BOULDER

The first block encountered at the 420s. With a perfect height, flat landing and excellent problems you can bypass all the other blocks without missing a thing—just kidding. When it comes to aesthetic settings for a granite boulder you will be hard pressed to find a better one.

☐ 1. **One Ton Ho V9** ★★
Start sitting and climb the arête.

☐ 2. **Scarface V6** ★★★
Start sitting on incut crimps and climb straight up.

☐ 3. **Public Property V8**
Start on *Scarface*, climb up and right to the sloping ledge.

☐ 4. **Incognito Speedo V9**
Start sitting on small crimps and climb the face to the left of the arête.

☐ 5. **Hank's Arête V5** ★★
The least desirable of Hank's problems but worth doing if you like bear hugging little bitty overhanging arêtes.

☐ 6. **Hank's Lunge V5** ★★★★
If your arms are short or you stand less than 5′ 7″ or you can't dyno you might as well find another problem. This gem will elicit more "It's a reach problem" than the red tape dyno at the gym. By the way, the *Lunge* is pure, undiluted, and classic bouldering.

THE MACE

From Hank's Boulder, head right, up a trail (faint 2-track) uphill about 75 yards.

☐ 1. **Reach Out V9** ★★
Stand start on crimps. Sharp.

☐ 2. **Mr. Harry V5** ★★★
Start standing on a high sloping edge. Great rock.

☐ 3. **The Mace V4** ★★
Step off the boulder and grab two flat edges. Make a move to the lip and topout.

Hank's Boulder

Hank's Boulder

THE LIGER

Located uphill from The Mace.

☐ 1. **The Liger V7** ★★★
Climb the arête.

☐ 2. **Will's Slab V10** ★★
This tall and beautiful slab was first climbed by Will LeMaire. The crux is at the top.

The Mace

The Liger

Grey Matter

☐ 1. **Rasta Font Trainer V7** ★
Start sitting, head left, then a hard mantle.

☐ 2. **Grey Matter V10** ★
Start sitting, on a good flat hold, and traverse the lip left to right.

Johnny and Hodgy Boulder

A squatty block on the way to the Can Opener and Puffing Stone. The block sits on the left side of the trail a little ways past the creek crossing.

☐ 1. **Johnny and Hodgy V5** ★★★
You can look at this problem and immediately know where the crux lies by the proliferation of chalk two inches below the top. Climb the left arête from a stand start utilizing the sloping arête and micro crimps on the face.

☐ 2. **V0** ★★★
The casual right arête, with good laybacks and not-so-good feet, is a fun warm-up or excellent project for the beginner. Not too high and with a dead flat landing.

Trailside Boulder

Just behind Johnny and Hodgy. A good place to warm up with many variations.

Todd Breitzke on Puffing Stone V6 Photo: Kyle Deutmeyer

Puffing Stone

Keeping the theme at the 420s is easy if you come prepared. If you don't, a little paraphernalia can be used on the boulders right side to get you in the mood for some self-flagellation.

☐ 1. **Puffing Stone Arête V2** ★
Start sitting on a jug. Climb the arête.

☐ 2. **Puffing Stone V6** ★★
Start sitting, matched on a low right-facing edge. Climb up and left. Great fun.

☐ 3. **F.A.S.T V8** ★★
F#%Hing Awesome Stoner Traverse, dude. Starts on the far right side of the east face almost in the darkest recess between the Puffing Stone and Balance Boulder (below *Cyrcadian Rhythm*) and follows the sloping lip right to left then way down onto the sloping middle holds, then back up to the lip and over on the boulder's left side. An easier version stays on the lip.

BALANCE BOULDER

The crème-de-la-crème boulder in the 420s. The boulder houses plenty of projects for the aspiring hardman with voyeuristic seating for the lacksadaisical climber. Problems described from left to right around the block.

❒ 1. Can Opener V11 ★★★
Southwest facing chalk-fest with a flat landing. The problem starts from almost laying down then follows the obvious caked holds to an exit either left (V11) or right (V12) into the open low-angle scoop. A stand up start exiting into the right scoop is V5.

❒ 2. Short Chubby Demon V6 ★★
The arête right of *Can Opener*. Basically a pull-on from a right hand sidepull and a small left-hand crimp and pop for the good hold up right.

❒ 3. Stickman Walking Over the Brooklyn Bridge V8 ★★
Start sitting and climb up the faint scoop.

❒ 4. Hickman Over the Poudre Bridge V8 ★★
Start as for *Stickman* and head left.

❒ 5. It's Ice V4 ★★★
Start standing on two pinches. Throw for the lip.

❒ 6. One Man Army V9 ★★★
Start standing with a right hand pinch. Jump left hand to the lip. Awesome rock.

❒ 7. Cyrcadian Rhythm V13 ★★★
Stand start on a good undercling and sidepull jug. Climb up the perfect rock to a hard throw at the end, careful to avoid a dab. A Dave Graham first ascent.

THE WARM-UP BOULDER

The Warm Up has everything a boulderer desires except the steepness offered on the Balance Boulder. The main problems are described below with a plethora of eliminates and contrivances and sds to be done as well.

❒ 1. SW Face of Warm-Up V3

❒ 2. The Warm Up V2 🌀 ★★
Climb up the chalk-infested overhang on the far left side of the north face. Start from the good holds below the overhang. The lower one starts the harder it gets.

❒ 3. Bisher Traverse V7 🌀
Climb the low left to right seam across the north face ending on the northwest arête.

❒ 4. North Face V1/V3 🌀
Two or three straight up problems on good edges head up the north face. These problems make for good progressive warm-ups.

❒ 5. NW Arête V2 🌀
Climb up the arête from the end of *Bisher's*. One can climb either side of the arête at about the same grade.

❒ 6. West Seam V1 🌀
A great low-angle problem that follows the open corner.

❒ 7. South Face V0-V4 🌀
A number of problems climb this side of the block but do not warrant best stature.

❒ 8. Tsunami V7 🌀
A left to right traverse left of *The Perch*. The problem starts on the left sloping hold at chest height and moves right to the next sloping hold then up to the pinch on the arête. V6 if you start closer to the rounded arête.

❒ 9. The Perch V6 🌀 ★★
Just around the corner from *The Warm-Up* is a low start to a bad left-hand edge then sloper to reach the top.

Balance Boulder

Balance Boulder

Warm-Up Boulder

The Can Opener

SHARMA DYNO

☐ 1. **What's Left of the Bottom of My Heart V12** ★
Climb the short prow using heel hooks.

☐ 2. **Sharma Dyno V9** ★★★
Start high on a right hand pinch and a left-hand sidepull. Put up during Chris Sharma's only visit. The sit start is V11.

SCUBA STEVE BOULDER

☐ 1. **Scuba Steve V7** ★★
Start on two underclings. A difficult opening move.

SHARMA TRAVERSE

☐ 1. **Sharma Traverse V6** ★★
Start on the left side, traverse the lip. Of a similar grade starting on the flat edge in the middle of the wall.

Sharma Dyno

Scuba Steve

Sharma Traverse

Past the 420s

T-Bone Arête

Walk south from the Balance Boulder on a social trail, crossing fallen trees and some slabs for 50 yards, to find this boulder on the right.

☐ 1. **T-Bone Arête V8** ★★
Start sitting on a flat hold, climb the arête.

Trailside Boulder

A bouldering trail continues southwest, passing a sculpted cliff on the right. Please stay on the climber's trail (marked by cairns) that avoids private property by veering right between two boulders.

☐ 1. **V6** ★★
Start sitting. Climb the arête.

Crusher Boulder

The trail splits 75 yards beyond the Trailside Boulder. Head left, towards some houses.

☐ 1. **Crusher Slab V0**
Climb the slab.

☐ 2. **Crusher V7** ★★
Start sitting. Climb the overhang to a hard move out left.

☐ 3. **Dead Moose V10** ★★
Start sitting. right hand on a good edge, left hand low. Make a huge move up and left to a sloper, then straight up.

Toaster Boulder

Just beyond Crusher on the right.

☐ 1. **Yosemite Arête V1** ★★★
Climb the striking left-leaning arête.

☐ 2. **Tollbooth Willy V8** ★★
Start matched on high crimps, dyno to the lip.

☐ 3. **Toaster V4** ★★
Start sitting, climb the interestingly featured overhang.

T-Bone Arête

Trailside Boulder

Crusher Boulder

Toaster Boulder

Toaster Boulder

TILT BOULDER

Uphill and towards the cliff 50 yds from Crusher.

☐ 1. **Ben's Face V3** ★★
Climb up the face.

☐ 2. **Ben's Goofy Face V5**
Start sitting, matched on a jug and climb the vertical face.

☐ 3. **Jousting at Windmills V9** ★★★
The sit start to *Tilt*. Start sitting, matched on a jug and head right, following the crimpy seam out the overhang.

☐ 4. **Tilt V7** ★★★
Start standing on two crimps. Make a hard move out right and follow the seam out the overhanging dihedral.

☐ 5. **Fire Pit V8** ★
Around the corner from *Tilt*, start on a left-facing sidepull and climb the vertical face.

CRAZY CODY BOULDER

Just beyond Tilt, in the cave to the right.

☐ 1. **Crazy Cody V7** ★★★
Start standing on a good hold. Climb the arête.

Tilt Boulder

Crazy Cody

Jamie Emerson on Tilt V7

FLATTOP BOULDER

☐ 1. **Will's Problem V5**
Start sitting on a flat edge. Climb the face.

☐ 2. **Goldrusher V7** ★★
Start standing on two crimps. Climb through flat underclings between two trees.

☐ 3. **Arête V3**
Chossy arête.

☐ 4. **V7**
Start standing on a left-hand edge. Head up and right.

☐ 5. **V7**
Start standing on a jug and head straight up on crimps.

☐ 6. **V5**
Start standing on a jug and head up and then left into the scoop.

☐ 7. **Pegmatite V4**
Climb the pegmatite edges up the face.

☐ 8. **Wipeout V9**
Start sitting on edges. Low.

DIVERGENCE BOULDER

☐ 1. **V2**
Climb the edges on the left side of the face.

☐ 2. **Divergence V9** ★★★
Start standing on two small crimps. A hard move to an undercling. Classic. The sit start, down and right, is V10.

Flattop

Flattop

Flattop

Divergence Boulder

CLOUDWALKER BOULDER

Facing Divergence, walk around to the right and into this massive cave.

Cloudwalker

☐ 1. Cloudwalker V10 ★★★

Start standing with a good foot out right. Make a hard first move, then into easier crack climbing and finish the difficult slab. A beautiful and difficult cave.

☐ 2. Cloudwalker Low V12

Start matched on the foot rail out right. Climb into the stand.

☐ 3. Centerfold V10

This problem is located at the top of a large slab directly in front of Tilt, on the same boulder as Cloudwalker. Climbs out a small limestone-esque roof.

MERLIN

A lone roadside boulder worth a visit.

Merlin

MERLIN BOULDER

☐ 1. Project

Climb the crimpy face.

☐ 2. Merlin V7 ★★★★

Start sitting on the incut sidepull. Classic. Clocks in at V5 from a stand start.

Fred Knapp on Merlin V7   Photo: Jim Thornburg

GANDALF AREA

Located 4.7 miles up the road from the 420s and across the river, slightly downstream from the parking lot. This is the large talus field just across the road. Against Humanity faces the parking area, hidden in the trees and slightly downstream from the parking lot.

AGAINST HUMANITY

Against Humanity

❐ 1. **Crime V9** ★★★
Start on the obvious left-facing feature, move left into flat underclings. The sit start from down low and right is called *Dump Truck* V10.

❐ 2. **Against Humanity V7** ★★★★
Start on the obvious left-facing feature and climb up on the flake, heading right to top out. Awesome. The low start on underclings is V8.

❐ 3. **Project**
Start on *Against Humanity* and head right through terrible slopers.

GANDALF WARM-UP

From Against Humanity, walk right on a social trail 10 yards.

Gandalf Warm-up

❐ 1. **Arête V4**
A sit start that climbs the arête.

❐ 2. **V6**
Start on a left-hand sidepull and a right-hand undercling. Climb left through the left-facing sloping feature.

❐ 3. **V4**
Start as for #2 and move right through the seams.

❐ 4. **V3**
Start on a sloping jug.

❐ 5. **Crack V1**
Nice warm-up crack.

GANDALF

From Against Humanity, walk right around the boulder and uphill on a faint trail 30 yards.

Gandalf Warm-up

❐ 1. **Gandalf V7** ★★★★
Stand start on a triangular hold. Classic.

❐ 2. **Black Swan V12** ★★
Sit start down and left and climb crystals into *Gandalf*.

❐ 3. **Free Flow Style V9** ★★★
Start on a jug an move into underclings. Make a hard dyno to a jug. Finish left on *Gandalf*.

❐ 4. **Orbital Resonance V10** ★★★
Start on #3 and head left into *Gandalf*.

❐ 5. **Project**
Climb the right arête.

Gandalf

As Hard As They Come

The backside of the Gandalf Boulder. Walk around right.

❒ **1. Courting Doom V9** ★★
Stit start move left and climb the arête.

❒ **2. As Hard As They Come V9** ★★
Start sitting, matched on a big undercling.

❒ **3. One Armed Scissor V10** ★★
Start on #2, head right.

Tractor Beam

From AHATC, walk straight uphill 40 yards into the talus. Faces downhill, toward the river.

❒ **1. Tractor Beam V7** ★★★
Start on a sloping side pull and head up. Great problem.

Geoff's Crack

Just left of Tractor Beam on a massive boulder.

❒ **1. Geoff's Crack V9** ★★
Climb the thin seam. Originally done without the arête, which makes it easier.

Dihedral With Underclings

Uphill and right from Tractor Beam is another large boulder.

❒ **1. Dihedral with Underclings V12** ★★
Start at the bottom on good holds, climb up and left.

❒ **2. Shapes and Sizes V11** ★★★
Start in the back of the roof, climb awesome holds to a good jug and head left, making a massive dyno to a sharp jug.

❒ **3. Shapes and Sizes Right V10** ★★★
Climb #2 to the good jug, then head right on pinches. Topout up the arête.

As Hard as They Come

Tractor Beam

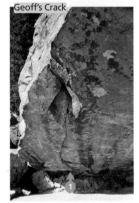
Geoff's Crack

Dihedral With Underclings

Herman Feissner on Cat Eye V3   Photo: Craig Luebben

HORSETOOTH RESERVOIR

Horsetooth Reservoir with its myriad selection of superb problems easily ranks as one of the best bouldering areas in the state. The Dakota sandstone boulders littering the hillside at Rotary Park are unsurpassed for quality and enjoyment. With the long ridges and boulders facing north, south and west the bouldering from January to December never ceases. For a change, venture over to the slabs of the North Quarry or The Scoop Area. The soft Morrison Formation sandstone at the North Quarry lends new meaning to thin and technical; or enjoy the Land of the Overhangs quality roofs and dihedrals. Pay special attention to some of the ultra-classics that John Gill established like *Pinch Overhang* and the *Right Eliminator* at Rotary Park—an area unequaled for classic problems. Current classics like the *Moon Arête* at Rotary Park make a worthwhile project. No matter what area one goes to, Horsetooth always satisfies those bouldering cravings.

Directions: The following areas (Duncan's Ridge, Piano Boulders, Rotary Park, North Rotary, The Scoop Area, Land of the Overhangs and North Quarry) can all be reached by taking Drake Road west from Fort Collins, going south on Taft Hill and driving up (west) on County Road 38E to the reservoir. Exact mileage from the intersection of Taft Hill and County Road 38E is given for the bouldering areas below.

Duncan's Ridge: Turn right on CR 23 and cross Spring Canyon Dam. 2.2 miles. Walk down on the lakefront.

Piano Boulders: Stay on CR 23 for 2.4 miles. The boulders are on a ridge up and right (east) from the road.

Rotary Park: Turn at the intersection with CR 42C and cross Dixon Canyon Dam. Five miles on the left.

North Rotary: Same parking area as Rotary Park. Problems are on northern ridge.

The Scoop Area: Park at Sunrise Day Use Area. 6 miles on the left. To reach the ridge walk south from the parking area on a trail until it drops into a quarried area (easiest way to get below the ridge). Drop down below the ridge and continue south along the ridge for roughly 150 yards to the southern most end of the Scoop Area.

Land of the Overhangs: 6.7 miles on the left is a parking lot before reaching Soldier Canyon Dam. Pop over the ridge to the west.

North Quarry: If you have an annual pass for your vehicle, park at designated sites in the southeast corner of 25G and Lodgepole (at the dirt road entrance to Lory). The signed trailhead (Satanka Cove) will be on the east side of the dirt road, just as you enter the park (and past the parks pipe-gate). Follow the Satanka Cove trail down to the obvious quarry walls on the north side, within the cove. If you don't have a parks pass, you must drive up to the parks entrance station (visitors center), or the self-serve pay station if the entrance is not manned, and obtain a day pass. Parking, restrooms, water, etc. can also be found at the visitors center.

Fees: Piano Boulders, Rotary Park, North Rotary, The Scoop Area, and North Quarry are now all fee areas. Pay your $7 to Larimer County via proper self-pay stations or kiosks.

Bennett Scott takes a sunset burn on The Eliminator Boulder   Photo: Andy Mann

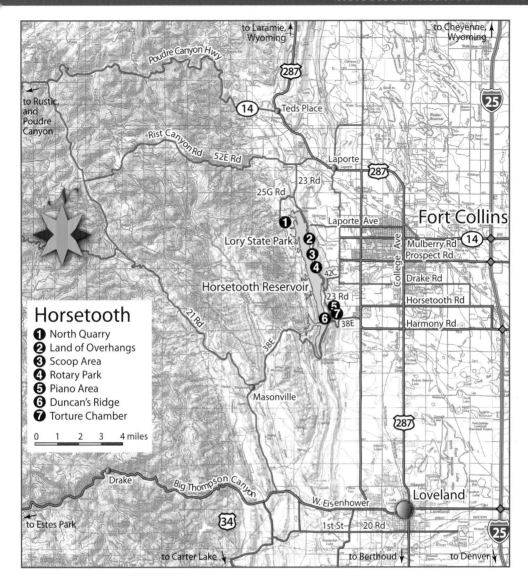

Horsetooth

1. North Quarry
2. Land of Overhangs
3. Scoop Area
4. Rotary Park
5. Piano Area
6. Duncan's Ridge
7. Torture Chamber

0   1   2   3   4 miles

DUNCAN'S RIDGE (NOT PICTURED)

On the northwest side of Spring Canyon Dam is another ridge of rock with a few separate boulders nearest the dam. Many cracks and dihedrals line the ridge and can be bouldered, although a toprope is recommended. All bouldering near the dam is closed. Routes 100 feet from the dam are open.

PIANO BOULDER AREA

Just up the road and on the right from Duncan's Ridge is a large boulder separated from the ridge with a few fun problems lining the ridge. Many short problems climb the small blocks constituting the ridge. No dogs allowed.

PIANO BOULDER

This is the second large boulder reached from the parking area that has broken off from the ridge. Left about 40 feet from here is a nice V3 arête on the ridge.

❑ 1. Piano Traverse V5 ★★
The traverse of the boulder from the south side moving left to the north is the one to do but many straight up problems exist.

❑ 2. Low Traverse V5 ★★
Just below the *Piano* on a short block is a right to left traverse on bulbous holds and ending with underclings.

❑ 3. V0 ★★
A small roof with jugs surrounding a crack is 10 yards south on the ridge.

THE SLAB

Further to the south from The Piano is a tall slab with a crack splitting the face. The arête right of the crack is V0. The crack is also V0.

❑ 1. Bootie V1 ★★★
The slab left of the crack with gratuitous edges.

Piano Boulder

The Slab

ROTARY PARK

Horsetooth's most renowned boulderfield with tons of classic to ultra classic problems first done by John Gill in the late 60s. The separate boulders and ridges are littered with excellent problems ranging from butt scraping affairs to over 20 feet tall. This is undoubtedly the place to go at Horsetooth.

A. TALENT SCOUT

Just below the Bolt Wall is an excellent boulder with a few thin problems on its northwest face.

❑ 1. Standard Route V3 ★
On the far right of the face is a route which has become harder over time.

❑ 2. Talent Scout Roof V6 ★★
A Gill problem that avoids the left arête and uses only the minute crimps and underclings on the face. A difficult move to gain the upper face is the business. *Powerglide* (V8) is a variant of *Talent Scout* just to the right. *THC* (V10) is a sit start to *Powerglide* involving henious crimping.

❑ 3. Left Arête V0 ★
Climb the arête using the best holds available.

Talent Scout

B. BOLT WALL

The southern most wall at Rotary Park defined by a vertical wall capped by a large roof with a crack leading out its left side.

Bolt Wall

❑ 1. Face It You're a Flake V0 😊
At the far right of the Bolt Wall area is a problem climbing through a small roof.

❑ 2. Corner Cling V0 😊
Just right of the vertical wall is a crack in the dihedral.

❑ 3. Cat Eye Face V3 ★★★ 😊
A thin problem through the middle of the face past a sloping pocket (the *Cat Eye*) that finishes by surmounting the roof out left. Escape right and downclimb after the eye for a safer outing.

❑ 4. West Bulge V0 ★ 😊
Climbs the slightly overhanging bulge around the corner from the *Cat Eye*. Many sit down starts boost the grade up to V5.

❑ 5. Pin Scar Finger Crack V1 ★
The crack in the dark dihedral can be done by using the face holds, which keeps it easy. Otherwise climb only the crack for a far harder variation.

❑ 6. Tendonitis Traverse V7 ★
Start stemmed near the crack and traverse the crappy holds left across the bottom of the face. High jugs are off.

❑ 7. Bolt Wall Standard and Left V0-V2 ★★★ 😊
The tall face left of the crack has superb problems up to the top. Very highball with a bad landing on the large boulder adjacent the face.

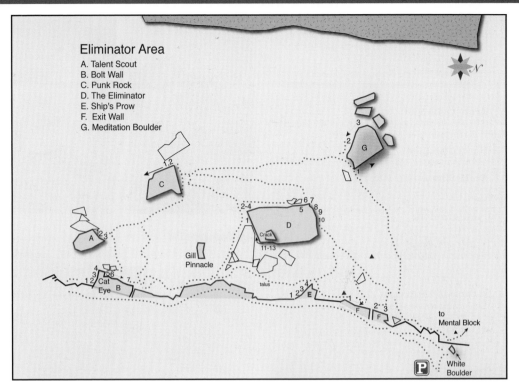

Eliminator Area
A. Talent Scout
B. Bolt Wall
C. Punk Rock
D. The Eliminator
E. Ship's Prow
F. Exit Wall
G. Meditation Boulder

C. PUNK ROCK

A short boulder just northwest and down the hillside towards the lake from the Talent Scout.

☐ **1. Punk Rock Traverse V5** ★★
The high traverse of the boulder from left to right.

☐ **2. Kelley Traverse V9** ★
The low traverse going from left to right. A squatters delight.

GILL PINNACLE

The tall upright, rectangular boulder sitting alone and north of the Bolt Wall offers a Gill problem with a couple of reasonable moves. A good place to sit and watch people flail on The Eliminator.

D. THE ELIMINATOR

The boulder at Rotary Park! There are enough frightening and powerful problems on this block to keep one busy for years. Superb stone and classic moves are the name of the game on this boulder just north of the Gill Pinnacle.

☐ **1. Moon Arête V10** ★★★
On the south face's left arête is a desperate slapping and crimp affair. Some consider the grade to be V9. The sit start is Sitting Moon V12.

☐ **2. Right Eliminator Prow V4** ★★★
Climbs on the right west arête instead of dashing out left to the jugs.

☐ **3. Right Eliminator V3** ★★★
A jump-start reaches the good jug just left of the arête and then up and left. R.E. Sit V11 starts sitting on the right side of the arête and climbs up and right into *Right Eliminator*.

☐ **4. Right Eliminator Left V4** ★★★
Classic beyond one's dreams. A Gill arrow leads one on the right path. Start by muckling on to the selection of bad holds then up to a jug and the top.

Punk Rock

The Eliminator

5. Left Eliminator V5 ★★
Classic and difficult. Possibly a good combination. Get ready for a big move from the starting hold to gain the crack out left.

6. Meathook V?
Figure this one out from the dirt or climb *Cheathook* (V8) from stepping off the adjacent block and starting on the terrible underclings.

7. Arête Crack V2
On the far-left side of the west face is a crack that climbs up then across a horizontal break then to the top.

8. North Slab Right V1 ★
Climb the right side of the wall without using the good ledge.

9. North Slab Center V1 ★
Starts with the right foot on a section of black marble then up. A V7 version climbs the face without hands.

10. Left Crack V0
On the north face is a crack on the left side. Climb it.

11. Corner Lunge V1 ★
Aka: *Slappin' the Ho Dyno*. A sit down start that busts up and right to the lip. A nice problem *Beached Whale* V2 climbs from a sds left on slopers and out the small roof.

12. Mammen Traverse V9 ★★
Climbs from the crack out right and finishes on the corner.

13. Cave Crack V3 ★
The obvious crack on the south face and within the slot created between The Eliminator and the adjacent boulder.

E. Ship's Prow
Just down and left (south) from the downclimb to Rotary Park is a chunk of rock with a distinct arête forming a prow.

1. Curving Crack V0
Actually not on the Prow but slightly to the right is a crack traverse going from left to right.

2. Standard V2 ★
Just right of #3 is a fun problem.

3. Finger Ripper V3 ★★
Climbs the middle of the face right of the arête.

4. Gill Reach V1 ★
The undercling problem over the roof.

F. Exit Wall
Just south of the downclimb before reaching the Ship's Prow is a steep wall with good holds.

1. Chicken Traverse V4 ★
Climbs across the wall and ends around the corner.

2. Stack This Crack Jack V1
A variant using only the wide crack.

3. Chicken's Delight V0 ★★
Climbs the chickenheads up the face.

G. Meditation Boulder
Well down the hillside from the Ship's Prow and north of Punk Rock is a lone boulder with a few moderate problems.

1. Meditation Traverse V2 ★
The traverse that climbs completely around the boulder.

2. Meditation Roof V2 ★
Climb through the roof for a good outing.

3. Low Traverse V4 ★
Another low traverse. Climbs left to right under the roof.

Ship's Prow

Exit Wall

Meditation Boulder

North Rotary Park

A. Tiger Rock
The boulder touches the south side of Mental Block. The proximity of these problems to one of Rotary's finest boulders seems to rob Tiger Rock of the traffic it deserves.

1. Tiger Rock Traverse V4 ★★
Climb from left to right starting from a mantel position.

2. Tiger Face V2 ★
Ascend straight up from the pocket and edge.

Tiger Rock

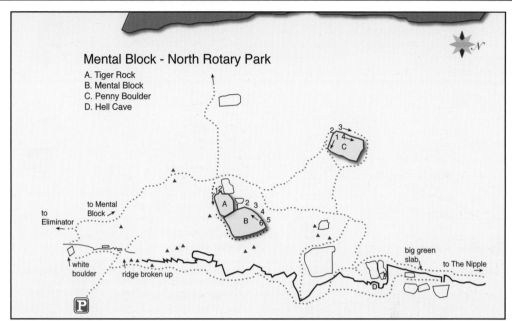

Mental Block - North Rotary Park

A. Tiger Rock
B. Mental Block
C. Penny Boulder
D. Hell Cave

B. MENTAL BLOCK

The bouldering gods only make a few boulders worthy of ultra classic stature. This is undoubtedly one on them. The boulder is north of the downclimb and set away from the ridge approximately 50 feet. With its bad landings and nightmare-like mantel finishes, what else could one ask for.

☐ 1. Pinch Overhang V5 ★★★★

Pretty much a one-move wonder, but what a move it is. Start on the right-hand pinch and jump off the ground to the sloping hold below the lip. Pulling on statically is V7.

☐ 2. Standard V4 ★★★

Classic like you always want it. Climb the secure edges on the arête to a moderate top-out.

☐ 3. Corner Lock V4 ★★

Start on the chest high edges and lock to the vertical seam hold then the top.

☐ 4. Willie's Lunge V3 ★

A dynamic problem that starts on the good holds down and left from the incipient seam of *Corner Lock*.

☐ 5. North Roof V4 ★★

Climbs the furthest left face on the north side of the block.

☐ 6. Mental Block Traverse V9 ★★

A traverse that starts on the north face and climbs right around the arête and finishes on *Pinch Overhang*. A fun V7 starts on the northeast corner, and traverses under the roof to finish on #3.

C. PENNY BOULDER

Downhill and north of the Mental Block is this superb boulder with good traverses and face problems.

☐ 1. Right Traverse V3 ★

Start below the double dyno holds on the southwest face and go right.

☐ 2. Double Dyno V1 ★★

Throw like the dickens from the bomber holds on the left side of the southwest face to the top.

☐ 3. Penny Boulder Traverse V3 ★★

Traverse the west face from right to left using any available holds.

☐ 4. Silver Dollar Traverse V? ★

The low traverse of the west face. Used to be V8, now undone since a crucial hold broke.

☐ 5. Ironsides V2 ★★★

Climb the amazing iron patina. A joyous affair! A nice V1 is just right.

Mental Block

Penny Boulder

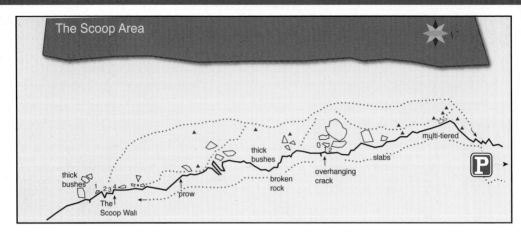

The Scoop Area

D. HELL CAVE

This dirty, glass and spray paint filled cave is north on the ridge and above the Mental Block. The crag looks like a devil worshipers or paint sniffers hangout. Hell Cave is not pictured.

☐ **Reach Overhang V6** ★
The difficult problem left of the crack that surmounts the roof.

NORTH ROTARY

This part of Rotary is north of Hell Cave approximately 60 yards on the ridgeline. A few outstanding slabs grace the ridge. Not pictured.

☐ **1. The Nipple V3** ★★★
A superb slab with good holds and feet to begin, then watch out!

NORTH SLAB

Just north of *The Nipple* is a quality slab with a slightly overhanging section on the left side. North Slab is not pictured.

☐ **1. North Slab Right Overhang V2** ★★
Starts the same as *Big Egos* and climbs straight up. Not pictured.

☐ **2. North Slab Left Overhang V2** ★★
Begin just left of *NSRO* and climb up the arête staying off the holds where *NSRO* climbs. Not pictured.

☐ **3. Big Egos, Little Dicks V7** ★★
Starts on a bomber high edge and traverses the face to the left on to the north slab. Expect a crux move getting situated on the north slab.

☐ **4. Leaning Seam Left aka Phhht V0** ★★
Start on incut edges just left of *Leaning Seam* and mantle like you mean it. Watch that the feet don't explode off the face.

☐ **5. Leaning Seam V0** ★★
Climb the seam on good layback holds and nice feet.

☐ **6. North Slab V0** ★
Just right of the seam is a fun slab.

THE SCOOP AREA

This is the next area north of Rotary Park. The problems in this area are somewhat limited but a few of the slabs are outstanding. Gorgeous white sandstone, technical problems, and a beautiful meadow leading down to the reservoir are the reward for visiting this unusually quiet stretch of rock.

WEST PROW

Walk south down the ridge past a prominent finger crack that faces west until a distinct prow sticks out from the ridge with a few roofs along its expanse. West prow is not pictured.

☐ **1. The Dihedral V0** ★
Climb the double dihedral system and escape out right before the overhanging crack.

☐ **2. Leaning Arête V2**
Bad fragile rock just left of the double dihedrals.

THE SCOOP WALL

This is the obvious white stone approximately 50 yards past West Prow at the far south end of the aptly named Scoop Area. A large amount of small boulders and thick bushes are just to the right of the scooped white section. The problems in and around the polished scoop are excellent and very technical.

☐ **1. Master of Disaster V5** ★★
Start on the undercling just right of *The Corner* a few feet and make a long move up and right over the bulge. Going to the left from the undercling is a fun V2.

☐ **2. The Corner V0** ★
Just around the arête from #3 to the right is a fun dihedral.

☐ **3. The Scoop V3** ★★★
Climb straight up the white scoop on thin edges and sloping feet.

☐ **4. Standard V0**
Just around the corner to the (left) from *The Scoop* is a gritty face/arête problem.

☐ **5. Doxology V11** ★★★★
Climb the gorgeous wall just right of #1. Starts on good holds on the right side and traverse left to a huge move to a sloper. Topout straight up.

Scoop Wall

Horsetooth Hang Organizer, Cameron Cross, tries Cheathook V8 at Rotary Park Photo: Andy Mann

LAND OF THE OVERHANGS

Located north of the Scoop Area and before Soldier Canyon Dam on the west side of the road. The ridge holds numerous problems in the V0 to V1 range with a couple of more distinguishable problems as one walks back to the north.

BEACH ROCK

On the northern part of the ridge. A section of rock with a slabby west face and hefty amounts of chalk lining the base below an arête. Beach Rock is not pictured.

❒ **1. North Face V0** 🌄
Climbs the rather dirty north face. A sds makes the grade V2.

❒ **2. Black Arête V1** ⋆ 🌄🌄
Climb the black face just right of the arête.

❒ **3. West Slab V1** ⋆ 🌄
The slabby face just left of the wide dihedral crack.

THE OVERHANG

The Overhang is located south on the ridge from the parking area. A severely overhanging roof with chalk across its head-height holds defines it.

❒ **1. V0** ⋆⋆
The splitter crack on the left side of the wall.

❒ **2. V0** ⋆
Climbs the jugs just right of the crack.

❒ **3. Bachar Lunge V3** ⋆⋆
A dynamic problem that throws from the obvious, lone flake at the base of the overhang to a super pod then up the face.

❒ **4. Lip Traverse V5** ⋆⋆
A traverse from left to right, through the pod, and ending on #2.

SHIP'S CORNER

Just to the south 10 yards from The Overhang is a part of the ridge with a couple of dihedrals forming two fun problems. Ship's Corner is not pictured.

❒ **1. Left Arête V2** ⋆⋆ 🌄
Climb the arête under the roof to a long reach and good holds.

❒ **2. Hank's Hang V0** 🌄
Climb up the slab to the right of *Left Arête* and end on a finger crack on the wall's upper section.

The Overhang

NORTH QUARRY

North Quarry parking and access from Lory State Park:
If you have an annual pass for your vehicle, park at designated sites in the southeast corner of 25G and Lodgepole (at the dirt road entrance to Lory). The signed trailhead (Satanka Cove) will be on the east side of the dirt road, just as you enter the park (and past the parks pipe-gate). Follow the Satanka Cove trail down to the obvious quarry walls on the north side, within the cove. If you don't have a parks pass, you must drive up to the parks entrance station (visitors center), or the self-serve pay station if the entrance is not manned, and obtain a day pass. Parking, restrooms, water, etc. can also be found at the visitors center. North Quarry is not pictured.

❒ **1. Sunshine Face V2** ⋆⋆
A perfect vertical face with an escape off left or a hasty downclimb.

❒ **2. Drill Marks V0** ⋆⋆
An excellent slab follows the drilled groove.

❒ **3. Motion Picture Slab V3** ⋆
The slab above the engraving *Motion Picture*. A running start makes it a little easier and stupid.

❒ **4. Arête Motion V0** ⋆⋆
The arête moves around the right corner. It's all in the feet.

❒ **5. Desert Crack V2** ⋆ 🌄
Climb the crack to mid-height then escape left. Straight up is filthy and quite insane without a toprope.

❒ **6. Leaning Dihedral V2** ⋆ 🌄
The left-leaning dihedral with good flakes and edges. Bad feet are all too obvious from the skid marks. Not a good idea to continue up the high part of the wall.

❒ **7. Little Arête V1** ⋆
The short arête right of *Leaning Dihedral*. Bad feet epitomize the start to easier moves.

❒ **8. Cinch V6** ⋆ 🌄
The furthest northeast (right) problem just left of the hanging cables. Unclimbable in spring. Starts on a sloping shelf and somehow gains the right-facing dihedral. Another tall problem is left.

Carter Lake

Naomi Guy footloose on Wilford Prow V3   Photo: Andy Mann

CARTER LAKE AREAS

Carter Lake is a vast bouldering area with many classics, old and new. The featured sandstone has two wonderful bouldering areas (North/South Dam Area and Biglandia) and an extensive number of problems for every level. These areas differ substantially even though separated by only a mile. The North/South Dam Area is a jumble of discontinuous ridges and sporadic lichen-striped boulders lining the hillside above Carter Lake. During the spring snowmelts, one of the Front Ranges best boulders — Kahuna Boulder— is nearly submerged under the cold water. The Dam Areas are south and west facing and stay particularly dry and comfortable through the winter months. Many outstanding new problems have been developed at Carter over the past few years, particularly at Biglandia, which was rediscovered in 1995. At Biglandia the miniature flatirons jut up every few yards to form excellent bouldering walls. The north-facing walls are relatively cold throughout the winter and stay comfortable through the spring and fall.

Note: An daily entrance fee or an annual pass is required. Biglandia has the presence of massive, hungry rattlesnakes.

Directions: *Carter Lake is located west of Berthoud. From Berthoud take State Route 56 west for 3.0 miles from the intersection of US Route 287/56 to Road 8E. A brown sign for Carter Lake is on the right side of the road. Go left on Larimer County Road 8E, which splits 0.5 mile after the Carter Lake Entrance Station.*

Biglandia: *Drive over the dam 1.2 miles to Carter Knolls on the left side of Road 31. Cross the road and either walk around the front side (nearest the dam) via a grass-covered road or behind on a dirt road and over the middle of the ridge. From the grassy road contine north around the rocky ridge and into the valley. From here the Big Betty Boulder is down by the drainage approximately 175 yards, and the Redneck Wall can be seen on the right. Access the walls by following a game trail at mid-height on the hillside. Watch for huge rattlesnakes and expect some serious bushwhacking.*

North Dam Area: *Go right (north) on Larimer County Road 31. Parking is directly before (on the south side) the dam and on the right. The Fawn Hollow Trail is on the opposite side of the road. Walk along the trail until even in elevation with the ridge (cairns may be in place) and walk a short distance to the ridge. Many of the boulders are visible from the ridgeline.*

South Dam Area: *Go straight at the intersection (Road 8E and Road 31) for 0.2 mile and park in the lot on the right side of the road. The boulders at the south end of the Dam Area are visible from the parking lot.*

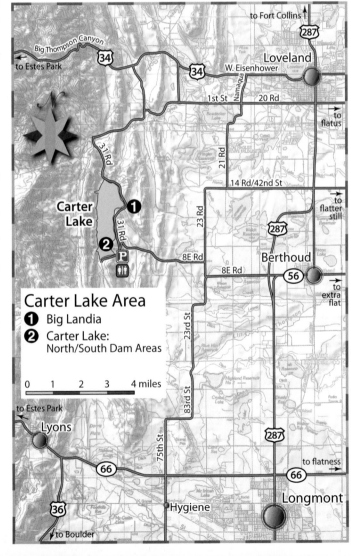

Carter Lake Area

❶ Big Landia

❷ Carter Lake: North/South Dam Areas

0   1   2   3   4 miles

BIGLANDIA

Approach: Park at Carter Knolls. Cross the road and either walk around the front side (nearest the dam) via a grass-covered road or behind on a dirt road and over the middle of the ridge. From the grassy road continue north around the rocky ridge and into the valley. From here the Big Betty Boulder is down by the drainage approximately 175 yards, and the Redneck Wall can be seen on the right. Access the walls by following a game trail at mid-height on the hillside. Watch for huge rattlesnakes and expect some bushwhacking.

BIG BETTY BOULDER

This is the lone boulder at the base of the hillside. It offers fun slab problems going straight up, as well as a V5 traverse that circles the entire block.

Big Betty Boulder

THE REDNECK WALL

Biglandia's highest and most striking feature. It is distiguished by its triple crack systems and continuous 25-30 degrees of overhang.

❏ **1. T-Neck V3** ★
Start low on the left arete and climb right around the arete to finish on V-Neck.

❏ **2. V-Neck V2** ★
A jug haul up the shorter left side of the wall and just left of the third crack system. Jump off.

❏ **3. Redneck Traverse V7** ★★
Start just right of #2 and climb left to the arete. A crux iron cross leads to the left finish.

❏ **4. Hot Cum Bath V6** ★★
Finger jams and bad hand jams lead to the jug on *Cream- Filled Man Boy*, then way up to the top. The leftmost crack above a bad landing is called *Sucks You Left* V6. Dangerous!

❏ **5. Cream-Filled Man Boy V6**
★★★
Start in the right-hand of the middle cracks and move up and left, firing to a jug at mid-height. From here either jump off or top-out at roughly 35 feet.

The Redneck Wall

THE MUDWEISER WALL

This yellow wall is just right of its much worthier neighbors, the Abdo Wall and the Rotund. Approximately 70 yards left of The Redneck Wall.

❏ **1. The Mudweiser V10**
Start low and left, then blast right through the glue.

❏ **2. Horatio Handjob V2**
The hand crack on the wall's right end. The top-out is frightening.

Mudweiser Wall

THE ABDO WALL

The striking green and brown wall just left of the Mudweiser and criss-crossed by small seams.

❏ **1. Pinchaloaf V4**
A grungy sit-down pinch problem on the wall's far left.

❏ **2. Abdo Cave V8** ★★
Start very low on slopers, go straight out to the ramp, then finish left on chossy jug/ flakes. A harder finish (V10) has been done going straight up the black bulge and into *Abdo Man's* high finish.

❏ **3. Abdo Man V3** ★★
A sit down start off the jug ramp, then climb up and left on good incuts. The top-out is right.

❏ **4. The Vertical Lawn V7**
Same start as *Abdo Man* but move right to gastons and edges. Finish on *Abdo Man*.

Abdo Wall

THE ROTUND

A steep, lichen-streaked wall just left of the Abdo Wall.

❏ 1. The Rotund V7 ★★★
A left to right traverse that climbs high through the middle of the wall.

❏ 2. Ponts De Lyon V4 ★★
A sit down start that climbs to the purple plates in the bulging central wall. Many variations exist.

RESERVOIR DOGS WALL

A steep brown wall approximately 65 yards left of the Rotund.

❏ 1. Reservoir Dogs V6 ★
A long right to left traverse. The finishing moves up the steep brown wall are worthy.

THE CHUMP

The steep diamond-shaped brown wall just left of the Reservoir Dogs Wall.

❏ 1. The Chump V6 ★★
Ascend the middle of the wall on crimpers. Drop from the jug at the lip. A link-up V8 has been done from the first half of *Charlie Horse* into this problem.

❏ 2. Old Nag V2
The right (north) arete of the wall on pockets to a bad top-out.

❏ 3. Charlie Horse V9 ★★★
Climbs from the right arete going left on crimpy, technical moves.

PERCADEATH WALL

A wall between The Chump and Bitch Slap Wall. A pit is at the base. Not pictured.

❏ 1. Traverse V8
A left to right traverse across the wall.

❏ 2. Perci V4
Climb up the wall left of #3.

❏ 3. Percadeath V4
Straight above a dug out pit.

BITCH SLAP WALL
AKA THE WARM UP TRAVERSE

The longest traversing wall and the last wall on the ridge before the barbed-wire fence. Bitch Slap Wall is located approximately 200 yards left of the Charlie Horse. It is reached most easily by walking along the lower hillside until coming to the fence, then following the fence line.

❏ 1. I'll Make You My Bitch V6 ★★
A traverse from right to left through the horizontal jug at mid-height.

❏ 2. The Bitch Slap V7 ★★
Traverse the wall either direction staying low the whole way.

❏ 3. Sky Pilot V2 ★★★ 🔲
A classic problem on the left end up the highest, cleanliest part of the wall.

The Rotund

Reservoir Dogs Wall

The Chump

Bitch Slap Wall

Carter Lake
North Area
A. Call It Crock
B. Skunk Rub Boulder
C. Extension Boulder
D. Spice Roof Area
E. Monster Boulder
F. Little Debbie's Boulder
G. Kahuna Boulder
H. Giant Pebble Boulder
I. Low Life Boulder
J. Mars Boulder

South Area
(starts at Crap Traverse)

NORTH / SOUTH DAM AREAS

A broken ridge of sandstone with sporadic boulders lining the hillside stretching a little over a half mile. This massive boulder field has problems first climbed by Steve Mammen and more recently rediscovered by eager boulderers. The result is a substantial increase in classic, highball problems.

NORTH AREA

The most concentrated area at the Dam Areas with problems ranging from V0 to V10. Take the Fawn Hollow Trail south from the north parking area approximately 200 yards and reach the ridge by hiking west from the trail (look for cairns). An easy downclimb from the ridge brings one to the Spice Roof Area and a view of the Monster Boulder, Mars Boulder, Little Debbie's and the Kahuna Boulder down by the lake.

A. CALL IT CROCK

Just above Skunk Rub Boulder and before reaching the upper ridge is a separate boulder with problems on the west face. A traverse that climbs right to left from the undercut is V5. The west-facing arête is V5. A V3 is right, utilizing the low right-facing dihedral. Not pictured.

B. SKUNK RUB BOULDER

Reached via the lower trail system, approximately 40 yards from Extension Boulder, this severely undercut boulder has a traverse skirting the entire lip.

❏ 1. **Skunk Rub V4** ★★
Lip traverse the low roof from left to right, finishing by using a great sloping pocket on the prow just around the corner.

❏ 2. **Daily Chuck Dose V6** ★
A two-move power problem that climbs out the bowels of the overhang. Finishing on *Skunk Rub* can be V8.

Skunk Rub Boulder

C. EXTENSION BOULDER AKA SERGEANT WOODY

On the lower ridge south of the Spice Roof approximately 45 yards. The wall is distinguished by its landscaped base to protect from water runoff, as well as a 19-foot tall face above.

❏ 1. **Sergeant Woody V7** ★★
Traverse the wall from right to left, finishing either on *Rocky Top* or further left. Maybe harder since holds have broken.

❏ 2. **Verdon Face V0** ★ 🌀
The south face on pockets with absolutely no resemblance to the *Verdon's* perfect holds.

❏ 3. **Sunshine V6** ★★
A sit down start on the southwest arête that climbs through positive, small crimpers before topping out on *Pocket Pussy*.

❏ 4. **Pocket Pussy V3** ★
Use the same jugs as *West Face* but bust right and top-out on the arête or climb right around the corner.

Extension Boulder

❒ 5. Tall Boy aka Natural Ice V6 ★★★

Stay on the west face (up the tallest part of the wall) and just right of #6. Sometimes cheap beer helps. Considered quite the sandbag.

❒ 6. West Face V3 ★★★

Climbs the flake/pocket system up the 19-foot tall part of the face above the landscaped stones. A classic highball problem.

❒ 7. Meatrope V10 ★★★

Seven feet right of *Rocky Top*. Climbs 16 feet on absolutely horrendous crimps.

❒ 8. Rocky Top V4 ★★

Climb up laybacks and pockets on the wall's left edge. Slightly harder with a sit down start.

❒ 9. Pete's Gritstone Wall V5 ★★

Around the south corner from Extension Boulder is a smooth, slabby wall. Start low on bad laybacks and highstep and pop to the lip. A frustrating scrunch-like sit down goes at V10.

❒ 10. Spooky Tooth V3 ★★

Highball, aesthetic face on the big wall right of *Pete's Gritsone*.

D. Spice Roof Area

Just south 15 yards from the downclimb off the ridge is the Left Roof Band—an undercut slab with excellent problems for warming up. The wall directly left has numerous V0s. The Spice Roof is right of the Left Roof Band.

Spice Roof

An overhanging bulge with bad rock on the lower section (many broken holds are evident).

❒ 1. Spice Roof V6

Out the right arête of the prow on sloping holds and heel-hooks. Missing the finishing dyno would be catastrophic.

❒ 2. Wilford Prow V3 ★★

A classic out the middle of the hanging prow. The stone is friable so climb like a butterfly.

Spice Roof

Left Roof Band

A nice undercut face with a horizontal break running the length of the low vertical face.

Left Roof Band

❒ 3. Seam II V3 ★

A thin problem on the wall's right side that utilizes small underclings.

❒ 4. Undercling V5 ★★

Five feet right of #5 and out the middle of the roof to a horrendous balance/power move over the lip. Substantially harder than it appears.

❒ 5. Seam V2 ★★★

Climbs the perfect flakes on the roof's left side.

Monster Boulder

E. Monster Boulder

The biggest, baddest boulder at Carter. Defined by its thick girth and talus strewn across the north face. Problems are listed from right (west) to left (north).

❒ 1. Lake Arête V2 ★

At the beginning of *Train In Vain* #2 (the middle of the west face) is a committing problem with serious potential for a broken back. Multiple spotters and pads are recommended.

❒ 2. Train In Vain V10 ★★★

A classic traverse that starts on the west face and climbs all the way through *Traverse du Jour*.
(Variation: *Born Slippy* is a V8 left to right traverse, from left arête reverse *Train in Vain*.)

❒ 3. Dispuntia Dudes V6 ★

Reasonable moves and an airy 15-foot top-out cap a thin gaston crux move at the beginning of the northwest arête.

❒ 4. Splick V5 ★

A serious affair on thin laybacks followed by a gentle top-out.

❒ 5. Krum V4

Left of *Splick*. A beached whale exit at 16 feet makes this the scariest problem on the boulder.

❒ 6. Traverse du Jour V7 ★★★

Begin on the northwest arête, then work up and left until you can roll around the northeast arête.

❒ 7. Days of Whining Posers V7 ★★★

Up the middle of the north face from the obvious eight-finger edge nine feet off the dirt. A deadpoint move from the large edge is the crux and is followed by more crimping and a committing, although reasonable, 17-foot top-out.

❒ 8. Pete's Arête V3 ★

Another airy problem up the northeast arête. A tad dirty pulling over the top.

❒ 9. Nobody's Face V1 ★

On the south face is a near-vertical problem that climbs up a brown face via opposing sidepulls. A really bad landing.

Andy Mann on Kahuna Roof V6 Photo: Andy Mann Collection

Little Debbie's Boulder

F. LITTLE DEBBIE'S BOULDER

On the lower hillside below the Monster Boulder and a little to the north. The problems face the lake. A V10 traverses right to left beginning on #2 and finishing on #6.

❒ 1. **Crapulator V2**
Out of painful underclings and straight up to a wide, lichen-covered lip.

❒ 2. **The Tension V7** ★
A three move powerfest. Start under the roof on the right side of the wall and reach up left to a bad undercling/sidepull. Throw over the roof to a big sloper then exit right.

❒ 3. **Dynoman V8** ★★
Start on a pair of sharp crimps, up to an atrocious left-hand sidepull then launch to the jug below the lip.

❒ 4. **Left Dynoman V6** ★
From the terrible crimps just right of the small adjacent rock pull into the far right slopers of the horizontal crack. Throw to the jug on *Dynoman*.

❒ 5. **Squeeze Job V4** ★★
Starting off the rock climb to the horizontal sloping crack then straight up to a massive rail.

❒ 6. **Sloper Chief V5** ★★★
One of the classic boulder problems on the Front Range. Start directly right of the small rock at the base of the wall and right of the black water streak. Traverse left on sloping holds to the pod and then up. Exit right.

❒ 7. **V7** ★
Start on the right side of the undercling pod and climb the rounded arête.

❒ 8. **V5** ★
On the north-facing wall is an undercling pod that climbs up through a shallow seam via strenuous gastons and laybacks.

IN BETWEEN BOULDER

The boulder that forms a small chasm with Little Debbie's Boulder north side. An easy V1 crack problem climbs the wall facing Little Debbie.

THE DOUGHBOY BOULDER

Nature has given Carter a new addition to the stellar bouldering by depositing a 20-foot block right next to the all-time classic Kahuna Boulder. What used to be a clod sticking in the hillside is now a new classic block.

Doughboy Boulder

❒ 1. **V2** ★
On the left side of the east face is a short problem exiting to the left onto a large ledge. A straight up variation bypassing the safe lower exit is V4 and higball with a possible bad landing but worth the adventure.

❒ 2. **Doughboy V7** ★★★★ 😊
Twenty feet of the best damn bouldering you will do! The problem climbs the gorgeous northeast arête from the big hole on the east face and hugs the sloping arête to good edges up high.

❒ 3. **V3** ★★★ 😊 😊
Climb the offset shallow corner on the north face.

G. KAHUNA BOULDER

The large overhanging boulder on the lakefront with some of the best problems on the Front Range. Super project out the overhang right of *Kahuna Roof*.

❒ 1. **Kahuna Roof V6** ★★★★ 😊
Ultra classic. A must do! The middle line on the boulder. A V8 direct start begins off a small left-hand undercling and right-hand crimp. A super project, utilizing the mono, awaits on the far right.

❒ **Kahuna Roof Variation V7** 😊
Do the first move of *Kahuna Roof* then bust right on slopers and over the top.

❒ 2. **Super Chief V11** ★★★★
A spectacular problem. On the left before rounding the corner to *The Layback*. Start on a sloper and small crimp to another sloping hole then dyno up to a small edge then to more sloping holds. A V8 called *Snake Eyes* is just left before #3 and climbs through the two small pockets from a squat position.

❒ 3. **The Layback aka Beach Crack V3** ★★★★
Start low on the northwest corner of the block and work up and right to jugs.

Kahuna

4. Big Pickle V6 ★★ 🔘
Superb vertical face left of #3 using a layback and small indescript edges.

5. V5 ★
A low start problem on the east overhang. Starts on a big jug and entails good heel hooks and powerful moves. Grovelly top-out.

Kahuna

Giant Pebble Boulder

Mars Boulder

H. Giant Pebble Boulder
Down the hill and north from Little Debbie's is this blazing, lichen-covered boulder.

1. South Face V0
The easiest way up the right, south-facing wall.

2. The Ultimate Con Job V4
Climbs the blunt bulge left of the *South Face*. Starts with the left-hand pocket and finishes with a dynamic move to the top.

3. Southwest Corner V2 ★★
Climbs the gorgeous lichen-covered dihedral in the middle of the south face up thin edges.

4. The Weeping Crescent V6 ★★★
On the backside (north) wall a classic traverse climbs from right to left. Starts underclinging on the northwest arête.

I. Low Life Boulder
Just north of the Kahuna Boulder on the lakefront.

1. South Face V0-V1
Climbs a multitude of holds to the top.

2. Barbed Wire V3 ★
The holds are far from sharp as the lake meticulously polishes the holds every year. Starts as a sit down.

J. Mars Boulder
This boulder is located north approximately 30 yards from the Monster Boulder and is an excellent warm-up area that stays out of the sun until mid-day.

1. The Arête V3 ★
A sit start problem on the far right arête. Bad crimps and feet are the rule of the day.

2. Mars Traverse V5 ★★ 🔘
A traverse from right to left with good holds and feet that climbs out of the cave and finishes on a small left-facing dihedral above the talus.

3. Worm-up V0 ★
Starts from the lip in the middle of cave and up to bomber edges.

4. Mantelope V2 ★
Mantle the flake/jug, and then find some good pockets. A sit start climbs through terrible crimpers at V5.

5. Pockets, Pockets V2 ★ 🔘
Starts on a good left-hand layback, then climbs to good pockets.

6. Crimpage V3 ★ 🔘
Up the lichen face just right of the traverse finish on small, hard-to-see edges.

7. Traverse Finish V2 ★ 🔘
Start low and right of the left-facing dihedral and climb left on layaways above the talus. Finish through the dihedral.

Giant Pebble Boulder

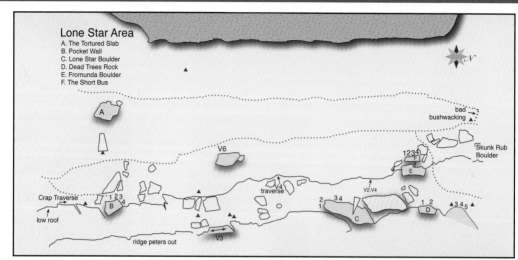

Lone Star Area
A. The Tortured Slab
B. Pocket Wall
C. Lone Star Boulder
D. Dead Trees Rock
E. Fromunda Boulder
F. The Short Bus

LONE STAR AREA

This area of boulders consists mainly of sections on the upper and lower ridge and is found just south and uphill from the Skunk Rub Boulder. A couple of separate blocks on the hillside are below the lower ridge.

A. THE TORTURED SLAB

Directly west and down the hillside from the *Crap Traverse* is an indistinct boulder with three slabs on its west face. From right to left the grades are V0, V1 and V0. These problems are seldom done but fun.

☐ **1. Crap Traverse V3** ★★

A long traverse from the far left through multiple rests and corners in the middle of the Dam Area ridge and just south of the Pocket Wall. A large deformed pine tree stands at the far left end. An excellent area for warming up. There are many V0 to V1 problems that climb straight up the entire face and a sit-down V4 is in the small cave on the wall's right side.

B. POCKET WALL

Just north from the *Crap Traverse* on the lower ridge is a north-facing wall with a seam and pockets.

☐ **1. Slabbing Westward V3**

A lichen-covered problem on the west face that climbs hard to see pockets and edges.

☐ **2. Northwest Pockets V2** ★★

Climb the perfect pockets to a small, right-facing dihedral and the distant summit. A little highball.

☐ **3. The Gimp V8**

Maybe harder since it broke. Climb the face immediately right of the seam and use the big pocket to vile crimps and a hard dyno to snatch the lip. Handholds in the seam are off-route.

☐ **4. North Seam V3** ★★★

A superb problem that climbs the seam on the far left (north) wall. An excellent V5 traverse begins below *Northwest Pockets* and finishes up the seam.

☐ **V6** ★★

Thirty yards north and down from the Pocket Wall is a lone, burnt orange boulder with a right to left traverse. An incipient crack splits this short boulder located just above the trail.

Crap Traverse

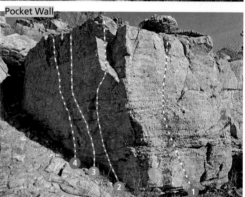

Pocket Wall

C. LONE STAR BOULDER
AKA THE MUSCLE BOULDER

Immediately south of the dead trees is a piece of the ridge with a crack that faces southwest.

☐ **1. Southwest Crack V1** ★

Climbs up and around the obvious crack.

☐ **2. Arêteach V0** ★

Climbs the wall left of the crack. A V2 sit down start can be done.

☐ **3. Lone Traverse V3** ★★

Starts left of #2 and traverses to the left above the lower horizontal gap. *Muscle Traverse* is V5 and traverses left to right from the far left edge of Lone Star and stops before *Southwest Crack*. The *Full Muscle Traverse* (V6) starts on *Muscle Traverse* and passes the crack.

❏ **4. V3** ★
Begin five feet left of the traverses on a low undercling and finish the end of the traverse.

❏ **Trivial Pursuits V0** ★★
Just south 10 yards from the *Southwest Crack* are some fun slabs on the ridge.

❏ **Lower Traverse V4** ★★
On the lower ridge and south from *Lone Star* is a left to right traverse that climbs under a small roof.

D. DEAD TREES ROCK
Walk above Skunk Rub to a small grassy area. Walk south past a wall littered with pockets and just beyond is the roof. Slightly farther south are the actual dead trees.

❏ **1. Roof Cave Crack V2** ★
Right of *Flakey Pull Roof*. A horizontal hand jam problem just off the dirt.

❏ **2. Flakey Pull Roof V5** ★★
This great steep problem climbs the huecoed roof just above (east) of Skunk Rub on the upper ridge. A V8 climbs out the roof immediately right and does not use the right face.

THE REAL POCKET WALL
Just north approximately 15 yards from the *Flakey Roof Pull* is a short wall with numerous pockets.

❏ **3. V3** ★★
Climb from the open dihedral around to the right and end on the slab.

❏ **4. V5** ★
Climb straight up the dihedral using an ultra-thin sidepull to gain the top.

❏ **5. V0** ★
From the low jug/pockets below the dihedral climb left and up the north slab.

E. FROMUNDA BOULDER
The boulder just west from Dead Trees that has a slot/hole on its bottom.

❏ **1. Death V2**
Undercling and jam out huge loose blocks on the rock's west face.

❏ **2. Fromunda V6** ★★
Start within the dirty chasm and climb to the huge pocket and up positive edges. A V2 starts on the pocket.

F. THE SHORT BUS
Directly west of *Fromunda* is a short boulder with a few excellent problems on its west face.

❏ **1. V2** ★
The problem that climbs the right arête. A V1 climbs the adjacent boulder's left side.

❏ **2. V4** ★
A low start off slopers then a tiny edge in the open dihedral and pockets above.

❏ **3. The Short Bus**

V8 ★★
A desperate sds from the hueco. Move right slightly on sloping edges then up the dihedral.

❏ **4. V5** ★
From the hueco move left to the arête using holds around the corner. An easy V0 is on the north face.

Muscle Boulder

Dead Trees

Real Pocket Wall

Fromunda

The Short Bus

Adie Drolet on the West Face Extension Boulder V3
Photo: Andy Mann

2 X 4 BOULDER

Located up and right (south) from The Short Bus. Not pictured.

❒ **1. V4** ★

Dyno problem up the middle of the block. Climbs through weird pockets to a hidden jug over the lip.

❒ **2. V2** ★

Start right on good edges, moving up and left to the 2x4 hold on top.

MIGHTY WALL AREA

This section of the Dam Areas is found to the south of Lone Star and well north of the South Areas boulders that are nearest to the south parking area. It consists of three main sections on the ridge with two boulders below (west) of the Mighty Wall.

A. PROW ROCK

The distinct prow 45 yards north of The Spaceship and south of Chain Rock with a deep gash/cave to the left (north).

❒ **1. Grumpy V1**

Climbs the corner two feet right of *Dishbutt* on pockets and edges and finishes up the prow to the left.

❒ **2. Dishbutt V5**

Climbs the sloping dishes on the faint, black-striped prow right of *North Pockets*.

❒ **3. North Pockets V1** ★★

The right wall that forms the corner on the northwest face. Finish either right or left.

B. CHAIN ROCK

A wall beginning immediately left (north) of Prow Rock.

❒ **4. West Face V1** ★★

Climbs the face using pockets and edges to the sides of the seam.

❒ **5. Chain Reactor V2**

Climbs five feet left of *West Face* on the arête's right side.

Prow & Chain Rocks

❒ **6. Cavus Maximus V1**

Start in jugs on the cave's right wall and climb to the right around the arête on positive edges.

❒ **7. Crack, Snapple, Pop V0** ★

Climbs the crack in the cave utilizing stems.

❒ **8. Chain Male V4**

Climbs the monos and pebbles to the left of the cave. The problem is on the southwest face around the corner from *North Face*.

❒ **9. North Face V0** ★

An easy problem up secure edges on the northwest face.

Little Boulder

C. LITTLE BOULDER

A great moderate boulder south of Crayola Rock and approximately 25 yards north of Chain Rock. There are numerous fun V0 variations on its tall northwest face. Defined by its solid, pink-streaked sandstone.

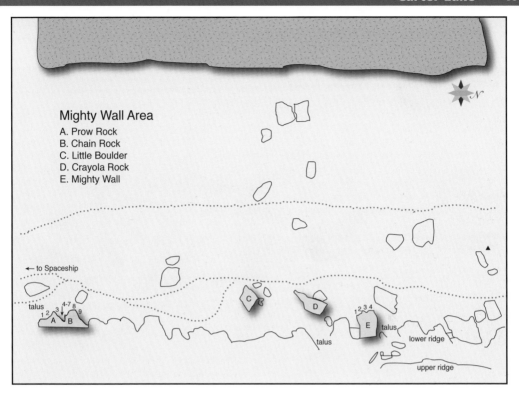

Mighty Wall Area
A. Prow Rock
B. Chain Rock
C. Little Boulder
D. Crayola Rock
E. Mighty Wall

← to Spaceship

talus

talus

talus

lower ridge

upper ridge

D. CRAYOLA ROCK

A colorful boulder with a fun traverse on the north face. Set below the ridge and just south of Mighty Wall. Some straight-up problems are also enjoyable.

❏ 1. Melting Traverse V2 ★★
The left to right traverse on the north wall. A few enjoyable variants exist as well.

E. MIGHTY WALL

Approximately 50 yards north on the ridge from Chain Wall is a tall wall with an orange face split by a thin seam.

❏ 1. Regular Route V3 ★★
A superb line of crimpers on the wall's right end, four feet right of the hueco. The top-out requires caution.

❏ 2. Silly Little Bulge V4
Starts in an undercling hueco four feet right of the seam. Climbs small, hard-to-see edges.

❏ 3. West Corner V3 ★★
Starts with difficult moves out the thin seam in the middle of the southwest face. A fragile top-out.

❏ 4. Dicey Prow V5
The arête on the wall's left end. A V6 with an ultra-thin sit down start has the same high finish.

❏ V0-V2
The tall wall directly right of Mighty has superior vertical lines.

Crayola Rock

Mighty Wall

SOUTH AREA

This area, above the south parking lot, is home to many classic problems, particularly those on Scenic Rock. This a good area for moderates with a few mid-range problems. This sector will remain warm and dry through most of the winter.

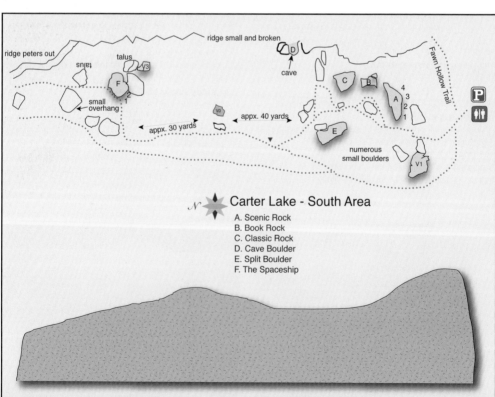

Carter Lake - South Area

A. Scenic Rock
B. Book Rock
C. Classic Rock
D. Cave Boulder
E. Split Boulder
F. The Spaceship

A. Scenic Rock

Scenic Rock—one of the best boulders on the Front Range—is easily identified from the south parking lot as the prominent overhanging block to the north. Take the middle of the three trails that split after the Fawn Hollow Trail begins, and walk uphill for 40 yards.

☐ 1. West Bulge V2
Start low and left on the boulder's west corner and up the blunt arête. The top-out is much easier to the left.

☐ 2. South Line V4 ★★★
Classic. Start on *Standard Route* and move left to the sloping horizontal and up to the top.

☐ 3. Standard Route V3 ★★★
The classic problem in the middle of the boulder that uses the hole to gain a painful finger lock, then the top.

☐ 4. Pocket Lunge V2 ★
Use the hole at arms reach with the left hand and dyno to the lip.

B. Book Rock

Above the Scenic Rock is a boulder with a V0 problem in the dihedral (#1) and a V1 (#2) on the left wall that climbs to the crack.

C. Classic Rock

Slightly above the Book Rock and almost on the ridge is a tall boulder with *Classic Crack* V0 on the west face. Another problem that starts left in a good pocket is also V0. Classic Rock is not pictured.

D. Cave Boulder

On the ridge west of Classic Rock about 15 yards is a small cave. The sit down start cave problem is V2 on less than perfect flakes.

E. Split Boulder

Fifteen yards to the south of Classic Rock is a broken boulder with three problems: a V0 on the north face and two V2s on the southwest face that tackle a tiny roof. Not pictured.

F. The Spaceship

A brown pinnacle approximately 80 yards north on the trail from Split Boulder. This separate block has a sharp brown and tan arête pointing southwest.

☐ 1. Southern Arête V0 ★
Climb the southwest arête.

☐ 2. Leaning Face V1 ★
Start on *Southern Arête* but go right around to the south face.

Big Block

Just above The Spaceship on the ridge is a small V3 roof hidden behind some boulders.

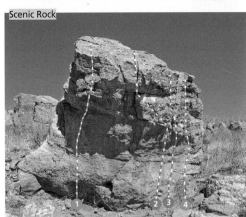
Scenic Rock

Book Rock

Cave Boulder

HERMAN FEISSNER

What inspires me to climb?

I'll be thirty-nine years old this May (2011) and after two decades of climbing I am more motivated than ever. Why? I simply love rock climbing. Honestly though, I didn't have much to offer on the subject of motivation or inspiration until Phillip asked me to write this short piece.

Photo: Jackie Hueftle

The last three years of my career have been among best for many reasons:

1. Patient persistence - I accepted my old age and decided to work with it rather than against it.

2. Luck - I welcomed my good health, decent genetics, and realized it was best to nurture steady improvement rather than seek out a 'quick fix'.

3. Relative to nothing - I accepted the best that I could do.

4. Because of the first three, I have more fun climbing than ever before.

I often see my peers forcing nature. "Huh?" you say. Well, it's important to recognize that, in nature, nothing is rushed. Things happen when it's time. When you are young, you don't understand. Everything comes easy so you just go go go. With old age, my slow pace, stubborn nature, and increased patience (in some ways), I learned to love the process and accept success and failure as equal teachers. One shows us that we have grown while the other instructs to keep trying. Both are important.

With my back to the wall and old-age holding a knife to my throat, it's been difficult to keep pushing. What has helped is the last three years of steady improvement through barriers I once thought to be impenetrable. More importantly though, I've stopped looking to everyone else as an indicator of how I'm doing. My only comparisons these days are to myself. As I said before – accept the best that you can do. Mindfulness of this simple thing will take you to new levels mentally and physically.

The end of my motivational message is to simply have fun. Next time you go climbing, ditch the agenda, turn off your brain, and just enjoy the company of your friends as well as the beautiful areas we are fortunate to have. These are the days where everything comes together and you attain the feeling. It's an enlightened state that I experienced during a recent trip to Switzerland. Some know. For the rest - the feeling simply can't be described. Seek it. When you find it, you'll know. You'll also find the inspiration to continue climbing no matter how old you are.

TOP 10:

1. *Right Eliminator* **V3 (Horsetooth Reservoir)**
2. *Power Glide* **V8 (Horsetooth Reservoir)**
3. *Center Route* **V10 (Morrison)**
4. *Moon Arête* **V9 (Horsetooth Reservoir)**
5. *Right Angry Man* **V10 (Lumpy Ridge)**
6. *Sap* **V9 (Lumpy Ridge)**
7. *Hollow's Way* **V8 (Flagstaff)**
8. *Left Eliminator* **V5 (Horsetooth Reservoir)**
9. *Deluxe Festival of Flesh* a.k.a. *Fleshfest* **V10 (Satellites)**
10. *Just Right* **V7 (Flagstaff)**

Estes Park

Dean Potter on Dilitheum Crystal V3   Photo: John Sherman

ESTES PARK

The bouldering in and around Estes Park is endless—vast boulderfields line nearly every road coming and going from the area. Ideal bouldering temperatures combine with the splendor of Longs Peak, the Park's glacial valleys and herds of voracious elk make this area a bouldering heaven. The huge boulderfield lining the base of Lumpy Ridge compliment the sporadic boulders of Rocky Mountain Park (covered in the mountain edition) to provide diversity on the weathered granite rocks. The current influx of new blood to the area has brought a substantial increase in first ascents and newfound areas. Classic problems on the Lumpy Ridge hillsides are as numerous as pine trees and aspen. No matter what area is visited the scenery keeps the psyche going through the inevitable changing weather.

LUMPY RIDGE

To the north of Estes is a giant ridge of intermittent cliffs towering above wonderful boulders hidden in the dense pines, aspens and rolling terrain. To the west from the main parking area is the Twin Owls Area with the Sap and Bolt boulder. Walk a little west from the parking area and the Little Twin Owls Area is a great place to warm up and has many offerings from difficult slabs to sloping nightmares. Further west down the trail is the Book and the Pear Boulders with distinct high problems, cracks and old easy slabs.

Directions: From the Hwy 34/36 intersection, take Hwy 34 north west and turn onto MacGregor Road (just past the shopping center with Safeway). Continue 0.75 mile to a bend in the road. Follow the road another half mile to the right and park at the new lot.

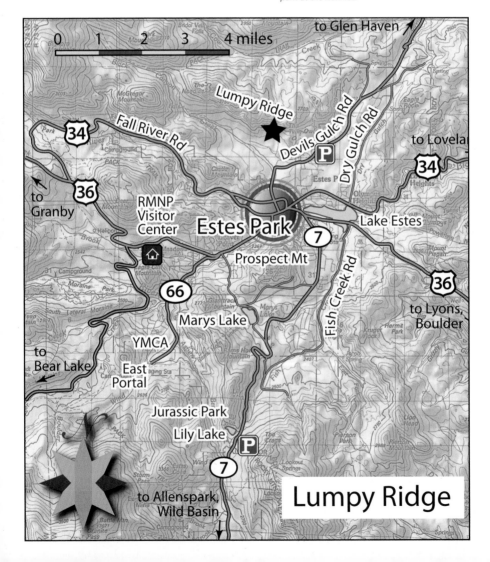

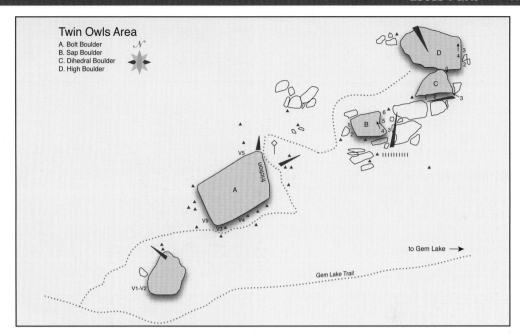

Twin Owls Area

A. Bolt Boulder
B. Sap Boulder
C. Dihedral Boulder
D. High Boulder

to Gem Lake →

Gem Lake Trail

TWIN OWLS BOULDERS

To reach the boulders walk west on the Gem Lake Trail. The Dihedral and High Boulders appear first, followed by the Sap and Bolt Boulder. A bouldering trail cuts back up and northeast.

A. BOLT BOULDER

The giant boulder right of the Gem Lake Trail sports a huge roof on it's upper west face.

☐ 1. Podophile V9 ★★ 😊

On the lower west face and right of the bolt line. Jump start to a left hand pocket to begin. A sit start was climbed by Tommy Caldwell at V11.

☐ 2. V0-V4 ★★ 😊

Numerous slab problems climb the 30-plus foot south face with a V3 on the far left face and a V4 up the middle of the wall.

☐ 3. V5 😊

The filthy problem on the north face above a flattened-out area. Just to the southeast from the Bolt Boulder is another large boulder with a couple of extremely highball problems (V1 to V2 on the slabby west face).

B. SAP BOULDER

Just off the Gem Lake Trail is a boulder loaded with problems. A cave on the west face, with a small boulder next to it, defines the boulders main problem.

☐ 1. Sap V9 ★★ 😊

Starts at the back of the small cave utilizing a preposterous heel/toe lock to get through the overhang. Finishes up and left from the lip of the cave. Hard for the grade.

☐ 2. Flaming Amigo V7 ★★ 😊

From the lower right side of the cave climb the arête to the finish of *Sap*. Sandbag status?

☐ 3. V1 ★ 😊

The jug haul on the far left side—on the opposite side (east face)—of the boulder from *Sap*.

☐ 4. V3 ★★★ 😊

Begin on the leftmost jugs and traverse right through the good edges and then up the crack/flake. Bad landing at the start. A straight up problem can be done right of #3.

☐ 5. V3

In the middle of the east face is a difficult two-move problem that starts as a sit down and finishes on the same jug system as #4.

☐ 6. V2

The rightmost problem. A little squeezed against an adjacent boulder.

Sap Boulder

Sap Boulder

C. Dihedral Boulder

Approximately 15 yards east of the Sap Boulder is a beautiful block with a difficult problem in a left-facing dihedral.

❏ 1. Glom V5
The leftmost problem starting on a right-hand undercling. Vicious topout. A V4 is between *Glom* and *PALN*.

❏ 2. Pop a Loose Nut V9 ★★
This is another of Lumpy's stupendous V9s. The left-facing dihedral with a crux reach to a topout right of #1.

❏ 3. V4
The right arête on the south face has a decent problem.

Dihedral Boulder

D. High Boulder

Just above the Dihedral Boulder is a tall block with superb slabs on the east face and one absolutely sick roof on the west face.

❏ 1. V4 ★
The sloping shelf that climbs out left to a reasonable top-out. The undone sit down start could possibly clock in as the hardest problem in the Estes Park area.

❏ 2. V0 ★★★
On the left side of the east face is a gorgeous slab with good holds.

❏ 3. V1 ★★★
Just to the right is another fine slab starting above a small boulder. Variations in the V1 to V2 range can be done off the small boulder up and right.

❏ 4. V0
The dirty traverse that climbs right on the horizontal break.

High Boulder

LITTLE TWIN OWLS AREA

From Twin Owls Boulders walk west to the old parking area past the information kiosk on the right trail that heads towards an outcrop approximately 125 yards away. The boulders in this area begin north of the old parking lot and extend to the west to the base of Little Twin Owls formation.

A. Melancholy Whale Boulder

Once reaching the Jaws Boulder walk to the southwest approximately 20 yards to a small boulder with a faint line of holds on an overhanging southwest-facing arête.

❏ 1. Melancholy Whale V8 ★
Climbs the sharp holds up and around the southwest arête.

Melancholy Whale

B. Jaws Boulder

The huge boulder just east of Little Twin Owls that has a roof near the ground on the southwest side of the boulder. Numerous sharp problems in the V0 to V4 range stretch across the north and south sides.

❏ 1. V2 ★
On the northwest face is a quick problem starting off a good edge and reaching the top.

❏ 2. V3 ★★
The traverse from left to right on the low line of jugs that finishes on #3.

❏ 3. V2 ★★
Start on the right end of the juggy traverse and move into the open scoop. A fine problem on good stone.

Jaws

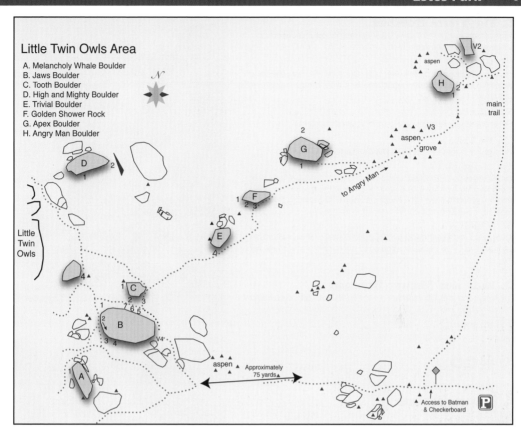

Little Twin Owls Area

A. Melancholy Whale Boulder
B. Jaws Boulder
C. Tooth Boulder
D. High and Mighty Boulder
E. Trivial Boulder
F. Golden Shower Rock
G. Apex Boulder
H. Angry Man Boulder

☐ 4. V4 ★

Start on an undercling flake and work like a fiend to the good edges straight up the face. This problem has become harder recently due to a broken hold. A V4 highball (full sandbag status) is right on the southeast arête.

☐ 5. V7

The sloping problem left of the jugs and seam of #6. Horrendously tenuous friction is required.

☐ 6. V0 ★★

Just left of the seam is an easier variation with the same finish as #7.

☐ 7. V1 ★★

On the north face start at the bottom of a seam and move up and left to incuts and a slabby top-out. A V7 on atrocious holds is to the right.

Jaws

Rylan Marshall on Pop a Loose Nut V9   Photo: Andy Mann

C. The Tooth Boulder

Adjacent and north of the Jaws Boulder is a triangular-shaped block with a slab on the southeast face.

☐ 1. **V2**
The vertical tweakfest on the west face. Quite thin for both the hands and feet. Use the left arête to reach the top. A V2 climbs the right arête of the west face.

☐ 2. **V0** ★★★
The slabby southwest arête. Also used as the downclimb.

☐ 3. **V0** ★★★
The slab just right of #2. Follows the small right-facing corner.

☐ 4. **Clingon V3** ★★
Just to the west of The Tooth Bolder is a distinct right-leaning crack closer to Little Twin Owls. A couple of difficult moves to get started then the problem eases up. *Dilitheum Crystal* V3 (opening photo) does the start of *Clingon* and climbs straight up.

☐ 1. **V1-V3**
Twenty yards to the northwest from *Clingon* is a tall wall with a horizontal crack splitting it. The problems climb up to the crack then exit to the right. They are not shown on the topo.

D. High and Mighty Boulder

Uphill approximately 50 yards and to the north from the Tooth Boulder is a tall boulder with a couple of problems on the southeast face.

☐ 1. **V2** ★★★ 🌄
The awesome highball problem that follows a small roof out right on the southeast face.

☐ 2. **V0** 🌄 ⚡
The blunt arête to the right of #1. Also fairly high.

E. Trivial Boulder

Follow the trail east from the Tooth Boulder for 20 yards. The boulder just left of the trail has a couple of V0 problems.

F. Golden Shower Rock

The name says it all. Just northeast from the Trivial Boulder is a tall boulder with two outstanding problems on its south face.

☐ 1. **V6**
On the west face is a small overhanging arête that leads to a crack out left. This problem broke recently and is substantially harder than before.

☐ 2. **V2** ★★ 🌄
The left-facing seam on the left of the south face. Fairly hard to get situated on the face. A long reach gains the top-out jugs.

☐ 3. **V2** ★★ 🌄
The right seam on the south face. A difficult to find edge and pocket are key to gaining the reasonable top-out moves. A V4 is right on bad holds.

☐ 4. **V0**
On the north face is an obscure short problem that adds an extra bit of contrived fun to the boulder.

Tooth Boulder

High and Mighty Boulder

Trivial Boulder

Golden Shower Rock

G. APEX BOULDER

To the northeast approximately 25 yards is a boulder with a small roof splitting its south face.

Apex Boulder

❑ 1. **The Apex V2** ★★
The south face problem is well worth doing. Follow the roof out right.

❑ 2. **V0**
On the back of the boulder is a quick hit.

Due east from the Apex Boulder and in a young aspen grove is a big boulder with a couple of aspens standing in front of its southwest face. If tall slabs get the juices flowing try it out.

❑ 3. **Gill Face V3** ★★
Tall commiting slab facing Apex boulder before reaching Angry Man Boulder.

H. ANGRY MAN BOULDER

Just around from the tall slab and north is a severely overhanging boulder covered with slopers and pounds of chalk.

Angry Man Boulder

❑ 1. **Left Angry Man V7** ★★★
A sit start off the lowest slopers and terrible heel/toe scum. Move immediately left on more slopers then throw to the wafer-thin top-out and an easy mantel.

❑ 2. **Right Angry Man aka Livid Man V10** ★★
Almost as good as the *Left* but far more demanding and difficult. From the same starting section and a better, but very bunchy heel hook, throw to an improbable sloper and continue right on terrible crimps and more slopers.

Just uphill and approximately 15 yards from Angry Man on a short block resides an east-facing finger crack. It goes at V2 if you can stick the first move.

Justin Jaeger on Right Angry Man V10   Photo: Andy Mann

BOOK BOULDERS

The Book Boulders are located by walking west on the main trail for 15 to 20 minutes past the old parking lot. The trail splits at the beginning but stay on the lower trail. The boulders are trailside after the sign for the Rocky Mountain National Park entrance.

A. WORLD'S GREATEST BOULDER

Not quite good enough for such a lofty title. The closest boulder to the trail with a crack splitting a small overhang.

☐ **1. V1** ★★
The right problem on the northwest face. Follows an open seam/pinches either up right or left. A scrunchy sit down makes it V2.

☐ **2. V2** ★★
Obvious overhanging crack facing the trail. A sit start makes this a good V4.

☐ **3. V3** ★★★
Starts the same as #2 but busts left to a sloping arête and then a flake to finish. A sds makes it V4. Finishing the problem by eliminating the top left flake boosts the grade to V6.

☐ **4. V0**
The slab beginning off the thin flake on the ground.

☐ **5. V0**
Start as for #4 but move left up the slab.

☐ **6. V0**
Just left of the tree is another easy slab.

☐ **7. V0**
A superb jug haul on the left side of the slab.

☐ **8. V2** ★
The right arête on the south face that does not use the jugs on #7.

☐ **9. V2** ★★
The crack/layback on the south face. A V6 or harder climbs the southwest corner just left.

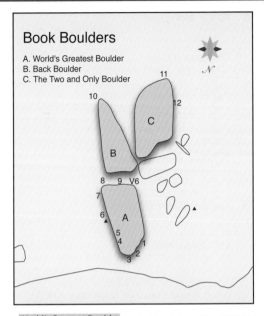

Book Boulders

A. World's Greatest Boulder
B. Back Boulder
C. The Two and Only Boulder

World's Greatest Boulder

World's Greatest Boulder

B. BACK BOULDER

The boulder just south of Book Boulder. The slabs on the east face are good V0 friction practice.

☐ **10. V1** ★★
The overhanging fin at the far south end of the boulder.

C. THE TWO AND ONLY BOULDER

The boulder next to Back Boulder.

☐ **1. V2**
A sit down start up and right on the blunt southwest arête.

☐ **2. Pepsi Mantle V0**
On the southwest face make a big jump to the lip and mantle over.

PEAR BOULDERS

Continue west on the main trail and pass through a gate. Walk another couple of minutes and pass the sign for The Pear—staying on the left trail rather than on the one headed uphill. The Pear Boulders are seen to the right of the trail 25 yards after the sign for The Pear.

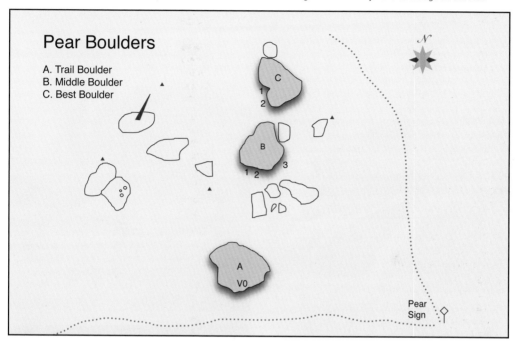

Pear Boulders

A. Trail Boulder
B. Middle Boulder
C. Best Boulder

Trail Boulder

Middle Boulder

A. TRAIL BOULDER

The closest boulder to the trail has a number of V0 problems on its south face.

B. MIDDLE BOULDER

Just up and north from the Trail Boulder is a gorgeous boulder that has a flat south face with a sloping shelf at mid-height running diagonally up and left.

❏ 1. **V8** ★★★

Classic! Jump start at the right end of the sloping shelf and work up and left to the arête. Hard sloper moves and throws are what this problem is all about.

❏ 2. **V4** ★

Head straight up from the right end of the sloping shelf on sharp crimps and balancy topout.

❏ 3. **V1**

On the northeast face is a fun problem up the right-leaning arête. Starting low and left from a sit down start boosts the grade substantially.

C. Best Boulder

One of the most beautiful boulders on Lumpy Ridge, this is the upper of the three boulders. The two problems on the southwest face are even blessed with a flat landing.

☐ 1. **V5** ★★★★
Starting in the scoop on a large jug, move left then straight up to a fragile edge and the top. Straight up from jug is V?. A desperate sds has also been done.

☐ 2. **Thundercling V9** ★
On the right of the scoop is a desperate problem utilizing a micro-crimp and layback to gain good holds and the top. An easier variation utilizes a right-hand edge around the blunt arête.

Best Boulder

To reach the next three boulders, walk to the climber's trail for The Pear. Walk up this trail for 150 yards (the main Pear boulders are to the left) and head due east 100 yards.

Scoop Boulder

A smooth boulder with a black scooped-out east face. A seam splits the right side of the east face.

☐ 1. **The Seam V6** ★★ 🌀
Climb the right-leaning seam on the east face.

☐ 2. **V1**
The northeast arête, up jugs to a mantle finish.

☐ 3. **V0-V2** ★
A selection of slabs can be done on the west face. Expect thin edging for tips and boots.

Scoop Boulder

Horizontals

Just northeast 25 feet from Scoop Boulder is a boulder with a horizontal crack across the northwest and south faces.

☐ 1. **V1** ★ 🌀
The left problem from a low start under the roof on the northwest face.

☐ 2. **V1** ★★ 🌀
The right problem under the roof that climbs to the southwest arête then up the short slab.

Horizontals Block

Highly Horizontal Block

Highly Horizontal Block

Uphill to the north 20 yards is a block with horizontal cracks along its south face.

☐ 1. **V0** ★
The right side of the south face off the good undercling flake. Exit around the corner to avoid a terrifying top-out.

Scrunch Block

Just to the right of Highly Horizontal is a small block with a steep southeast side. Scrunch Block is not pictured.

☐ 2. **V0** ★
The easy slab directly right of Highly Horizontal.

☐ 3. **V2**
The right-trending seam by the big pine just to the northwest of Scoop Boulder.

THE CUBE

A beautiful block with problems on every side. The Cube can be used as a warm-up boulder but you need to feel comfortable on high problems that begin at V2. Perfect landings and memorable problems define this extraordinary block.

Directions: Walk west on the main trail, skirting the kiosk on its left. Continue along the trail (a wooden fence is left of the trail) past the sign and gate for entering Rocky Mountain National Park. After passing through the gate continue past the Pear Trail (heads up to the right) and past three blocks on the right. The trail stays headed west and goes up a slight incline with erosion steps. Pass a faint drainage coming in from the cliffs then follow the left side of the drainage towards Thunder Buttress. The Cube is found approximately 250 yards up in the woods and on the hillside directly below the low large roof on Thunder Buttress.

The Cube South Face

SOUTH FACE

A tall slabby face with a small tree blocking access to the tallest section of the face.

❑ **1. V2** ★ 🔵
On the left side of the south face is an arête dividing the south and west faces. Long reaches and friable feet are the rule. Sounds delectable.

❑ **2. V3** ★★ 🔵
Start just right of the tree and move right to a good set of edges. Move straight up to the high seam and micro edges. Escape right to the small huecos.

EAST FACE

The most uneventful section of the block. Not pictured.

❑ **3. V0** 🔵
On the left side of the east face is a small bulge to start then ledges to the top.

❑ **4. V1** ★ 🔵
Start low on a big left-facing sidepull then up to an obvious sloper below the roof. Exit left of the roof.

NORTH FACE

The cold side of the block, facing Thunder Buttress.

❑ **5. V2** ★★
Start on the corner between the north and east faces, then follow the arête to a long reach over the lip.

❑ **6. V3** ★★
Just right of #5 is a high set of edges. Start on these edges and throw to the right-leaning arête. Hidden edges appear to soothe the worried mind. A V8 link can be done starting on #7 and traversing in from the right.

❑ **7. V1** ★★★ 🔵
A superb line climbing up the middle of the north face from the jugs at arm's reach. Utilize holds in the left-facing dihedral and exit either right or left at the top. Classic!

❑ **8. V7**
Climb the extremely small sloping edges right of #7.

❑ **9. V3** ★★
Starts with a jump to the sloping shelf on the right of the north face then up good edges.

The Cube North Face

WEST FACE

A golden face littered with edges.

❑ **10. V0**
Climb the left side of the face up good edges to the sloping top-out.

❑ **11. V4** ★★★ 🔵🟢
The direct line, up the middle of the west face, on positive edges. A fantastic vertical affair that requires far more technique and thought than power.

Matt Samet holds onto the V8 on Middle Boulder
Photo: Phillip Benningfield

Justin Jaeger on Best Boulders V9   Photo: Andy Mann

SPRING BOULDERS

These two blocks are located 200 yards west of The Cube. Walk on a faint game trail due west but head uphill ever so slightly. The first block with problems will be directly east of a spring and the other is easily seen 40 yards to the west.

SPRING BOULDER

The boulder right by the spring; it has not been well traveled but offers a couple of intriguing problems on the west face.

☐ **V0**

Several V0s climb the lichen-covered slabs on the south face.

WESTERN SPRING BOULDER

This block, with a tall white slab on the west face, is 40 yards west of the spring.

☐ 1. **V1** ★★ 🔘

Follow the right-facing dihedral up the tall slab on the west face.

☐ 2. **V3** ★★★

The traverse across the south face from right to left. Ends with a throw to the lip before the west face. An extension traverse continues along the thin seam on the west face.

☐ 3. **V2**

A low start on the left end of the seam on the east face to a sloping right-trending ramp. A traverse along the seam to #4 is hard.

☐ 4. **V1** ★

The right problem on the east face that climbs through the questionable white and black holds to jugs over the top.

Western Spring Boulder

THE FRENCH FRY

When it comes to getting psyched for a new boulder this beauty fits the bill. The boulder is shaped like a french fry but offers so much more than grease; you get tip-shredding crisp edges and fright as well. The south face is a mere 12 feet wide but the east and west faces are nearly 60 feet long and covered in edges made to bring smiley faces to the tips and pure joy to the day.

Directions: Be very, very patient when trying to locate this block! It is obscure and easy to miss on the massive hillside. The block is located below the left side of The Pear and can be reached from The Cube by walking due east along the hillside approximately 250 yards (look for the golden south face). The block can also be reached by walking up the Pear Trail 200 yards then west into the woods for another 150 yards.

FRENCH FRY SOUTH FACE

The golden 12-foot wide face with a gorgeous right arête. If you are inclined to first ascents, the arête will be a classic highball.

☐ 1. **V1** 🔘🔘

Climb the ledges on the left of the south face. Be ever mindful of loose and dirty rock.

FRENCH FRY EAST FACE

A 60-foot long gray and tan face with blank granite on the left and tons of problems from the middle to the far right section of the wall.

☐ 2. **V5** ★ 🔘🔘

The leftmost line, before the trees, with a flat landing. Starts with the right hand using the left starting hold on #3 then up and left. Expect extremely thin edges to a hard move to reach the top.

☐ 3. **V4** ★★

An awesome line starting off two positive edges then up to a right-facing sidepull then the high ledge and higher exit.

☐ 4. **V2** ★

Start on the ramp and climb the good left-hand edges and atrocious right-hand sidepulls.

☐ 5. **Cryin' Out Loud V5** ★★★ 🔘

Start low on two perfect crimpers then move right on progressively sharper and more painful edges and a difficult top-out.

FRENCH FRY WEST FACE

A long slabby wall with far more problems than listed here. All problems are 20-plus feet tall and lichen-covered.

☐ 6. **V1** ★ 🔘

The rightmost line starting right of the corner system and following the slabby ledges to the top.

French Fry Boulder

Camp Dick

Tika Anderson on A Seperate Piece V4 Photo: Jay Droeger

CAMP DICK

Although people have known about the granite boulders littering this valley for years, it wasn't until the summer of 2000 that anything decent was discovered. The untrammeled alpine setting and the high quality of the compact granite combine to make "The Dick" a superb bouldering experience, marred only by the scattered nature of the boulders. For those who don't mind a little hiking, the Omniglobe Area, in its idyllic aspen grove setting, has the highest concentration of problems. With countless boulders littering the dense, primordial forest that blankets the canyon, Camp Dick offers the promise of new bouldering for years to come.

"The Dick" is best during summer and fall, as it can be quite snowy even into June, and the shadier rocks on the southeast side of the canyon take a long time to dry. Though the drive from Boulder is only 20 miles, it's 20 of the steepest, windiest miles you'll ever drive, so allow yourself an hour to get there and another hour to hike/drive to the more remote areas.

Directions: Heading north on Broadway out of Boulder, take a left (west) onto Old Stage Road, the last light in town (all mileage is given from this point). Drive 4.5 miles to the junction with the Lefthand Canyon Road, then take a left. At 7.2 miles stay right on the road to Jamestown (don't go left to Ward), passing through Jamestown at 10.2 miles. At 16.9 miles the road ends at the Peak-to-Peak Highway. Turn right, follow the road down a large hill and take a left at the bottom of the dip (18.5 miles). If you pass the sign for Peaceful Valley on the left you've gone 50 yards too far (Peaceful Valley is located on the Peak-to-Peak Highway between Ward and Hwy 7). Follow the narrow paved road west into the valley, passing the Peaceful Valley Campground and the Camp Dick Campground before the paved road ends at the Buchanan Pass Trailhead (19.8 miles).

For the Trail Boulders (The Traverse, Warm-up Area, Omniglobe, Cock Block and Jumbotron), park here and follow the signs for the Buchanan Pass Trail. For the Roadside Boulders (Bolt Boulder, Pyramid Boulder, Fingerbanger Boulder and Moat Boulder), walk or drive west up the very rough four-wheel drive road, FR 114. This road can also be used to access the Trail Boulders.

Kevin Jorgeson sends UK Hockey Night V6   Photo: Andy Mann

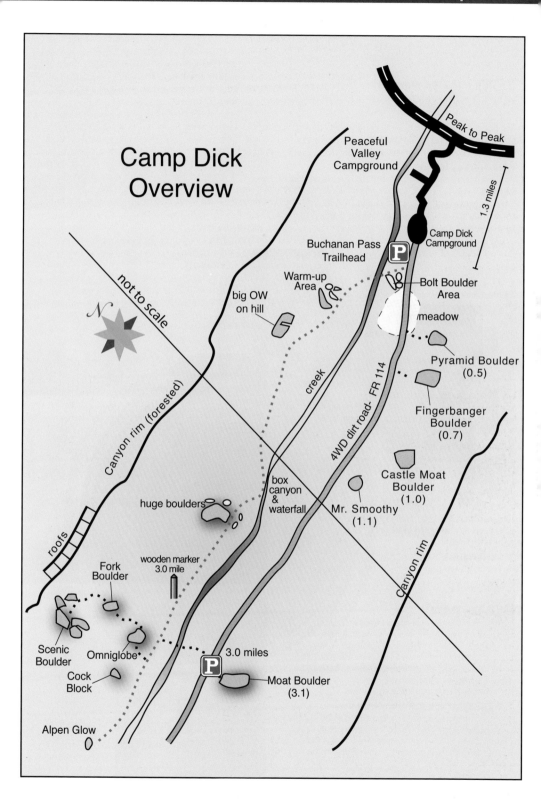

Camp Dick
Overview

Peak to Peak

Peaceful
Valley
Campground

1.3 miles

Camp Dick
Campground

Buchanan Pass
Trailhead

P

Warm-up
Area

Bolt Boulder
Area

big OW
on hill

meadow

not to scale

N

Pyramid Boulder
(0.5)

creek

Fingerbanger
Boulder
(0.7)

4WD dirt road- FR 114

Canyon rim (forested)

Castle Moat
Boulder
(1.0)

box
canyon
&
waterfall

huge boulders

Mr. Smoothy
(1.1)

roofs

Canyon rim

wooden marker
3.0 mile

Fork
Boulder

Scenic
Boulder

Omniglobe

3.0 miles

P

Cock
Block

Moat Boulder
(3.1)

Alpen Glow

BOLT BOULDER AREA

Head up the 4WD road from the parking just past the Buchanan Pass Trail. The boulders are on the right. This set of three blocks provides the easiest access with problems ranging from V0 to V7.

❐ 1. **Bolt Boulder Problem V5**
This fragile, loose, low-quality problem ascends the bolted line facing down valley (east).

BEHIND THE BOLT BOULDER

This is the tallest block with problems facing the creek.

❐ 1. **UK Hockey Night V6** ★★★ 😊🌀
Climb the left arête on the north face to the high ramp's right side then up.

❐ 2. **Legend of the Drunken Master V7** ★★ 😊🌀
Climb the faint corner right of the black streak with a huge move to reach the summit plateau.

❐ 3. **V4** ★★★ 😊🌀
Ascend the superb solid sidepulls to a straight up finish from a pinch.

❐ 4. **V2** ★ 🌀
Climb the shorter right side of the north face to a slopey finish.

❐ 5. **Roadie V0**
This easy slab problem sits directly adjacent to the road and climbs to a jug at mid-height then the top.

❐ 6. **V3**
The thin slab immediatley left of #5.

THE TRAVERSE BOULDER

A lone block that rests on the right side of the Buchanan Pass Trail after a brief 300 yard stroll west from the bridge over the creek.

❐ 1. **The Traverse V4** ★★★ 🌀
An excellent problem beginning from the slopers just left of the rounded sidepulls that lead up the block's middle. A V8 traverse begins on the boulder's far left side and continues through the V4.

❐ 2. **V3** 🌀
On the southwest side begin from a flat ledge or undercling or nasty kneebar and climb up the open "V," staying to the right to a jug at mid-height.

❐ 3. **Variations V2-V5**
Same start as #2 and contrive a multitude of entertaining problems.

WARM-UP AREA

This conglomeration of tall blocks is located 100 yards past The Traverse on the trail's right side. It is impossible to miss these boulders. Problems range from numerous V0 slabs to a couple of obscure traverses and sit-downs that reach V5 in difficulty. These blocks are certainly the best choice for novice boulderers; as well as those who are afraid of highballs, desperate affairs, and long drawn-out approaches.

❐ 1. **Tragedy of the Commons V9** ★★★
A long standing project finished up by Paul Robinson. Climb the 25-foot face starting down and left, move slightly right, and finish directly up the center of the face on small sharp crimps (ie: crux). This vies for some of the hardest moves executed at such a height.

Behind the Bolt Boulder

Warm-up Area

Warm-up Area

Tragedy Boulder

Roadside Boulders

Directions: If you have a burly 4WD vehicle and don't mind driving three miles an hour, then zero your odometer out at the start of the road (FDR 114) and redneck on up to the boulders—be aware that driving to the Omniglobe takes only marginally less time than hiking, and is easily twice as annoying.

The Pyramid Boulder

Well-hidden in a thick pine forest, this aptly named boulder is a good tick in the summer, as it stays well-shaded all day. Though not extensive, the bouldering here is excellent. Drive 0.5 miles up the road from the trailhead and park in a large meadow, directly across from a large block with an obvious offwidth crack, high on the canyon wall to the right (north). Walk 40 yards off the road due south along a faint track to reach the boulder. Pyramid Boulder is not pictured.

❏ 1. **V0**
Start matched on a ledge on the far left, gaston a crystal, and top out left. V2 if you start in the crack and grab the crystal with your left hand.

❏ 2. **Treetop Flyer V5** ★★★
Follow the right-leaning crack up the immaculate white face. Airy and involved.

❏ 3. **Mr. Clean V7** ★★
Harder from a sds start on the left (north) side, this prow can also be climbed on the right at V3. Cool moves on good, black stone.

❏ 4. **Le Banging du Fingers V3** ★
A pumpy, left to right traverse across the west face of the boulder, beginning on #3 and finishing far right on crimps. Somewhat mossy.

❏ 5. **Dicey and Dirty V2**
The high, licheny slab on the tall face right of #4. Use caution, especially up high.

❏ 6. **V0**
The detached flake veering right, then straight up.

Fingerbanger Boulder

This 20-foot high, square-shaped block is roughly 0.7 miles from the trailhead. Park on the right in a small campsite. The boulder sits 30 feet south of the road, offering decent, though crimpy, warm-ups on its south side and higher, harder lines on the impressive east face. A good, sunny hang with perfect landings.

South Face

❏ 1. **Pete's Party Pudding V1**
Take a small crimp with your right hand and fire over the lip.

❏ 2. **Matt's Dirty Fingers V3**
The faint seam in a black streak near the middle of the wall.

❏ 3. **Slopus, Slopus V0**
The slopey, rounded arête on the right side of the wall.

East Face

❏ 4. **V2**
The funkus left side. Climb past the diagonaling horizontal and onto the mossy slab.

❏ 5. **Drop Kick Murphy V4** ★
Up the obvious thin finger crack, moving right onto the bulge to top out. V5 from the lowest holds in the crack. Beware the loose chockstone!

❏ 6. **Slight of Hand V11** ★★★★
Shares a start with #7, then move left up crimps and pinches to the apex of the boulder.

Fingerbanger Boulder

❏ 7. **Le Fingerbanger V7** ★★★
Start on a crimp rail at head height where the boulder bends north, then slap your way past crimps on the rounded prow, moving left to finish. The exit has claimed at least two ankles!

❏ 8. **Pattycake V7** ★★★
From *Le Fingerbanger* start move right into the overhanging black scoop. V3 from a stand-up start on the block. Slopey, technical, excellent.

❏ 9. **Mantle Panties V1**
On the uninspiring west face of the boulder. Mantle two crimps at head height then punch it up the 20-foot mossy slab.

Trixie Tartasky on Drop Kick Murphy V4

CASTLE MOAT BOULDER

This monster is the biggest of the Dicks. At mile 1.0 it sits out of view up in the woods (about 75 yds) to the south of what is the obvious crux in the 4x4 road. This boulder has the potential for very high, very hard problems.

❑ **1. A Seperate Piece V4** ★★★★ 🔵🔵

Start on the detached block; mantle up through thin face holds. Mantle in a butter dish.

❑ **2. Finesse Test V5** ★★★★ 🔵

Mantle up through a right-leaning scoop. Suck it up and turn the lip straight up.

❑ **3. Bail Out V3** ★

Escape out right from *Finesse Test*.

❑ **4. Vanilla Gorilla V9** ★★ 🔵

Reach high and go up the slightly overhanging face to a series of good ledges with reachy moves in between.

❑ **5. Warm Up V2** ★★

Problem with good holds on the SW corner.

MR. SMOOTHY BOULDER

This is a funky, highly polished (read: blank) slab of rock about 1.1 miles up the road and past the Fingerbanger Boulder. It sits just off the road on the left and offers a trio of slabby but unique problems. Mr. Smoothy Boulder is not pictured.

❑ **1. Mr. Smoothy V3** ★

Follow the left-trending sloper rail.

❑ **2. Mr. Touchy V3**

The arête on the right side of the wall.

❑ **3. Mr. Feely V3** ★

The obvious crimpy face.

THE MOAT BOULDER

There is a distinctive swampy moat at the base of the north-west face of this gigantic block. The rock is every bit as good as on Fingerbanger Boulder. The highball V4 on its east face makes for a great excursion.

Directions: From the Omniglobe parking at 3.0 miles, walk up the road another 100 yards until you hit a series of log steps. Head left into the forest 20 feet from the steps to the obvious, square-cut boulder.

Castle Moat

Tika Anderson on A Seperate Piece V4

photo by Jay Droeger

Moat Boulder

❑ **1. Mikey's Traverse V0** ★

There is a boulder leaning against the back of the Moat Boulder. This is a right to left lip traverse of this boulder.

❑ **2. V4** ★★★ 🔵

One of the best problems. Begin in the middle of the east face and cruise left past plates and flakes to a stimulating finish.

❑ **3. V6** ★★

The crimpy, gymnastic prow formed by the meeting of the east and north faces. Hard on the fingers.

❑ **4. V5** ★★

The first problem above the moat on the front (north) face. Start on a slopey rail and jump to higher holds in the black scoop above.

❑ **5. V6** ★★

Begin above the right edge of the moat and step onto a glassy slab, then move up and right to a ramp behind a log leaning against the boulder. Slippery and technical, this problem is V3 if you start on the ramp.

❑ **6. V1**

The small, unremarkable slab right of the dead log.

Upper Trail Boulders

Directions: Drive up the hideously rocky four-wheel drive road to 3.0 miles and park where you can. Follow a small cairned trail northwest across the river to the Buchanan Pass Trail, where you intersect the faint track to the Omniglobe.

Otherwise, walk roughly an hour up the Buchanan Pass Trail, passing a 3-mile marker on a brown, three-foot-high wooden post on your right. From here, continue up the trail another 5-10 minutes, passing eight (count em', 8) diamond-shaped, blue trail markers nailed to the trees. Twenty feet before the ninth diamond head back and right on a climber's trail (look for small cairns) to the Omniglobe, which is one minute to the north. If you come across an obvious and very filthy 20-foot-high rock just left of the trail, you need to backtrack about 100 yards. The Cock Block is roughly 100 yards up-canyon from here (northwest) through the trees.

From the north face of the Omniglobe follow a faint track northish, then west up the hill to reach the Fork Boulder (2 min) and the Scenic Boulders (3 min).

The Jumbotron requires a bit more of an approach. Drive another quarter mile past the Omniglobe parking and park in the lot at the end of the 4WD road. Cross the creek via the bridge and head down-canyon (right) three or four minutes on the Buchanan Pass Trail until you reach a large clearing. Head 150 yards uphill (towards a talus field) along a faint trail (possible cairns) then head right (down-canyon) towards the grouping of big boulders just below the cliff line. Approach time from the parking lot: 20-25 minutes.

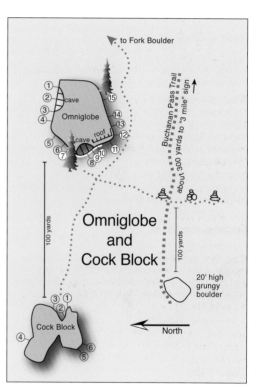

The Cock Block

With a handful of completed problems and potential for a few new classics, the Cock Block offers a good companion area to the nearby Omniglobe. Approach by hiking 100 yards up-canyon from the Omniglobe through the trees in a direction more or less parallel with the Buchanan Pass Trail. Patience may be required to locate this hidden block.

❒ 1. **V1**
Climb jugs up and right to a scary top-out.

❒ 2. **Dick V3** ★
Start on the right side of the cave and move up and left.

❒ 3. **Don't Call Me Dick V5** ★
Sds. Inspired by the VRG's Don't Call Me Dude, and nearly as classic to boot.

❒ 4. **Dick's Slab V4** ★★ 🌀
A great, highball slab problem.

❒ 5. **Dick's Other Slab V2** ★★
Another engaging slab for those of you with twinkle-toes!

The Omniglobe Boulder

This perfect cube of white and grey granite is surely one of the "Best in Colorado." From 20-foot-long cavey desperates to 20-foot-plus technical highballs on vertical, white stone, this boulder has it all—unparalleled bouldering in a secluded, forested setting.

North Cave

❒ 1. **The Dogfight V6** ★ 🌀
From a low undercling in the bottom left of the cave reel left out the chossy crack to the lip. A slightly contrived V8 moves straight up from the start of this problem.

❒ 2. **Put Some Hair Around It V8** ★★★
An exemplary boulder problem: powerful moves on perfect rock. Either begin low as for #1 (V8) or start standing up on good laybacks at chest height, punching past slopey ramps to the triangular apex of the cave. Can be started from #3 at V9.

❒ 3. **Schwagg V6** ★★
Almost as good as its neighbor. Sds low on the cave's right margin at a big pinch, then punch past crimps and a glued flake to a difficult lip encounter.

West Face

❏ 4. V3 ★
Begin just right of #3 and move past the double overlaps in the black streak, topping out just left of a patch of heather. Can also be started on #5.

❏ 5. V1 ★★★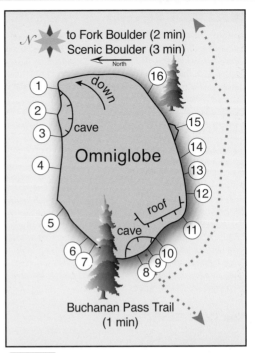
Begin at the downward-pointing "V" and work up the 20-foot tall white face on perfect incuts. Face climbing at its best!

❏ 6. V2 ★★
Start on a jug at waist height then grunt your way past a series of faint, left-facing liebacks. Tricky.

❏ 7. Theo's Problem V6 ★★
Start on #6 then climb the high, thin face next to the tree.

South Cave

Problems 8-10 can be finished out the hanging, black prow of *The Maxi Pad* for full value. Alternately, rock over right onto the ledge and either jump down or head up a V0 dihedral above (subtract one V-grade, you lightweight!).

❏ 8. The Maxi Pad V4 ★★
Sds at a good rail running across the south cave, then work left and up into crimps, traversing out the hanging prow.

❏ 9. Cleaner's Call V7 ★★
Start as for #8 and head directly up on tiny, painful crimpers to the sloping lip. Powerful.

❏ 10. Sweet Emily V8 ★
Sds matching on a three-foot high jug, three feet right of #9, then up past a pocket into slopers.

Southeast Face

❏ 11. V2 ★
Either start on a slopey rail directly under the right side of the large upper roof or begin four feet further right on an undercling. Thrutch your way past the bottom, then cruise straight out the right side of the large roof on perfect jugs.

❏ 12. V4 ★★
Begin as for #11 but head right onto a rounded prow after the opening moves, climbing carefully around a large, loose block to top out. Great moves in a great position.

East Face

❏ 13. V5 ★★★
The obvious thin crack that begins in a corner and runs up the right side of the prow. Technical, ferocious and scary.

❏ 14. Project ★★★
Directly up the east face on the tiny crimps that litter the seam-ridden, impeccable black stone.

❏ 15. Raggedy Man V4 ★★
Start on a small rock below the right-leaning ramp. Toss for the ramp then head up behind the tree. V6 from the lowest possible crimps.

❏ 16. Raggedy Ann V0+ ★
A decent little warm-up problem out blocky holds in a small corner behind the tree.

❏ 17. Dick's Arête V4 ★
A fun arête climb.

to Fork Boulder (2 min)
Scenic Boulder (3 min)

Omniglobe

cave

roof

cave

Buchanan Pass Trail
(1 min)

Omniglobe

Fork Boulder

Impeccable rock with potential for harder lines.

❏ 1. Ball That Jack V5 ★★★★

This problem climbs the obvious, over-hanging block that faces north on your way to the Scenic Boulders. Work past jugs and slopers into the faint scoop in the middle of the rock, then huck for the lip.

Fork Boulder

THE SCENIC BOULDERS

Part of the Upper Trail Boulders, these are located further west uphill from Fork Boulder and the Omniglobe. This complicated cluster offers a great range of moderates and desperates as well as an awesome view up-valley to the Indian Peaks Wilderness. The rock here is more metamorphic than granitic, lending itself to dynamic moves up solid squarecuts, on interesting gray stone.

THE PARALLELOGRAM

This is the small, slick-walled boulder forming the left wall of a corridor on the southeast side of the grotto. It offers fun moderates.

☐ 1. **Lip Traverse V1** ★
Traverse the lip of the boulder from left to right, then back. A good warm-up.

☐ 2. **Face V3** ★
Straight up crimps in the middle of the wall.

☐ 3. **Tree Jam V2** ★
Begin on holds near the aspen tree, then head up the right side of the wall. A hand jam against the tree trunk is considered "on."

THE UBER-PYRAMID

This gigantic 30-foot-high boulder/spire sits just uphill (west) of the Parallelogram, forming the right wall of the corridor.

☐ 4. **Big Richard V1** ★★
This 30-foot highball sits on the southeaast face. Begin low on a rail then work right and up to a high, licheny top-out.

☐ 5. **Little Richard V1**
Climb out the roof/prow in the corridor formed by the neighboring Parallelogram.

SCENIC BOULDER

This excellent boulder is the centerpiece of the area, both spiritually and geographically. It is the long, vertical to overhanging wall located at the back (west) end of the grotto, and offers a fine array of stiff problems.

☐ 6. **The On-Par Bouldering V0**
Three easier problems climb out the short left side of the south-facing, overhanging wave in the aspen grove.

☐ 7. **I Love Dick V7** ★★★
Yes, you do. Either start on opposing sidepulls at head height and reef up the middle of the wave, or begin low in a hand crack for the full V8 excursion. Bring lots of pads for the uneven, rocky landing.

☐ 8. **Project V?** ★★★★
Out the prow right of #7. Will be exceptional when completed.

☐ 9. **Swallow This V5** ★★★
Follow a thin finger seam in a left-facing corner, then realm up the beautiful face above. Technical and insidious.

☐ 10. **Easy Highball V2** ★
This would get an extra star if the rock were better. Begin right above the best landing on the platform and work past pinches and jugs—treat the holds gently!

☐ 11. **We Gotta Save Them Critters V5** ★★
Above the right margin of the platform, punch up the crack, bust right to slopey holds, then head straight up on edges. Scary.

The Parallelogram

DEATH GROTTO

This is the tight (read: dangerous) corridor just right of Scenic Boulder.

☐ 12. **Death by Dick V2** ★★
Climb the obtuse corner, with its perfect pink and white stone, on the corridor's right wall. Begin near the outside of the corridor and work left into the corner. Don't fall!

☐ 13. **Finessa V3** ★★
On the back side of Death Grotto. Start on jagged blocks and crimp your way up the orange veneer on the 13-foot face.

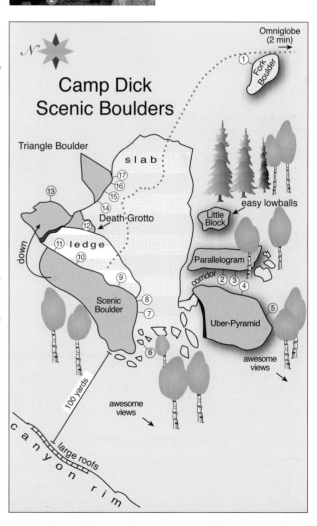

Camp Dick
Scenic Boulders

TRIANGLE BOULDER

This is the small, triangle-shaped block just below Death Grotto. It is the lowest, rightmost boulder in the cluster as you approach.

☐ 14. Warm-up Arête V0 ★

Realming up the crisp arête. Harder if done from the left side.

☐ 15. V1 ★

Begin in the middle of the face right of the arête, then work back to the arête at 10 feet. A fun warm-up on positive holds.

☐ 16. Little Jack Horner V0 ★

The obvious corner to the right. Harder if you start low, in the monkey pit.

☐ 17. Uncle Bumbly V1

Begin right of the corner, grab an incut on the left, heel hook, and wind your way up the fractured blocks.

THE JUMBOTRON

If your legs aren't tired by the time you reach The Omniglobe then pack up your pads and head on up to The Jumbotron, an isolated, house-sized block further up the canyon. This boulder sits in a sunny, warm spot, making it a good choice on colder days or when the wind is screaming down out of the high country. Potential for new problems seemingly abounds.

☐ 1. Get to the Point V3 ★★★

Start low and left and climb along the right-leaning roof to the point of the arête. This is the first problem you encounter upon reaching the boulder. Problems are described in a counter-clockwise direction from here.

☐ 2. V2 ★

Climb the arête up and left.

☐ 3. V4 ★★

Start in the back of the cave then move up and left.

☐ 4. Creaky Slab V3 ★

Realm up the highball slab on creaky, disconcerting edges.

☐ 5. V0 ★

Climb out the small roof via good jugs. This problem is a nice warm-up.

Note: #6 and #7 are in a hole on the northwest side of the boulder.

Death Grotto

☐ 6. Dead Teletubbies V5 ★★★

This is the obvious line of slopers out the left side of the hole, off-routing the left arête for your hands. Tricky.

☐ 7. Uncle Mike's Late Show V4

Aka "The Nasty Crimpy Thing." Climb straight out of the hole on painful sharpies. Ouch!

Note: #8 through #11 climb out of a similar hole on the other side of the boulder abutting The Jumbotron to the right.

☐ 8. Corner V2 ★

Tackle the easy corner on the left side of the hole.

☐ 9. Ken's Party Pudding V7 ★★

A hard, crimpy line that starts down in the hole just right of #8.

☐ 10. The Orifice V2 ★★★

A classic thuggy problem that climbs out of the hole on positive grips.

☐ 11. Dick's Party Pudding V4 ★

The rightmost line in the hole, moving straight up past sidepulls and crimps.

ALPEN GLOW BOULDER

A relatively easy block sitting alone in an alpine meadow with the most inspiring backdrop of the Dick repertoire. Problems range from V0 to V5 on cool swirly rock (individual problems not listed). A good block for those afraid of the "Dick's" usual highballs.

Directions: From the Omniglobe, continue up the Buchanan Pass Trail for a few minutes, into a meadow (1/2 mile). It is impossible to miss the boulder as it sits trailside.

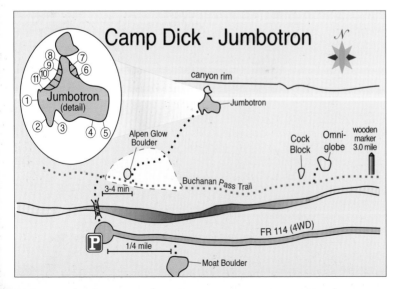

Camp Dick - Jumbotron

Allenspark

Ryan Fields on Chicken and a 40   Photo: Phillip Benningfield

ALLENSPARK

The granite near the mountain town of Allensark varies as much as climber's opinions. The Moss Boss is one of the hordes of granite blocks near The Ironclads: two cliffs filled with relatively short sport routes and surrounded by a mixmaster of 4x4 roads and private property near Highway 7. The redeeming quality of the Moss Boss is its seclusion, it's way highball, and the rock is pretty damn good, especially on the Moss Boss proper.

Directions: At the intersection of CO Highway 7/US Highway 36 in Lyons, zero your odometer. Go left on Highway 7 for 15.5 miles past CO Highway 72 and turn left on FR115 (Bunce School Road). Drive 1.0 mile total: pass a big sign for Historic Bunce School Road and stay left when the road splits at the start. At one mile, park if you have a passenger car or 4x4 up the road (216 Rd.) to the right — staying right as the dirt roads split every which way. Drive (or walk) a few hundred yards to The Ironclads and park. You will know you are at The Ironclads if the first climbable size cliff you see (30-45 feet) is littered with bolts. A large dome sits to the left as one faces the first Clad.

Now take a deep breath; finding the Moss Boss from here is an exercise in obscurity and patience. From the left side of the larger Ironclad head north (stay level with the Ironclad) for approximately 200 yards to the first ridgeline, then continue another 150 yards through a drainage and up to a rocky ridge. From the second ridge, you can easily see the larger Ironclad behind. Head down (right) along the ridge, staying on the north side for 300 yards past intermittent cliffbands (a large cliff is directly north as you head down) to a gnarly looking little crag covered in poop (the Guano Roof Area: good warm-ups on far left with problems all along the expanse from V0-V8). You can climb here but the atmosphere is not very amenable. Walk north another 150-odd yards and up a hillside to Moss Boss (chalk will be present on a few problems).

MAMMOTH RUB BOULDER
(AKA THE MOSS BOSS)

A lone monstrosity sitting to the north of the Ironclads and littered with slightly overhanging and committing highballs (20 to 30 feet) as well as difficult steep problems. If you are faint of heart you might bypass this baby for more palatable lowball problems found at nearby boulderfields like Lumpy Ridge or Camp Dick. For the industrious and curious boulderer, there are many smaller blocks in the vicinity, but boulders not considered rad enough for the Best.

Northwest Face:

This tall wall of striking, albeit occasionally crumbly granite faces north and west, making it a great morning destination in the summer. Because of nearby trees, it is also climbable in late-afternoon in the warmer months. At least two pads and two spotters are recommended for all the problems, though the more the merrier, as many problems have cruxes up high.

☐ 1. Cracker, Cracker V2 ★★ 😎

Start just left of the very licheny, left-trending crack (poor V1) on the far left side of the west face. From low incuts, move up orange and tan rock to a slabby finish in "toilet bowls."

☐ 2. Moss Boss V4 ★★★ 😎

Begin right of the crack in a scoop, make difficult moves to a sloping horizontal, then keep it together for continuous crimping up the high black streak. It helps to scope the topout from above, as locating critical edges can be a plus. A slightly harder variation climbs to the horizontal from the crack, then stays a bit left of *Moss Boss* on smaller, hidden crimps.

☐ 3. Skyler is the Man V8 😎

The central line up the west face, climbing the fairly grainy tan/white rock up the tallest part of the wall. Climb grainy rock on poor holds, using micro-crimps as intermediates to make long tugs for better holds. Sustained.

☐ 4. To Die For V6 ★★★★ 😎

A line that sort of became the definitive highball on the face, probably because of the quality of the moves and infamous high crux. Start just right of center on two shoulder-height crimps, then zig and zag your way up the wall, using any and all holds within reach, to a ballsy topout involving a long move off a poor sloping crimp and a pinch. Committing.

☐ 5. Death Flake V2 😎

Don't do this problem unless you want to get the chop. Start about three feet right of #4, move up into the flake via a strange backhand undercling, then layback, praying all the while, to a long pull for a jug near the top.

☐ 6. The Bulge V7 ★★ 😎

Begin about 10 feet left of the southwest corner of the boulder under the obvious belly with a black streak and orange lichen, as well as some small bushes. Easy opening moves lead to dastardly sharp crimps, nipples and nubbins out the bulge, with the holds getting better again as you get higher (i.e., past the point of no return).

☐ 7. 98 Percent, aka Allen V10/V12? ★★ 😎

Named in honor of Samet's asshole proclamation that "I've put up 98 percent of the problems here and I can say who gets to come here or not! Right? Cuz the next day all you guys kept repeating that, slagging me off and calling me Allen, cuz it was *my park*. Not that I didn't have it coming."

For the stand start, begin on two gastons in a scoop just left of the rounded southwest corner of the boulder. Body-tension on, and fire for a complete incut jug/horizontal. From here, move straight up and slightly left on the blank face via crimps, then top out carefully through slightly loose, licheny terrain. For the sit start, begin with your hands matched, low and around the south side of the rounded arête, bust left to a crimp with some Hilti Hit in it, pimp to the gastons, then make the toss. Hard and very core-strength and temperature dependent. The harder grade is for the sit start.

☐ 8. P-Diddy V5/V7 😎

This is the excellent, striking line up the rounded southwest prow/nose of the Mammoth Rub, and was one of the first problems to go down. Begin, ass in the dirt, with your hands matched on a flat jug. Up high, nice incut horns lead to a rest below the somewhat dirty finishing bulge (5.10—25 feet off the deck), or reverse the top of the crux and jump to the pads.

☐ 9. Mouth Breather V6 😎

Begin as for *P-Diddy*, but bust right immediately off of the jug, heading through the overhanging dihedral via a series of puzzling moves that, once figured out, come together in a kinaesthetically pleasing and surprisingly do-able sequence involving heel hooks, toe scums, and other tricks. Top out via the corner, taking care with loose holds up high.

South Face:

☐ 10. Sunshine Corner V2 ★★ 😎

This obvious line of weakness up the south face has fun, muscular moves, and is a good warm-up for the rest of the rock. Begin low in laybacks, crank up the corner to good holds over the apex, and gingerly pick your way up flakes and incuts to the summit. *Zoolander* (V6) begins in the corner, but move right off the initial laybacks, stretching high for a pair of nipples over the lip, then making technical, powerful moves to gain the face above. Exit via crimps.

Mammoth Rub Boulder

EAST ALLENSPARK/PEAK TO PEAK HIGHWAY:

The bouldering is near Peaceful Valley, but the Peak to Peak Highway is real close to the blocks. Of course the views, once you top out, take in the Indian Peaks Wilderness and scads of granite domes. The Key Slab is not for the faint of heart. The problems all venture 20-plus feet above the landings and require some route finding, as the chalk is washed off every time a meager rainstorm passes by.

Directions: At the intersection of CO Highway 7/US Highway 36 in Lyons zero your odometer. Go left on Highway 7 for 14.8 miles to a left on CO Highway 72 (Peak to Peak Highway). Drive 0.7 mile to a dirt road on the right (FR 217). Park here unless you have a 4x4.

The Dihedral parking is found less than 0.1 mile on the right of the dirt road at the first pullout (a small flat meadow—the Peak to Peak is still visible down the road) after the first steep section in the road (three 4x4 roads diverge then come back together). From the left side of the meadow, head down through the gully then uphill (NE) approximately 120 yards (cairns may be in place) to the north-facing dihedral, which is up one level on the cliffband.

THE KEYS SLAB AREA

Directions: Drive up FR 217 for 0.4 mile to the second campsite on the right and park. Head approximately 80 yards to the east into the woods to a 100-foot-long, 20-foot-tall gray slab.

THE DIHEDRAL

A distinct, overhanging orange corner located directly behind a viewing block.

☐ 1. **V4**
The left face starting from the low holds and finishing in the corner.

☐ 2. **V3** ★★
The best line up the well-featured corner.

☐ 3. **V6**
Sharp ass crimpers on the right arête finishing in the corner.

The Dihedral

THE KEYS SLAB

If you like slab climbing until your toes ache and your psyche is frazzled then this granite cliff will leave a smile on your face. Problems listed from right to left. All problems are highball!

☐ 1. **V3** ★★
The first slab encountered on the wall. The line heads straight up the wall, starting five feet left of the pine tree.

☐ 2. **V1** ★★
A superlative slab that follows the left-leaning seam to a long move high up on the slab. At least you're going to a damn good hold.

☐ 3. **V0** ★★
Another excellent slab directly behind the aspen tree that ends on a left-angling dike.

☐ 4. **V1** ★★
Climb the left-angling seam into the previous problem.

☐ 5. **V2** ★★
Up two tiers along the slab. Climb the horizontal edges just right of the wide crack (V0).

☐ 6. **V1** ★★
Left of the wide crack before the gray streak.

☐ 7. **V2** ★★
Immediately right of the gray streak, start on the big-ass hold with a no hands rest before the high crux.

☐ 8. **V0**
Climb the left-facing flake/corner up to the bushes.

☐ 9. **Less Conversation More Action V4** ★★
Elvis had this sentiment right, although he was talking about relationships. The upper slab starting on the low dike and moving slightly right above the tree. You will break your leg and rip the skin off your back if you fall off the high crux!

Keys Slab

Pierson Park

As hard as it is to believe, there is another excellent bouldering area just off the Peak to Peak Highway. Pierson Park has only been developed in the past few years, but the amount of problems fills more than a few days of flesh loss. The granite here is quite compact and the boulders range from frighteningly tall affairs with harder problems to more moderate heights and difficulty. Only the big three boulders in the main area are included here, but rest assured, the area is far more expansive with new lines sent on a regular basis.

Directions: From Lyons, head west on State Route 7 (toward Allenspark). Stay on Highway 7 past Allenspark to a right at Meeker Park on Boulder County 82 Road (Cabin Creek Road). Go right and continue for a mile to 82E. Stay on 82E over a cattleguard, then another 0.5 mile to a left for Pierson Park (FR119—a 4x4 road). Drive carefully for 1.4 miles to a left on 325 Road, then continue 0.4 mile to an undeveloped camping area on the right. Walk north and west on an old roadbed for approximately 500 yards to the Lower Three.

Upper Big Three

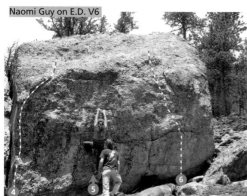

Naomi Guy on E.D. V6

Upper Big Three

The main attractions. Climb the left side to warm up for the steeper right side. This boulder has a sufficient number of crimpy problems to start a great session or end one (if you do all of them). Save energy for the Lower Three and The Sidecar.

❐ 1. **Crimpin' V4**

❐ 2. **Undercling Reach V2**

❐ 3. **Needles Redux V1**

❐ 4. **Abbey's Arête V5**
Just right of the crack on solid edges. Exit right.

❐ 5. **E.D. V6**
Bring your reach or power to get through the crimpy crux.

❐ 6. **Squatty Ned V5**

Around to the right are three vertical problems from V0-V2.

The backside of the boulder (The Golden Pillar) has three problems: two short V0s and a V5 that starts on the ground traversing up and to the right.

Behind this is a corridor that has 4 problems V0-V3—great to warm-up on especially on a warm day.

LOWER BIG THREE

THE SIDECAR

This is a great warm-up wall with eight worthwhile problems from V0-V7, and fairly good landings. Bring pads for *Chicken and a 40*.

Pierson developer Mike Frieschlag on a nice V2   photo by Phillip Benningfield

LOWER BIG THREE

☐ 1. **Chicken and a 40 V7** ★★★★
Ultra-classic highball with a mandatory dyno unless you are very tall and very strong. The V0 downclimb is classic in its own right.

MIDDLE BIG THREE

☐ 1. **Painful Hand Crack V4**

☐ 2. **Fish Out of Water V12**
The hardest line at Allenspark, done by Kevin Jorgensen.

☐ 3. **High Octane V6**

☐ 4. **Samet's Revenge V2**

☐ 5. **Horny V0**

Lower Big Three

Middle Big Three

Middle Big Three

Lion's Den & South St. Vrain

Kevin Smith on the mega classic Big Cat V4   Photo: Andy Mann

THE LION'S DEN

The Lion's Den was developed over ten years ago by Lyons locals Colin Lantz and Paul Pomeroy. With its quiet, scenic location high above the North St. Vrain River and scattering of good granite boulders, the "Den" offers a unique getaway for boulderers burned out on the Front Range's more traveled areas. Expect crimpy problems on good, crystalline granite and mortifying highballs, as well as fun moderates with soft, pine-needle landings. Though the area isn't vast it does offer potential for new lines. Expect some lichen and loose holds. The Den is best visited in the fall or spring, as the exposed position of the boulders leaves them open to gusty winter winds and sweltering summer heat.

Directions: From the town of Lyons head west for 4.0 miles on US 36 towards Estes Park from the light at the junction of Highway 7. Turn left at the Shelly Cottages onto County Road 80, which is signed for the Longmont Dam. Follow the dirt road 2.8 miles to its end and park below the white gate.

Pass through the gate and continue west on the dirt road about 7-10 minutes (0.5 mile), passing the River Wall and Button Rock Reservoir en route. Just above the point where the stream flows into the Reservoir notice a set of power lines that cross from the south side of the stream to the north side, then back again. Where the power lines cross back again find a faint track on the left, paralleling the road and heading up into the trees. This is an old original portion of the Sleepy Lion Trail (not to be confused with the marked trailhead for the new Sleepy Lion Trail, another 0.5 miles up the road).

Follow the trail up the steep hill past six well-defined switchbacks (home of the Switchback Boulders). The Paulaner Wall is just east of the fourth switchback (it has steps) on the hillside. The Prow is about 50 yards southeast and uphill from the sixth switchback, forming a northwest-facing mini-cliff with a large ponderosa in front of it.

The trail then levels out and heads southwest through a clearing to an excellent vista point, affording views of the valley below and the high peaks to the west. From here, cut left (eastish) onto an old ranching road and follow it 200 yards into a large clearing. The rock pile atop the hill to the east is the Lion's Den Proper. Total approach time: 30-35 minutes.

To reach the Lower Den walk east from the Lion's Den Proper until you encounter an old road leading north through the woods. The Caterwaul Grotto is roughly 100 yards north and downhill along this road and sits on the canyon rim.

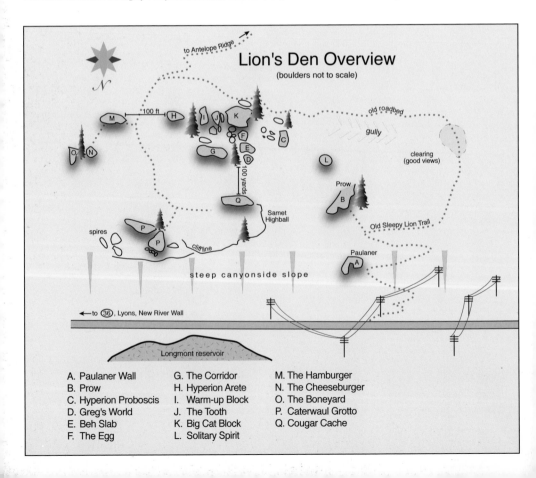

A. Paulaner Wall	G. The Corridor	M. The Hamburger
B. Prow	H. Hyperion Arete	N. The Cheeseburger
C. Hyperion Proboscis	I. Warm-up Block	O. The Boneyard
D. Greg's World	J. The Tooth	P. Caterwaul Grotto
E. Beh Slab	K. Big Cat Block	Q. Cougar Cache
F. The Egg	L. Solitary Spirit	

SWITCHBACK BOULDERS

These boulders offer an esoteric and highball venue on the steep hillside below the Lion's Den Proper. You can warm-up here, but it's not recommended. Best visited once you're in send mode. Don't forget your crash pad.

A. PAULANER WALL

So named because the problems were all put up with the help of three bottles of this fine lager by one who shall remain nameless ... Expect slightly licheny problems on stone ranging from unapologetic choss to good, varnished granite. (Note: Problems #1 and #2 are on the east of the two fins of rock.) Paulaner Wall is not pictured.

☐ 1. **Lager V2** ★
Climb the red face, moving left around the arête when convenient. Needs traffic.

☐ 2. **Pilsner V0**
Follow the dirty, right-trending crack to a blocky top-out. Jingus.

☐ 3. **Hefe V3** ★★ 😊
Climb the slabby face via the thin horizontals. Appealing stone and continuous, thin moves.

☐ 4. **Weizen V4** ★ 😊
Climb the right-leaning arête where the slab meets the overhang. Thin, friable, and strangely unnerving.

B. THE PROW

A trio of hard, stellar highballs make this isolated wall well worth the short, steep slog off the trail—if you fail to send, at least you can gawk at the awe-inspiring undone line up the clean, nubbin-studded vertical face. Bring lots of crash pads, cuz these problems are high!

☐ 1. **Poop Deck V0** ★★ 😊
Layback up the crack in the corner, moving left to finish.

☐ 2. **Project V?** ★★★ 😊
In the words of Colin Lantz, "Way highball—so thin, so high, so aesthetically perfect." The Braille trail on the vertical wall right of the corner.

☐ 3. **Walk the Gangplank V7** ★★★ 😊 🏃
Quite serious. Climb the nose feature just right of the Braille bumps, aiming for a rounded horn at mid-height.

☐ 4. **The Ice Lock V7** ★★ 🏃
Climb the sharp, incut seams up the orange patina on the hanging bulge feature, moving right into #5 to finish. The hard start, low and left, has yet to be freed.

☐ 5. **Hoosh Pot V4** ★ 🏃
Start as low as possible in the crack/fin feature and climb up to the bonsai tree, taking care not to use the large loose block by the tree. V1 from a high start.

☐ 6. **Blubber V0**
Also the downclimb. The easy corner out right.

The Prow

LION'S DEN PROPER

Though there are a handful of good outlying blocks in the trees both above and below the main area, the highest concentration of problems is found at the Den Proper, a dense maze of walls and blocks capping a scenic hillside. Problems tend toward the crimpy, so ration your skin wisely. The high, committing problems on the Big Cat Block are hard to beat, as are the strange but steep Hyperion Proboscis and the excellent Egg Boulder.

C. HYPERION PROBOSCIS

This lone block sits about 100 feet downhill and slightly northwest from The Egg on a sunny bench at the edge of the meadow, and is easily recognized by its phallic form.

☐ 1. **Hyperion Proboscis V6** ★★★
Sds on a good jug/flake to the right then pimp your way up the double arêtes. Thuggy and unique. See action photo for problem identification.

Mico Alejandro on Hyperion Proboscis V6 Photo: Mann

D. Greg's Dada

A short but fun wall 15 feet north of the Beh Slab.

☐ 1. **Greg's Dada V2** ☆

Up the seam/finger crack on the west-facing wall.

E. Beh Slab

Tucked in a notch just ten feet north of The Egg, this splitter blob of granite offers kind stone that recalls the texture of the Buttermilks in Bishop, California. The rock is exceptionally featured and solid, but the landings are bad to non-existent.

☐ 1. **Unknown V3** ☆ 🎯🎯

An interesting line up the scoops and edges on the tall northwest side of the boulder, over an uneven landing.

☐ 2. **The Mariacher Factor V3** ☆☆☆ 🎯🎯

Climb the west arête up to good horns. Buttermilkian.

☐ 3. **The Beh Slab V0** ☆☆ 🎯🎯

Follow the flake up and right into the scoop, step left to finish.

☐ 4. **Inside Moves V2** ☆ 🎯

Start on #3 but move right from the scoop to climb the arête on porcelain flakes.

F. The Egg

This aptly named chunk of granite is perched just west of The Corridor and just south of The Big Cat on a flat, pleasant bench. It offers good problems up crisp edges on very bulgy stone.

☐ 1. **Egg Roof V7** ☆

Sds in a finger seam in the small cave on the northeast side of the rock. Slap up for crystals, then thruct over as best you can.

☐ 2. **Over Easy V8** ☆☆ 🎯

Start under the faint prow on the west face on a good jug. Crimps gain a tiny right-hand crystal, and a slap left to finish takes you out over the bad landing.

☐ 3. **Poached V4** ☆☆ 🎯

Start on #2 but move right along the horizontal to a white-stained jug, then head straight up on tiny dinner plates.

☐ 4. **Scrambled V4** ☆ 🎯

Start up and right on the high terrace, matched in a good horizontal. Crank up the face on flat crimpers to a juggy finish.

G. The Corridor

This tall but solid wall offers a few good problems on funky jugs and dinner plates like those found at City of Rocks, Idaho. It sits uphill and west of The Egg about 40 feet and the problems face south, making this a nice place to catch morning sun and stretch out your fingers. Good landings abound.

☐ 1. **Schwank V1** ☆ 🎯

Climb the right side of the diamond-shaped block under the small roof, then stretch up over the roof for an incut bucket and finish out.

☐ 2. **Linoleum V2** ☆☆ 🎯

This proud line takes the scoop up the middle of the wall, heading for a faint seam to top out. V3 if you off-route the jug on the right.

☐ 3. **Hall Pass V1** ☆☆☆ 🎯

Face climbing at its finest. Start low in the layback crack in the good tan rock, then punch straight up the wall on bizarre, wavy stone.

☐ 4. **Late Bell V2** 🎯

The slightly loose problem on flake holds just left of the eastern arête.

☐ 5. **Main Line V1**

Climb the right-trending layback on the block directly behind #3. Awkward and unpleasant.

Greg's Dada

Beh Slab

The Egg

The Corridor

H. HYPERION ARÊTE

Not to be confused with Hyperion Proboscis, this funky little block offers a short but technical arête. It looks like a piece of bread sticking up out of the ground and sits just west of the Warm-up Block.

❏ 1. Hyperion Lunge V-Stupid
Run and jump up the center of the face, latching the grainy jugs at the lip.

❏ 2. Hyperion Arête V3 ★
The short, slabby arête on the right side of the face. Start low for full value. Tricky.

I. WARM-UP BLOCK

Though quite lowball, this little fin offers a handful of cruiser problems with perfect landings. Use caution topping out. This is a useful place to start climbing due to its central location and ease of access to the other rocks, as well as a safe place to get used to the Lion's Den variety of granite.

❏ 1. South Arête V0 ★
Climb incuts and dinner plates up the rounded south arête, aiming for a small seam at the top.

❏ 2. PW Traverse V4 ★
Start on #1 and cross the rock rightwards, staying low and finishing out on #5. Crimpy.

❏ 3. Moss Boss V1 ★
Start on a chest-high horn and go either straight up or move right to a crimp then up to good dinner plates. Fun.

❏ 4. Choss Boss V0
The easy hand crack splitting the east face.

❏ 5. Crack 'n Up V1 ★
This line takes the short finger crack in the black rock four feet right of #4.

❏ 6. Slab Master V1
Climb the layback seam in the pink rock from a sds, off-routing the finger crack to your left. Miniature.

J. THE TOOTH

This is the block/wall in the corridor just west of, and behind, the Warm-up Block. A pair of good moderates grace the slightly grainy stone.

❏ 1. Rollerball V0
Climb the rampy, south-facing arête on ball-bearing slopers.

❏ 2. Canines V2 ★
Start on a layback at chest height then reef up to good incuts on the rounded arête feature with the bright green lichen. Fun and aesthetic.

K. BIG CAT BLOCK

The highest, cleanest, and most aesthetic wall at Lion's Den, this exemplary chunk of stonker granite is also home to the area's scariest highballs, many of which top out at over 20 feet, sometimes over rocky landings. Expect crimpy and technical problems on immaculate, varnished stone.

WEST FACE AND SOUTHWEST ARÊTE

❏ 1. Scaredy Cat V3 ★ 🅐 🅑
This terrifying line takes the finger seam/layback on the left side of the west face, topping out at a tiny tree. Insecure.

❏ 2. The Big Cat V4 ★★★★ 🅐
The best problem at the Den. Climb the layback flake/finger seam directly over the good landing, heading for a water groove up high. Classic.

Hyperion Arête

Warm-up Block

The Tooth

Big Cat Block

❏ **3. Le Samet Corner V5** ★★

A real ankle-breaker. Climb the left-facing corner just right of #2. The crux comes high over the rocky landing.

❏ **4. Lion Bitch V6** ★★

Slap your way up the double-arête/prow via the good brown-red stone. Crimpy and technical.

❏ **5. Knee Bar Pussy V6** ★★

Climb the southwest arête of the wall, moving right into #6 to finish.

LOWER SOUTH FACE

❏ **6. Punch the Kitty V5** ★

Climb into the scoop on the south face then exit via tiny crimpers.

UPPER SOUTH FACE

❏ **7. Alley Cat V0** ★

The leftmost line on the upper part of the south face. Climb the clean corner into the white-stained crack. High and spooky.

❏ **8. Tigger V0** ★★

Climb the middle of the dinner-plate-covered wall directly under the pine tree.

❏ **9. Catfish V0** ★

Climb the left side of the eastern arête, moving left up high to finish in a positive layback crack in the black rock.

❏ **10. Cat Scratch Fever V2** ★★

This scary line takes the eastern arête to the black bulge, then moves right onto the bulge to finish out over the horrible landing.

L. SOLITARY SPIRIT

This is a tomato-shaped blob in the forest down and diagonally right (northwest) 50 yards from the *Hyperion Proboscis*. This boulder is small but aesthetic in a Font sort of way; it's probably a bad idea to come here at the end of the day as the holds are tiny and sharp.

❏ **1. Solitary Confinement V2** ★

The rounded east arête of the boulder.

❏ **2. Solitary Spirit V3** ★★

The aesthetic, scooped face via distant holds. Harder if you're short.

❏ **3. Seldom Seen V1** ★

A decent slab/mantle problem on the west face of the boulder.

THE LOWER DEN

This grouping of boulders has lots of hidden gems—if you have the patience to find them. Expect nicely textured granite and good, pine needle landings in a forested setting (Though a few problems in the Caterwaul Grotto have uneven, rocky landings). It's generally cooler down here than up at the Den Proper, as the cavey clustering of the boulders and a cool breeze off the Continental Divide keep temperatures down.

M. HAMBURGER

This rock sits 100 feet east of Lion's Den Proper, just across and down from an old logging road leading north to the edge of the canyon. It is an elongated, northwest-facing wall with a bulge on each end.

❏ **1. Happy Meal V3**

More like Unhappy Meal. Start in the horizontal crack and crank the awkward bulge on the left.

❏ **2. Hamburger V5** ★

Start on a good waist-high horizontal and punch out the bulge on crimps. The direct top-out gives full, awkward V5 glory, while bailing right subtracts an entire V-grade.

Big Cat South Face

Solitary Spirit

Hamburger

N. Cheeseburger

This is a unique little boulder, with slopers and "eyebrow" features, 100 feet northeast of Hamburger across a grassy clearing. It offers excellent moderates over perfect landings, and hey, it really does look like a cheeseburger!

❏ 1. Supersize It V1 ★
Out the crisp horizontals on the northwest face, just left of the tree. Fun.

❏ 2. Cheeseburger V3 ★★
Send the slopey horizontals just right of the aforementioned tree to a "Font-style" top-out.

❏ 3. Extra Cheese V3 ★
The direct southwest face, aiming for a pink smiley-face hold with your right hand and off-routing the ledge out right. V4 ★★ if you low traverse into it from as far right as possible.

❏ 4. Tom's Tavern V1
Sds and climb the squatty, grotty prow via crumbling jugs.

O. The Boneyard

This odd west-facing wall, just visible from The Cheeseburger, is 50 feet down and to the east in a stealthy grotto behind a large spruce tree.

❏ 1. Crackyard V0 ★
Climb the pleasant, arching crack on the left side of the wall.

❏ 2. Kevin's Arête V2 ★
Climb the pinkish arête between the two crack lines. Phunkee!

❏ 3. The Boneyard V3 ★★
Sds on locks and layaways and voyage up the funky crack above. Big hands and dirty jams take you over the lip.

❏ 4. Contrived Pile V4
The face right of the crack, off-routing the crack for some strange reason.

P. Caterwaul Grotto

To enter the grotto, follow the road down to the canyon rim and duck right into a corridor with a small pine tree. This is a nice place to get out of the sun or the wind, with a couple of classics to boot. Though many of the landings are good, a few problems climb directly over ugly blocks. Bring plenty of pads.

Corridor Problems

❏ 1. Sprayspot V3 ★
The water groove, crisscrossed by horizontals, on the right wall of the corridor across from #2.

❏ 2. Sprayflake V2
Five feet right of #3. Start on a horn hold in the horizontal then make a long reach over the bulge, eventually joining the chossy flake.

❏ 3. The Howling V4 ★★
The black-colored left wall of the corridor, behind the pine tree. Stretch to a jug then make your way up the wall as best you can.

❏ 4. Ichiban V4 ★★ 🌀
Start matched in the dirty (but juggy) horizontal then move up into underclings then back left along the lip of the roof.

Cheeseburger

The Boneyard

Corridor Problem Sprayspot

LOWER PROBLEMS

On the same boulder as *The Howling* but wrapping left and north downhill.

❑ 5. Sweetness V0 ★

A fun jug haul—sds on the good lip and move past the huecos.

❑ 6. Right Now V4 ★★★ 🐾🌙

A great highball! Continuous crimping on the tall black face above the evil, rampy landing.

❑ 7. Wrong Now V1

The ultra-licheny groove/nose below *Right Now*. Good landing, needs travel.

❑ 8. Sickness V4 ★

So utterly sick! Up the slabby red face via thin, sharp holds to gain the water scoops and a dirty top-out.

❑ 9. Steadman's Heffer V2 ★

This problem is on the small buttress out right and features a perfect, sandy landing.

Q. COUGAR CACHE WALL

This wall can be hard to locate, but it's worth the effort. It features varnished stone with a red patina and user-friendly, wind-sculpted holds. Head west 70 feet from Caterwaul Grotto to get here. The wall faces north and commands an excellent view of the valley. Many link-ups and variations are possible on this highly-featured gem.

❑ 1. Cougar Left V1 ★

The leftmost line on the wall via positive holds.

❑ 2. Bathtubs V0 ★★

A monster-fun jug haul. Sds off the landing block and work left three feet, then cruise back right into the bath-tubs and up.

❑ 3. Cougar's Crank V1 ★★ 🌙

Sds from the right side of the landing block then move straight up the wall on incuts to the funky little horn. V2 if you traverse in from the right on the diagonaling crack.

❑ 4. Cougar'n'a'bing'bing, Bling! V3 ★★ 🌙

From the undercling flake head straight up the bomber, red wall on small edges, off-routing the bathtub out right.

❑ 5. Cougar Cooze V1 ★

Start about three feet right of #4. Head for the diagonaling bathtub, then scunge your way over the lip.

❑ 6. Cougar Cache Traverse V3 ★★

This fine traverse goes both ways.

Corridor Problems

Cougar Cache Wall

Kourtney Nelson spotted by Sara Rich - Cougar Cache Wall

SOUTH ST. VRAIN CANYON

Like all the east/west canyons from the Front Range this long, curving drainage is packed with sporadic cliffs and boulders. The only problem is most of the rock is exfoliating crap with one good find for every fifty boulders. Numerous bouldering zones can be found and exploited in the canyon, but only the Ape City Boulders and a couple of sporadic blocks seem to come close to decent.

Directions for Ape City, Hidden Valley and Unhidden Hill

Ape City: *From the intersection of CO Highway 7/US Highway 36 Stop sign in Lyons head west up highway 7 for 5.3 miles and Mile Marker 28. Park on the left side of the highway and ford the river just downstream. The first block is just uphill with a triangular wall facing the river. Other blocks can be found by walking to the uphill side from the first block then up the drainage on a faint slippery path, which threads in and out of the wet drainage and leads to the other boulders.*

Hidden Valley: *From the above intersection drive 8.6 miles to a large left hand pullout big enough for ten-plus cars. Cross highway just down from the 30 MPH sign then go right into main drainage following an intermittent trail through the rocks. Follow this trail for 700 yards (less than 10 minutes) always staying in the rightmost drainage. Follow the occasional cairn past a broken bottle shooting range then continue up the trail as it leaves the drainage and follows the drainage on the western hillside (not steep at all). The drainage splits again and stay on the western hillside then cross drainage to a lone boulder sitting above the drainage and facing due south.*

Unhidden Hill: *Same parking as Hidden Valley. Easy access during late fall. Cross the river at the parking and head upstream along the river below a talus field until the Riverside Boulder is seen on the first level above the river (two minute approach).*

Note: *All the north-facing slope boulders are best climbed during the fall as the river crossing is safe, the temperatures are conducive to good friction, and the poison ivy is dead, dormant, or withered and harmless.*

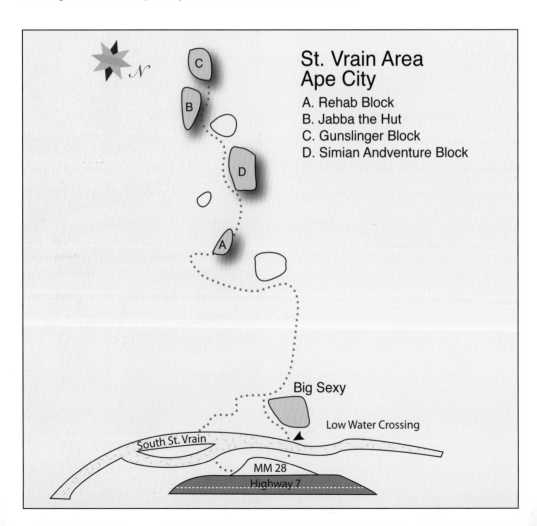

St. Vrain Area
Ape City
A. Rehab Block
B. Jabba the Hut
C. Gunslinger Block
D. Simian Andventure Block

THE BIG SEXY BOULDER AKA MM28

This big and beautiful block lies directly at the start of the trail up to Ape City proper. It sits on relatively flat ground one level above the streambed.

Big Sexy Boulder North Face

☐ 1. **Spraypaint Silverback V7** ★
On the stream-facing side, start on the right arête with your right hand on a decent sloper at seven feet and left hand out and lower on a foot-hold-like crimp on the face. Tension and slap up and left on the arête until reaching the sloping but blocky top of the feature. Mantle and top out the rest of the slab slightly right of the arête.

☐ 2. **Angerbeast V7** ★
Just right of the very blunt left arête of the stream-facing side, start with a high reach to the crimpy not-so-sweet spots on the highly sloping rail directly in front of two small saplings. Dead point to the obvious sloping feature a couple feet above. Ascend the obvious ledges straight up, using friable sidepulls over the left side of the high arête [careful!] to eventually gain small stabilizing holds with your right and good 'thank-god' holds on the left side of the arête with your left to pull the easy mantle.

Big Sexy Boulder South Face

☐ 3. **Big Sexy Slabs V0-V3** ★
Many large undercling and side-pull flakes exist to ascend the compelling downstream face of this large boulder. Again, bring a brush to clean holds in situ, though the most obvious features have been cleaned.

☐ 4. **Coconut Brassiere V0** ★
Layback the sharp arête that points directly upslope/away from the river.

☐ 5. **Curiosity Killed the George V?**
On the blank upstream face, sprint and scramble up the steep slab, catching an unlikely, but ok, sloping hold on the bottom edge of the obvious dip in the center of the face and match to mantle out. While this hold seems more unlikely to hang than the more squared sections of the boulder's lip, the six less inches of vertical needed to obtain these grips seems critical.

APE CITY

Rehab Rock

Ape City is a cool little spot to chill in the summer because it faces north. Sometimes the river is hard to cross. Do not try to cross the river if the water is too high or running too fast. Some problems are tall so bring pads and spotters. Most problems have seen only a few ascents so they may seem a little dirty. Watch for the poison ivy in the summer. Many other problems have been done, but only the best ones have been listed here.

A. REHAB BLOCK

Jabba the Hut Boulder

☐ 1. **V2** ★
Start low on jug, move right to arête and up face.

☐ 2. **V4** ★
Start on opposing gastons. Move to layback edge, then long move to edge out right.

☐ 3. **V1** ★
Move up slab to top.

B. JABBA THE HUT BOULDER

☐ 1. **Jabba V4** ★★
Stand start, move up and right.

Gunslinger Boulder

C. GUNSLINGER BOULDER

☐ 1. **Gunslinger V7** ★★
Left crimp, right sidepull. Move up arête to right-hand jug, then out left to jug.

☐ 2. **Illegal Cowpoke V8** ★★
Essentially a variation: start sitting as for *Gunslinger* and use crimps, slopers, and gastons to build your feet and ascend the slabby face trending to the right of the arête. The arête itself is not 'off'; one must naturally avoid the holds on the left face.

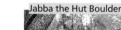

D. SIMIAN ADVENTURE BLOCK

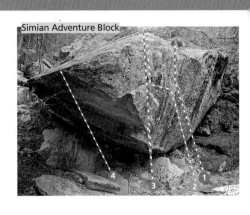

Simian Adventure Block

❒ 1. Liza's Lockoff V9 ★★★ 🎱

Climb the 'rail' problem proper-style, from the lowest start through the direct top out. Sticking and matching the lip is the crux, though it has been said that wishing Chuck's kid sister a happy birthday will bring good luck. A good edgy gaston out right will help you roll over with confidence. This problem should be a clean bet for even the most egregious dabber.

❒ 2. See No Evil V8 ★★ 🎱

Start as for #1 and slap and slope your way up to the terminus of the rail, pick out some tricky feet, and power out left to a juggy sidepull meeting with the top out of *Simian Adventure*.

❒ 3. Simian Adventure V5 ★★★ 🎱

Start with the left hand on crimp pinch and the right on a sidepull. Get a heel placement and go to a good jug. Surf left, then lunge to flake. Top out by going straight up.

❒ 4. Banana Slap V10 ★

A few feet right of *Sgt. Fury*, start standing at a good left sidepull and a sloping crimp and dyno through this steep over-hang to the sweet spots on the sloping lip. Top out straight or by traversing a few feet to the left. The grade will depend highly on your height and dyno ability.

❒ 5. Sargeant Fury V3 ★

Sds at the flake. Pull over bulge.

HIDDEN VALLEY

A nice spot to get away from the vehicular traffic and practice some mean slab and crimping skills close to the ground. The boulder described here is the best one found so far but other boulders are up the right drainage 140 yards; in the left drainage less than 200 yards west from the Pink Boulder are a couple of small and uneventful developed blocks.

PINK BOULDER

A clean 10-foot pink granite boulder covered in edges. Two small blocks sit in front of the south face and a dilapidated fort is next to the boulders' west face.

Pink Boulder

❒ 1. South Face V1 ★ 🎱

Climb the south face all the way to the top.

❒ 2. V1 🎱

Work up perfect pink edges.

❒ 3. V3 ★★ 🎱

Climb the blunt southeast arête starting with the left hand on a good edge at bottom of mini right-facing corner and pop-ping to a good edge on the arête. To the top!

❒ 4. Soooo Haaaard V8 ★★ 🎱

An incredibly heinous vertical affair that is way freakin' harder than it looks. Atrocious, tricky feet to start, with the right hand on an excellent flat edge on the east face and a super-thin edge for the left. Try and stick the first move then pray you can figure out the reachy top move, all in a ten-foot span.

❒ 5. V2 ★★ 🎱

Right side of east face starting on low jug and finishing on the northeast arête.

UNHIDDEN HILL

The sister boulderfield to Hidden Valley. The boulders at the base of this talus field were established recently. The Riverside Boulder is the best as far as bad landings go, although a few pads and attentive spotters will keep anyone from rolling down the hill into the river. Doesn't it sound great so far?

RIVERSIDE BOULDER

An attractive newly developed boulder with a clean, fairly tall northeast arête. Many holds abound on the faces with low starts available for the industrious sort.

Mike Freischlag on Riverside Boulder Photo: Krong

❏ 1. **East Face V5**
A one-move wonder starting off chest-high sidepulls with little bitty feet. Dyno to a sloping left-hand hold then use the good edges and jug on the face.

❏ 2. **V1**
Climb the left-leaning corner utilizing good laybacks.

❏ 3. **It's All On V3** 🌀
Climb up the northeast arête using all the good holds on the east and north face.

❏ 4. **It Ain't Over Till It's Over V4** 🌀
Climb up the left side of the north face starting from the low jug using the arête and good north face holds.

❏ 5. **Break It to Me Roughly V6** 🌀
This is what will happen to your coccyx if you don't have plenty of pads and good spotters. Not a suggested problem for the faint of heart. Start low on the left-leaning and sloping arête and finish by moving left to *IAOTIO*.

Scott Neel on Banana Slap V10 Ape City   Photo: Andy Mann

Bennett Scott

When I first moved to the Front Range I was a total gumbie with stars in his eyes. Coming from Ohio, this was the place for *real* rock climbing. All those misconceptions brought on by the media, gave me the delusion that I was walking into a different dimension where the real rock climbers roam. I also heard that Colorado was totally tapped. All the classics were found, chalked, polished destroyed, rebolted, than pooped upon all over again. Nothing was left to explore or develop. I didn't care though, I just wanted to climb the hard beautiful stuff and have fun running around the woods with friends. Eventually I climbed something that somebody said was a first ascent. "Nahhh," I retorted, "this is Colorado, some old guy did it years ago." But sure enough I had derived a sequence through uncharted territory, and the rest is history. Nothing feels as worthy anymore unless its a FA. I waste countless rainy snowy days wandering around Northern Colorado, hoping and dreaming I will find a piece of stone that motivates me to climb it. Grades and difficulty took a back seat to the discovery and creation of new movement on new stone with nobody around to care. I can't imagine living anywhere else in the US. Yeah it sucks sometimes, but in the end my friends and I can climb FA's every weekend without repeating a problem. Everytime I thinks it's all been climbed, I find a motivated searcher who took his dose of optimism and set out to get as lost in the mountains as I do. The amount of rock on the Front Range is finite, but I hope it lasts until I'm returned back to the dirt.

Top 7:

1. **Pinch Overhang V5 (Horsetooth Reservoir)**
2. **Bolt Wall V0 (Horsetooth Reservoir)**
3. **Standard, Mental Block V4 (Horsetooth Reservoir)**
4. **Kahuna Roof V6 (Carter Lake)**
5. **Ghostdance V6 (Millenium Boulder)**
6. **Germ Free Adolescence V5 (Eldorado Canyon)**
7. **Right Eliminator, Horsetooth**

Fred Knapp on North Shelf Block   Photo: Jim Thornburg

MOUNT SANITAS

An amazing mountain laced with beautifully colored sandstone boulders. Superb conditions can be found on Sanitas throughout the year. The mountain is named for the old Boulder Sanitas Sanitorium. Sanitas means health, and with the excellent hiking, running, bouldering and scenery it has certainly become a provider of health.

Directions: From Broadway in Boulder drive west on Mapleton Avenue past the hospital and park for Mt. Sanitas. Take the trail headed north (left) and go up and west over a small aqeuduct around Mt. Sanitas on an obvious landscaped trail. The boulders are on the right after the steep, landscaped section. Note: Use designated climbing approaches and be ever careful of the eroding hillsides. Vast amounts of hard work have been done to protect this heavily traveled area. Boulders are listed from the first encountered as one hikes up the trail.

SANITAS PROPER
The first wall covered in chalk and close to the trail.

❒ **1. V0** ★
Traverse the bottom of the wall either way.

❒ **2. V1** ★★ 🌀🌀
A tall face in the middle of the wall. Good laybacks and edges lead to the arete or continue higher to the top on the face.

SOUTH SHELF BLOCKS-LOWER WALL
The wall just left of Sanitas Proper. A tree hugs a small wall with a long, low traverse across its face that follows a distinct horizontal crack.

❒ **1. V1** ★ 🌀
The face directly right of the tree that climbs above the crack splitting the wall.

❒ **2. V1** ★
Traverse, in either direction, the line of jugs that form the crack in the face.

SOUTH SHELF BLOCKS-UPPER FACE

❒ **1. V1** ★★
Start at the lowest angle rock between South and North Shelf Blocks and traverse right.

❒ **2. V0** ★★★ 🌀🌀
The gorgeous line up the tallest part of the face. A true classic for the grade.

NORTH SHELF BLOCK-UPPER BLOCK

❒ **1. V2** ★★
Traverse the entire expanse of North and South Shelf Blocks from left to right. Cruxes are found at both ends.

❒ **2. V1** ★
The leftmost face problem avoiding the shallow pocket and climbing just right of the arete.

❒ **3. V0** ★★ 🌀
The face a couple of feet right of #2 that climbs through a chalked chockstone.

❒ **4. V1** ★★ 🌀
Just left of the tree is a nice straight-up problem.

❒ **5. V0's**
Two problems are right of the tree before the low-angle stone between North and South Shelf Blocks.

THE TURD BOULDER
A lone block on the east face of Sanitas. Walk over the ridge from the left side of North Shelf Block and go south. A distinct steep boulder is on the hillside. Problems are contrived and range from V4 to V8. Other problems are in the vicinity on tall faces.

Sanitas Proper

Lower Wall

Upper Block

Lynn Hill on The Turd Boulder   Photo: Fred Knapp

Twin Fins

These boulders are a short distance up the trail from North Shelf Block. The fin closest to the trail has very easy problems on secure holds. The back fin climbs on some questionable rock, but the crimp problems are fun.

Front Fin
The taller fin close to the trail.

Front Fin

☐ **1. V0**
A short face that starts off an excellent undercling on the left side of the wall.

☐ **2. V0** ★★ 😊
The obvious crack splitting the wall.

☐ **3. V1** ★ 😊
The face right of the crack.

☐ **4. V0** ★
The rightmost problem on the face.

☐ **5. V2** ★
Traverse the wall from right to left.

Back Fin
The fin east of the Front Fin with small edges.

Back Fin

☐ **1. V0**
The leftmost face problem.

☐ **2. V2** ★★ 🌐
Climb up the middle of the face on a thin line of crimps that lead to a big, flat edge and the loose top-out.

☐ **3. V2** ★★ 🌐
The face just left of the arete. Stay on thin edges and move up to the good edge that is found on the previous problem.

☐ **4. Traverse V4** ★★
Traverse from right to left staying low. Small crimps and bad feet.

CORNER ROCK

Up the trail a short distance is a small boulder with a blunt arete.

❏ **1. V0** ★
The problem on the face left of the blunt arete.

❏ **2. V2** ★
A sds that finishes going left after getting situated on the face.

❏ **3. V0**
The right problem. Can be used as the downclimb.

Corner Rock

CLASSY WALL

Just around the left corner of Corner Rock is a superb face with a multitude of possibilities. Most problems on this face are V0 to V1, with some dyno eliminates on the right side checking in a little harder. The traverse, usually done from right to left, is V1.

Classy Wall

P² TRAVERSE

An obscure butt-dragging traverse in the V3 range has long existed on the micro wall just above the trail.

P² Traverse

RIDGE GAP WALL

The final bouldering wall with clean problems. A short, flat hike up the trail from Corner Rock brings one to this long wall. A well-chalked V-shaped block in the middle of the wall defines the face.

❏ **1. V1** ★★
Traverse the wall from left to right. Try to keep your feet off the ground.

❏ **2. V0** ★
The leftmost face problem on the wall.

❏ **3. V0** ★★
The face that climbs up utilizing the V-shaped block.

❏ **4. V0** ★
A tad harder than the other straight up faces. Follows the seam with decent laybacks and shallow jams.

Ridge Gap Wall

LAST PROBLEM

A V2 highball just past the Ridge Gap Wall offers the last chance for decent bouldering on the way to the summit.

Lynn Hill on Last Problem V2   Photo: Fred Knapp

Jody Hansen on Hollow's Way V8   Photo: Brian Solano

FLAGSTAFF MOUNTAIN

Flagstaff is one of the best and most popular bouldering areas in the state. With views of Boulder, excellent trails and picnic areas it serves as a quick fix to city life. The coarse Fountain sandstone has allowed hundreds of wonderful, although sometimes painful, boulder problems to be established over the decades. Flagstaff problems are the products of many outstanding and devoted boulderers. Pat Ament, Jim Holloway, Bob Williams, Jim Michael, Skip Guerin, Christian Griffith, Jim Karn and others have climbed wonderful problems by attaching their emaciated bodies to the micro-crimps, pebbles and coarse slopers. Considering many of the oldest problems have thwarted the ever-increasing strength of modern boulderers it stands as a testament to their difficulty. Such disgustingly sick problems as *Trice, Over Yourself, Direct Just Right* (just plain gross), and *Reverse UCT* are but a sampling of the most difficult and finger wrenching nightmares. The mortal classics on Flagstaff start with such marvelously fun and easy problems as *Y Right* on the Upper Y Traverse, *Monkey Traverse*, King Conquer's layback, *Southwest Overhang* on Beer Barrel, and many others. For those boulderers playing in the ever-pleasant realm of V3 to V5, problems like the ultra classic *Hagan's Wall* will satisfy your cravings. Be sure and think about *Consideration*, the *Right Side* of Red Wall, First Overhang and *Gill Direct* at the Amphitheater. Taking a jaunt up the V scale you might be faced with *Smith's Overhang, Just Right,* and *Hollow's Way.* With problems all over the scale, a boulderer can enjoy the pine-covered hillsides and relative peace found in and around the beautiful boulders throughout the year.

Mileages are given from the first ranger (fee collection) kiosk located on the east side of the road near the Panorama Point overlook.

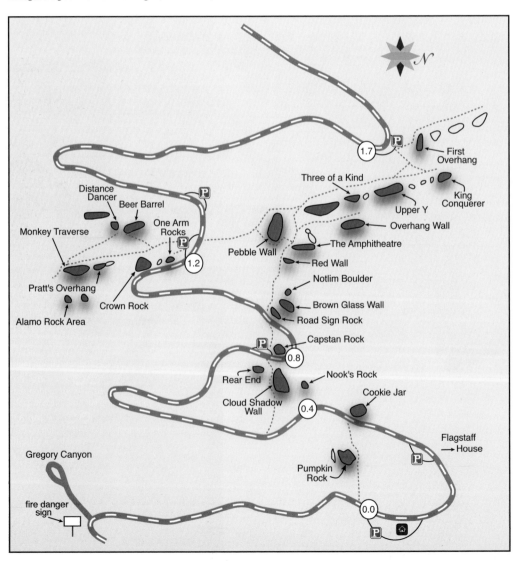

PUMPKIN ROCK

The first boulder found on Flagstaff that offers decent climbing. The boulder sits in a large meadow to the left of the first ranger (fee collection) kiosk. Pumpkin Rock is a very popular toprope boulder, although all of the routes/problems have been climbed sans rope.

❐ 1. West Face Left V3 🔟🔵

Climb the face directly right of the toprope problems. An Ament problem from the 60s.

❐ 2. Yellow Hammer V6 ★★ 🔟🔵

Just right of #1 is a tufa-like feature, a huge move, and a terrible landing!

❐ 3. West Face Right V1 🔟🔵

The next face right has another Ament problem. Fragile rock. A sds adds some flavor.

COOKIE JAR ROCK

The Cookie Jar is directly uphill from Pumpkin Rock. A well-beaten trail leads to the road and the Cookie Jar sits adjacent to the road on the opposite side. Driving from the kiosk the boulder is 0.3 miles up the road on the right. A number of good problems can be found on this boulder and are usually toproped.

❐ 1. Russian Nose V1 ★

The overhang to the left of the crack.

❐ 2. Cookie Jar Crack V0 🔟

Considered a toprope due to its height, but the ease of the problem allows for a confident ascent.

❐ 3. The Shield V1 🔟

The face directly to the right of the crack dissecting the boulder on the south side.

❐ 4. Commitment V2

On the right side of the north face a nice bulge can be surmounted.

❐ 5. Jackson's Pitch V2 ★★ 🔟

Next to *Commitment* is another bulge that starts with an undercling move to good edges.

❐ 6. Kor's Corner V0 🔟

A big right-angling dihedral next to the road.

❐ 7. Northcutt's Roll V? 🔟🔵

On the southeast face is a steep lichen-striped wall.

❐ 8. Rough One V2

Located just below Cookie Jar. A short overhang leads to an open dihedral.

CRYPTIC BOULDER

This boulder is on the right as you head down from the guardrail as for the preferred approach to Nook's Rock.

❐ 1. Cryptic Magician V7 ★★ 🔟

Start squeezing at almost full wingspan on the rounded northeast corner. Bump into hard-to-see underclings and crimps to a thin but reasonable topout. Cryptic!

❐ 2. Cryptic Tips V5 ★

Start on obvious matched holds on the east face and go straight up by crimping the be-jesus out of pebbles!

Pumpkin Rock

Cookie Jar Rock

Cryptic Boulder

NOOK'S ROCK

A well-hidden boulder located up the road from the Cookie Jar. It is 0.4 miles from the kiosk. There are two ways to reach it. Either park at the overlook past the first kiosk and walk the trail up Flagstaff (Nook's Rock is directly above the trail after crossing the road from Pumpkin Rock. The preferred parkin-spot is at Capstan (0.8 miles from the kiosk). Walk downhill next to the Brown Glass Wall and Nook's Rock is at the base of the hill before the Flagstaff Trail.

❏ **1. Westside Traverse V7** ★★
A long problem with stacks of tiny slopers and pebbles that traverses across the west face. It is best done from left to right. Try not to rest against the tree when the pump starts coming. New beta has the problem coming in at V9 from a sds way down on the left and finishing even further right.

❏ **2. Wimpie's Revenge V0** ★
On the west face is a straight up problem next to the pine tree. Other choices abound for contrived face routes.

❏ **3. South Face V0** ★★
Numerous fun slab problems that are attempted sans hands.

❏ **4. The Scoop V0**
Just to the left of *Butt Slammer* and starting off a small boulder. This problem climbs easy terrain.

❏ **5. Botslayer V10**
Begin on a jug on the left side of *Butt Slammer*. Jog to a crimper with the right hand and end with a big move out left to a rockover. A sds goes at V11.

❏ **6. Butt Slammer V?**
As this disintegrating pile of rock continues to clean up, it remains a proud, and undone, severely overhanging problem with difficult moves. Climb at the risk of busting your arse. *Slut Bammer* V6 starts down and right and surfs up and left along the sloping arete to the apex, and rocks over. Spooky!

❏ **7. Northeast Undercut V2**
A rather sharp affair. Climb the filthy wall, which faces the road. A broom is handy for cleaning the top-out.

❏ **8. Window Shopper V11** ★
Sharp problem on the northeast face. Starts on the far left side close to a small block and moves up and right on sharp crimps and wicked slopers. A decent short problem called *Dont Touch the Glass* V7 climbs the face on the right side from a stand start.

❏ **9. That Flakes It V1 or V4** ★★
A small rock that faces Nook's Rock. A motherlode of chalk defines these problems. Either climb the leftmost rail to the top (V1) or pull onto the overhang in the middle and make a hard throw (V4).

JIM HALL BOULDER

This long overlooked boulder is 47 feet south of *That Flakes It*. Walk up a small footpath (not the Flagstaff Trail) to a short boulder (this path leads up to Cloud Shadow, it is defined by the immense amount of broken glass and trash that mindless drunks pitch off the Cloud Shadow boulder). Many short enjoyable problems can be found on the hillside surrounding this boulder.

❏ **1. The Jim Hall Traverse V5** ★★
Start on the bottom left jugs and traverse the lip holds around to a finishing grovel on the west face.

❏ **2. Battaglia's Bottom V7**
Start on the right side of the flake a few feet off the ground, halfway along #1. Make a really long move to the lip of the boulder and finish up and right through a tooth hold.

❏ **3. The Pillar V2** ★
Directly right of *The JH Traverse* finish is an overhanging pillar. Climb the good incuts up the left side. Not pictured.

Nook's Rock

Butt Slammer

That Flakes It

Jim Hall Boulder

CAPSTAN ROCK

Capstan is located on the left side of the road 0.8 mile from the kiosk. A pull-out, new landscaping and immense amounts of chalk highlight this boulder. This boulder is a pocket-lover's dream. Many topropes exist on this rock but the near endless choice of holds allows the boulder to be downclimbed in a number of places. One through three are not pictured.

☐ 1. North Face V0
A tall problem that starts in the road and climbs to the summit.

☐ 2. Northeast Mantle V0
A mantle problem found on the northeast corner.

☐ 3. Northwest Edges V1 ★★
Climb the edges to the summit. Be ever so careful at the top as the sloping finish is disheartening.

☐ 4. West Face V1 ★★ ☺
A fun, long problem up the face. Good holds abound but reaches are necessary.

☐ 5. South Crack V2 ☺
Climb the pin-scarred crack up and right. *Sarabande* (V0) is an extension on the South Crack that climbs to the summit.

☐ 6. South Overhang V2 - V6 ★★
A multitude of contrivances fills this small overhang just to the right of the crack. Good footwork is imperative for the reaches and throws.

☐ 7. Just Right V7 ★★★
Arguably the best problem for the grade on Flagstaff. Starts on the opposing pinches and punches up and left then a dynamic move reaches the obvious pocket. The top-out is frightening with long reaches and thin edges. A direct sds start has broken since it was established long ago and remains Flagstaff's best hard project. *Just Wrong* V8 bypasses the left seam/hold and throws directly to the pocket then up. Many other harder and historic variations exist as well.

☐ 8. Diverse Traverse V2 - V5
Starts at the sloping jug at the base of *Just Right* and moves left. The further along the wall one traverses the more difficult the problem. An excellent traverse for contrivances.

☐ 9. The Oxman Arete V10 ★★
Starts as a sds between #7 and #10 on a crystal and a slopey pocket, power up into a crimper rail at the sloping lip and surf back along left on tiny crimpers and top out #7. Starting the same and throwing right into #10 is a stellar V8.

☐ 10. The Trough V0
The bulge just right of *Just Right*. It ends in the trough above *Just Right* and is actually part of the downclimb off the boulder.

Justin Roth on Just Right V7 photo: Andy Mann

CORWIN SIMMON'S ROCK

This boulder is situated on the left side of the road before reaching Capstan Rock. The lack of chalk may attest to the popularity of these problems. Crown Simmon's Rock is not pictured.

CLOUD SHADOW

Cloud Shadow holds some of the best problems on Flagstaff from long traverses to short power problems. Problems are listed from the left of the wall to the right. One point to consider at Cloud Shadow is the hundreds of holds to choose from. Contrived problems on this boulder can keep a boulderer busy for years. At the far left end is a small overhanging block next to a thin gap between Cloud Shadow and an adjacent boulder (The Alcove). Numerous problems also exist in this area.

To get to Cloud Shadow park at the Capstan Boulder (0.8 mile from the kiosk) and walk to the hairpin turn and go over the guard rail on its right. A gravel trail leads down the hillside. Skirt left when a long boulder appears from behind the trees to the left.

❒ 1. Launching Pad V4

The farthest left problem. The easiest way to find this problem is go left two problems from *Hagan's Wall* (a continuously chalked line between the two small boulders just right). Small edges are the business on this sharp problem. A low direct start, *Soon to be Souvenir* V8, climbs through the glued pink pebble from a poor toothy crystal and a bad undercling.

❒ 2. Dandy Line V7 ★

Directly left of *Hagan's Wall* is a dynamic move from two small holds. Starts off the boulder left of #3. Disintegrating.

❒ 3. Hagan's Wall V5 ★★★

A classic problem. Starts contorted to reach the first holds. Once situated on the wall with an edge and pocket, throw to the sloping edge then again to the pebbles and up. A few variations exist to this problem. Low start is V10.

❒ 4. Shadowline V9

Starts just right of Hagan's and joins *Hand Traverse*. Crimpy! A kindred line known as *Yo Jimbo*, which once climbed though similar territory, has now broken into oblivion.

❒ 5. Hand Traverse V2 ★★

Climb the ramp that goes up above the gently overhanging wall where *Shadowline* climbs.

❒ 6. Cloud Shadow Traverse V4 ★★

Many variations exist on this traverse. The higher traverse on good pockets is easier. Start at *Consideration* and traverse the wall as far as possible then up. At the obvious pocket (at chest height and roughly in the middle of the traverse between *Consideration* and *Hagan's Wall*) a one-move wonder called *William's Pull* (V4) matches in the pocket and reaches a large solution pocket up and left. A super low traverse can be done at V7, and linking *Reverse UCT* into this is a V11, called *Trolling for Mank*. Contrivances abound!

❒ 7. Contemplation V1 ★★ 😎

Start to the left of *Moderate Bulge* and traverse up and left on a shallow crack. Pull up and over the high bulge.

❒ 8. Moderate Bulge V0 ★★ 😎

Left of *Consideration* is a large hole eight feet off the deck. Undercling this hole and reach to the downsloping shelf—good edges—and pull up and to the right.

❒ 9. Undercling Traverse V9 ★★

This is a very popular problem. Start at *Contemplation* and undercling like crazy past the small holds under the bulge then finish groveling up *East Inside Corner*. A reverse of *UCT* has been done that finishes up *Consideration* (V10).

❒ 10. Consideration V4 ★★★ 😎

Start on the deep sideways pocket below the hole on *Contemplation* and reach up and slightly right to a flat edge on the wall. Match and pull through to the sloping shelf. Starting this problem with the right hand in the hole and pulling up to the same holds is called *Reverse Consideration* V4. Both of these problems are high quality and a blast.

❒ 11. Trice V12 ★★ 😎

The hardest couple of moves on Flagstaff. Start left hand on the thin crimp/layaway down and right of *Consideration* (the last holds before diving under the bulge on *UCT*)—the right on an undercling under the bulge and pull up to an improbable and extremely shallow pocket. From there an invisible edge resides up and left of the pocket, then up to the rail. *AKR* (*Another Karn Route*) is a variation that pulls to the shallow pocket with the left hand then throws with the right to the top rail. *Epochalypse* (V13) does *Reverse UCT* into *Trice*.

❒ 12. Bob's Bulge V5 ★

Start on the holds under the bulge and slap up and over to the bottom of the sloping shelf then toe hook and climb left. Start on #11 is *Holloway Direct* V7.

❒ 13. East Inside Corner V0 ★

Climb the open dihedral at the far right end of Cloud Shadow.

THE PEDESTAL BOULDER

At the far right end of Cloud Shadow (facing the boulder) is a small bulbous boulder with a few fun problems.

❒ 1. The Roof V1 ★

A short overhang problem starting on *Pedestal Traverse* and pulling straight up and over. Other variations exist.

❒ 2. Pedestal Traverse V2 ★

Start at the bottom of the chalked sloping ramp and climb up and around right using the high discontinuous flake/crack.

❒ 3. V0 ★★

An easy, short problem climbs straight into the finish of #2.

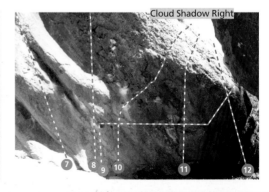

Cloud Shadow Left

Cloud Shadow Right

Jamie Emerson makes the third ascent of Trice V12 (thirty years after the first) Photo: Andy Mann

THE ALCOVE

On Cloud Shadow's north face. There is a tight gap with problems all around it. Approach left of *Hagan's Wall*.

☐ 1. East Overhang V2 ★★
Climb the crack to a difficult mantle-like finish. *Alcove Dyno* V7 makes the five foot dyno just left at the corner.

☐ 2. Curmudgeon V7 ★★ 🌀
Start down and right of #1 on a right-facing sidepull and climb small edges to the top. All feet are on, but the vertical crack and the handholds associated with it are off.

☐ 3. Sailor's Delight V1 ★★ 🎯🌀
The epitome of off-the-deck. Facing the gap look up and left to a large roof. That's it!

☐ 4. Allegro Bulge V2 ★★
The problem right of the gash in the gap.

☐ 5. Crack Allegro V1 ★★
The open gash on the right wall of the gap.

☐ 6. Stranger than Friction V6 ★★ 🌀
Located on the roof behind and north of The Alcove. Sds on the detached pinch down and right, roll left through the roof and finish left or direct through the groove above the roof. *Pulp Friciton* V6 goes straight up from the starting block pinch using it for feet as well.

☐ 7. Pawn V5 ★
Right off the road at the Cloud Shadow turn next to a yellow diamond reflector in a pine tree is a short arete, the detached block down and left is off. Hard top-out.

REAR END ROCK

This south-facing boulder is found by turning right (the opposite direction to reach Cloud Shadow) after dropping down the hill from the guardrail. Walk past a stand of pines and the problems appear. The problems face down hill toward the Flagstaff Trail and a dead tree lies near the base. Like all of Flagstaff, other varations exist.

☐ 1. Left Bulge V5 ★★
The difficult face left of the crack. Jumpstart and slap up the sloping holds on the face. *Tongue in Cheek* V9 starts matched on the undercling. A thrutchy V5 sds is way down and left and finishes on the arete four feet to the left.

☐ 2. The Crack V4
The problem that pulls through the flared, sharp crack.

☐ 3. Gluteus Maximus V6 ★
Climb the bulge on the right from opposing sidepulls.

ROAD SIGN ROCK

Across the road from Capstan is a short boulder with drilled pockets (the pockets face the road).

☐ 1. Road Side Traverse V4 ★
Traverse the pockets from left to right. Shorter problems pull up and over before completing the traverse.

☐ 2. Northwestern Overhang V3 ★★
The opposite side has a problem that climbs slopers to positive pebbles. A V6 stays direct on tiny flat pebble crimpers.

☐ 3. Bucket V4 🌀
A problem on a steep block adjacent to the Road Sign Rock. Big pods define the face up to the dirty and difficult top-out.

The Pedestal Boulder

The Alcove East Overhang

Stranger than Friction

Pawn

Rear End Rock

Road Sign Rock

BROWN GLASS WALL

Below the Road Sign Rock is a massive boulder. Nearly every problem in this vicinity is highball and has atrocious landings. Topropes may be necessary. A few decent lines to V3 climb the boulder just left of #1.

☐ **1. Stem Rise V1** 😊 🎿

To the left of Brown Glass is another face problem starting with a giant stem off a boulder adjacent to the face. Vast amounts of lichen and choss are the name of this unpleasant game.

☐ **2. Back Extension V2** ★★ 😊 🎿

Directly to the left of the *Crack Slot*. Climbs the severely overhanging face with good edges, although the crux is off a hollow edge, 15 feet up and upside down. Danger! Use a toprope.

☐ **3. Crack Slot V2** 😊 🎿

On the left side of the wall is a deep gash up a steep wall.

☐ **4. V Crack V0** ★★ 😊 🎿

An easy crack in the middle of the wall. A thin flake at 2/3 height creates a substantial fear factor.

☐ **5. V1** ★★ 😊 🎿

Climb the chalked face immediately left of *Briggs'* through a pod/flake section just past the horizontal break at 2/3 height.

☐ **6. Fear on Layaway V4** ★ 😊 🎿

Another sketch-fest that starts as #5 and moves right into the top-out of #7.

☐ **7. Briggs' Bridges V2** ★ 😊 🎿

A bold problem on the right side of the wall. It climbs the arete up positive edges and pebbles. A terrible and uneven landing on roots.

☐ **8. Brown Glass Overhang V6** ★ 🎿

Low sds on the west face that powers into a juggy arete and trends right.

NOTLIM BOULDER

As you walk down the hillside from the Road Sign Rock you will see an indiscreet boulder out to the left and even with the Brown Glass Wall on the hillside. The wall facing down-slope has one of the most aesthetic and difficult lines on Flag.

☐ **1. Botsy's Way V5**

A grungy little V5 climbs out the cave to the left from a sds.

☐ **2. Hollow's Way V8** ★★ 🎿

A shallow dihedral with micro-crimps and bad feet leads to the top-out. A bolt has been placed on the top for those not desiring a dose of high bouldering.

☐ **3. Right Dihedral V2**

The disgustingly dirty dihedral around the right corner from *Hollow's Way*. Not recommended.

Brown Glass Wall

Brown Glass Overhang

Notlim Boulder

Pratt's Overhang

MONKEY TRAVERSE & RED WALL AREA

The parking lot for this area's boulders is located 1.2 miles up the road from the kiosk. Since this area is undoubtedly the most popular for climbers, hikers, picnickers and resident Boulder oddballs, additional parking is just up the road on the right.

ONE ARM ROCKS

Immediately left of the parking lot (facing away from the road) and adjacent to the pay station. A jumble of rocks that got their distinction from protracted bouts with one-arm mantles and crimping. This is an excellent area to use two hands!

☐ 1. Smith's Face V0 ★★
Climb the slab with one damn arm if you can. Using both arms is V0. Bad, bad footholds to start.

☐ 2. One Arm Arete V1 (two hands) ★
Immediately left of the overhang is a thin problem up the arete.

☐ 3. One Arm Overhang V3 (one armed)
On the short overhang left of the *Right Hand Mantle* is a problem that steps over the roof while climbing with only one arm. A one-armed sit start would be rather taxing. V0 using both hands.

☐ 4. Right Hand Mantle V2 (one armed) ★★
Probably one of Ament's best known mantle problems. Climb the wall facing the road up and left to, you guessed it, a one-arm mantle. V0 with two hands.

One Arm Rocks

CROWN ROCK
Directly behind the One Arm Rocks is a massive boulder/slab. Individual problems are not listed and the rock is not pictured. A good place for beginners to practice friction.

PRATT'S OVERHANG
This boulder is located by walking south away from the parking lot and the relative security of the car. New railings and closed trails fill the entire hillside. The boulder is approximately 150 feet from the parking lot and faces west; standing looking away from the boulder and downhill is the Beer Barrel. The Monkey Traverse is just past Pratt's, another 30 feet. Problems are listed from the left to the right.

☐ 1. Pratt's Mantle V2 ★
The sloping shelf on the left side at arms reach. Get a hold and mantle like you mean it.

☐ 2. Aerial Burial V3 ★★
A double dyno from the lowest edges below *Pratt's Mantle*.

☐ 3. Pratt's Overhang V2 ★
The gash to the right has a problem that climbs up, through, and nearly inside the open crack.

☐ 4. Smith's Overhang V7 ★
Folks begin this many different ways. The true problem starts low before the glued undercling. This problem is extremely difficult and sharp. A spotter is recommended as the ground can demolish an open hand in the inevitable, explosive fall.

☐ 5. Gill Swing V4 ★
Starts on a down-facing edge and swings all the way past the crystal to the top. Hard.

☐ 6. Crystal Corner V2 ★
The same start as the *Gill Swing* but uses the obvious crystal to gain the top.

Jim Garber takes a sunset lap on Monkey Traverse V4

Monkey Traverse Crag

The unequivocal reigning king for the most popular boulder.

☐ **1. West Overhang V1** ★★

In the middle of the traverse is an easy, although highball problem. Classic.

☐ **2. Million Dollar Spider V2**

Climbs the loose flake just right of the open groove/dihedral. This problem has a bad landing and begs for an attentive spot.

☐ **3. Shallow Slot V4** ★

The far right problem that laybacks the right-leaning crack. Gritty on top!

☐ **4. Monkey Traverse V4** ★★★

Classic. Long, pumpy, fun and a little scary at the end. A low traverse that avoids all upper holds can be done at V10 or so.

Monkey Traverse

Beer Barrel Rock

Beer Barrel is the first boulder west reached from the trail leading across the meadow from Monkey Traverse. A picnic table is close to its east face.

☐ **1. East Slab V0** ★

The low-angle slab with a wide groove splitting its expanse. Used as the downclimb for all the problems.

☐ **2. Southeast Arete V5** ★★

On the southeast arete is a set of slopers at waist height. Climb through these slopers to small edges. A undercling sds with a key kneebar is *Beached Whale* V6.

☐ **3. Poling Pebble Route V5** ★★

The pebble is gone but sharp crystals and bad feet remain. A classic problem for the grade. Just left of #2.

☐ **4. South Face V0** ★★

Pure fun on nice edges. A long reach over the top-perched boulder finishes the enjoyment.

☐ **5. Southwest Corner V0** ★★★

Top ten for Flagstaff. Climbs the overhanging flake system at the far right of *West Traverse*.

☐ **6. Hritz Overhang V3** ★

So close to the *Southwest Corner* you could kiss it. Slightly contrived but well worth it. Climbs the pocket and sloping pebble just left of the flake system. A nice V8 is just left.

☐ **7. West Traverse V4** ★★★

A forearm burn not easily matched on Flagstaff. Finish #5.

☐ **8. Double Clutch V8** ★★★

On the northwest corner, grab the big jug rail, step your feet high, and huck for the broken/slopey jug below the lip.

☐ **9. NE Corner V6** ★★

This great problem starts where the west side traverse ends. Work across a few moves on the north side with bad feet until you can get to two edges on the northeast lip of the slab. From here make some big and insecure moves on slopers.

☐ **10. Beer Barrel Traverse V9** ★

Start on the underclings below #2 and traverse clockwise into the finish of #9. For those who have done it all!

Beer Barrel Rock

Nick Sherman on Shallow Slot V4 photo: Brian Solano

DISTANT DANCER PINNACLE

The boulder directly downhill (west) from Beer Barrel. A glue-encrusted hold on the far right side defines the boulder.

❒ **1. West Overhang V1 - V4** ★

This face has multiple problems. A traverse coming from around the right arete and finishing up the far left jugs is V3. The crack in the middle of the face has a difficult jam move, V4. Other straight up problems are V1 to V2.

❒ **2. Red Horn Overhang V1** ★

Climbs the far right low arete then veers left and up to the right of *West Overhang*.

❒ **3. Distant Dancer V6** ★ ★

Better off top-roped. This line takes the south face head on.

Distant Dancer Pinnacle

V5 TRAVERSE BOULDERS

❒ **1. V5** ★

A right to left traverse across two boulders 15 yards due south from Beer Barrel. The problem faces south. Difficulty can be adjusted by limiting footholds at the start. Not pictured.

TREE SLAB

This outstanding slab has four fun problems. It is located slightly down and right (south) from the Distant Dancer Pinnacle.

❒ **1. Slab Traverse V1** ★★

A traverse that skirts the lower section of the slab. Good footwork is imperative.

❒ **2. Classic Line V0** ★★

Behind the tree is a superb slab that climbs through the appropriately named "banana" hold, a foothold lacking any semblance of texture. Good pockets and edges lead up to nice pebbles. Downclimb the left (north) gully.

❒ **3. Layback Crack V0** ★★

Located slightly right of the tree. Tall and moderate. Down-climb the gully on the left of the slab.

❒ **4. V1** ★★

A tall problem slightly right of *Layback Crack*.

MISCELLANEOUS VALLEY

Down the hillside and west from Distant Dancer is a conglomeration of boulders that line the hill back towards the parking lot. To reach the boulders simply turn around from the Tree Slab and walk down and then right.

❒ **1. Arete V5** ★★

Below *Phantom Face*, go past small formations and find a boulder with many pebbles and a blunt arete. It is the last boulder before the drainage. Sds from an undercling slot just off the ground and climb the arete through a nice sloper finishing up and left.

❒ **2. Farming V4** ★★

Sit as for #1, move right, then up the slopey lip further right.

❒ **3. V0** ★★

An ultra-classic jug haul on the first boulder seen after walking down from Tree Slab. Not pictured.

❒ **4. Phantom Face V1** ★

Left of #3 is a tall slab on the right side of the big slot between two boulders. Underclings lead to small pebble pulling and friction moves. A tad on the bold side. Not pictured.

❒ **5. Short O V0** ★

Left of the *Phantom Face* on the next boulder's far right side. This boulder is well-chalked and can be identified by a small boulder lying next to it.

Tree Slab

Miscellaneous Valley

Miscellaneous Valley

Miscellaneous Valley

❑ 6. Traverse V2 ★★★

Starting the same as #5 is an excellent traverse on good holds. Finish up and left on slightly sloping edges. An excellent pump. A nice V2 climbs up direct into the finish from good holds.

❑ 7. V1 ★

The discontinuous seam just left of #4. Layback the offset arete to reach the top jugs.

❑ 8. Left Bulge V0

On a boulder just north of *Short O*. The bulge left of *Leaning Jam*.

❑ 9. Leaning Jam V1 ★

The easy, left-leaning crack on the boulder's left side.

❑ 10. Right Bulge V?

The bulge right of *Leaning Jam*. It was originally B1+ but the rock has felt nature's affects. A grovelly and lichen-covered bulge that was probably a good problem in the Pleistocene.

LITTLE ROCK

This is the boulder again left (north) of the boulder that contains *Leaning Jam*. Little Rock is not pictured.

❑ Fun Lieback V0

Climbs the shallow crack.

SOUTH END COVE

Uphill from the far right side of the Monkey Traverse are two right-leaning crack/slots slightly hidden from view as one looks up from the trail.

❑ 1. Left Hand Crack V1 ★

A bad landing is in store if the grovelly top-out goes badly.

❑ 2. Right Hand Crack V2 ★★

A sloping pinchfest. The better of the two cracks.

LITTLE SPUR ROCK

Forty odd feet right of South End Cove.

❑ 1. Little Spur V2 ★

Starts on the big undercling and climbs up the laybacks and shallow jams.

❑ 2. Spur Face V0 ★

Just around right is an easy problem that finishes on *Little Spur*.

❑ 3. V2

Twenty feet right is an overhang that starts on underclings and continues to a right-angling arete.

AID CRACK WALL AREA

A toproping wall that is found by walking down the main trail from the Monkey Traverse approximately 50 yards until a separate trail begins to meander left through the multiple miniature flatirons. *William's Mantle* is found on the left before the trail goes left and uphill and heads to the Aid Crack Wall. The first large wall seen up the left trail is Aid Crack Wall. Vast amounts of chalk highlight the Aid Crack (on the wall's left).

AID CRACK WALL

❑ 1. Shane's Traverse V2 ★

A long traverse starting on the lower right part of the wall and ending before the Aid Crack. Pebble pulling and solid layback reaches tell the story. A tad on the squatty side.

❑ 2. William's Mantle V1 ★

On a small boulder before heading up to the Aid Crack Wall. A pine stands in front of the boulder and right of the slick-looking mantle holds. Better done as a face climb. The mantle is substantially harder.

❑ 3. Ament's Bulge V1 ★

Just up and right on a separate boulder from *William's Mantle*. A fun, quick problem. Two moves of pebble pulling left of a chossy seam.

Aid Crack Wall Area

South End Cove

Little Spur

THE ALAMO ROCK AREA

Mainly a toprope area with a number of fine boulder problems gracing its lower flanks. This rock is best reached by walking south between Crown Rock and Pratt's Overhang. A well-worn trail heads south—stay on the lower (left) trail when it splits. A small boulder along the lower trail with graffiti spray painted on it is a good landmark. Continue south and Alamo Rock appears on the left after another 40 yards or so.

BULGING WALL

Attached to the bottom of Alamo Rock's west face. The wall is well chalked with pockets, jugs and a crack.

☐ **1. Bulging Face V1** ★★
Left of *Dalke* is a classic straight-up problem. Try not to climb into *Dalke Finger Crack*.

☐ **2. Dalke Finger Crack V1** ★
The crack on the left of the wall.

☐ **3. Rib Right V0** ★
Right of the crack is an easy face.

THE RIB BOULDER

A square boulder lying below the west face of Alamo Rock.

☐ **1. The Crease V0**
Jug haul central up the west face. Follows a left-leaning flake.

☐ **2. Arete It V1** ★★
Starts on good underclings on the right of the arete. Superb.

☐ **3. Face It V1** ★
An easy face climb just right of *Arete It*.

☐ **4. V2** ★
An overhanging problem within the slot down and right of *Face It*. Climbs the arete via good pinches.

THE CANDEL AREA

Be patient trying to find this secluded area. Head around the right side of The Alamo and go up two levels in the miniature flatirons. On the walk to the Candel Area pass a dead tree against a short bouldering wall—a distinct crack splits the left side of this boulder called Fingers Boulder. The Sunshine Slab is a south-facing gray wall at the lowest southern reaches of Candel Area.

FINGERS BOULDER

The first boulder encountered in The Candel Area.

☐ **1. Finger Arete V2** ★★
Left of the crack is an extremely good opposing crimp/layback problem.

☐ **2. Fingers Fingers V1** ★
The crack splitting the boulder.

☐ **3. Right Finger V2** ★★
A thin face problem beginning right of the crack and finishing before reaching the crack. Much harder from a low left sds.

WELDON'S BOULDER

By following the hillside south and dropping down another 200 yards is one of the mountains most obscure classics. It will take some effort when trying to locate this boulder. A few good warm-ups and moderates are on the left side of the boulder.

☐ **1. The Great Escape V7** ★★
Sit start on the arete from incut crimps and work right into the giant pod, fire straight up the face and finish slightly left in the groove via one delicate and scary top-out.

Bulging Wall

The Rib Boulder

Fingers Boulder

Weldon's Boulder

THE JUG

Slightly downhill (south) from Fingers Boulder is a large boulder facing west and defined by a beautiful red streak on its lower face.

❏ 1. The Ramp V1 ★★

A 22-foot-tall gray slab attached to the left side of The Jug. A classic problem with committing moves well off the deck.

❏ 2. Legacy of the Kid V1 ★★

Highball and classic with the discomfort of a loose flake at the crux. The grade assumes an early exit, as straight-up is harder.

❏ 3. Red Streak V0 ★

A tall red-streaked face that starts on small edges and climbs into progressively bigger holds up and right.

❏ 4. Right Red V0

Just to the right of *Red Streak* and almost around the corner.

❏ 5. Southwest Face V0 ★

Around the corner from *Red Streak* is a slab littered with pebbles.

The Jug

Muffet Rock

MUFFET ROCK

A hueco covered wall to the right of The Jug. It faces west and has numerous contrived problems in the V0 to V2 range.

SUNSHINE SLAB

This is a low-angle gray slab found at the farthest southern part of the Candel Area. It is downhill slightly from The Jug. Facing south it is an excellent boulder to climb in the winter. A number of pines stand in front of the wall. These problems are very tall. Formulate a plan for a careful retreat.

❏ 1. Bush Route V0 ★

On the left side of the slab.

❏ 2. Aerial Ballet V0 ★★

Slightly right is a tall slab with delicate footwork.

❏ 3. Difficult Route V2 ★★

A fairly delicate face just right of *Aerial Ballet*. A few of the pebbles appear on the verge of detaching from the wall.

❏ 4. Michael's Face V2 ★

A thin outing behind the tree closest the slab.

❏ 5. Nubbin Wall V0 ★

Big solid, pebble pulling.

❏ 6. Cave Hang V0 ★★★

Hidden in a slot approximately 20 feet right of Sunshine Slab is this excellent problem. A good fragile sit down start is V5.

❏ 7. Overhanging Prow V4 ★★

A classic problem that climbs a small prow facing the Sunshine Slab.

Sunshine Slab

Cave Hang

Overhang Prow

RED WALL / GREAT RIDGE

THE PEBBLE WALL

From the parking lot for the Monkey Traverse Area cross the road and walk north on the Flagstaff Trail. Do not follow the switchbacks, which begin after 40 odd yards, but walk towards a large boulder slightly hidden behind some pine trees—The Pebble Wall. Around the right, going north, past a small gap between Pebble Wall and a little boulder is North Rocks (two boulders sitting next to one another). Just past North Rocks, and again to the right (north), is Red Wall. Uphill (west) from North Rocks is The Amphitheatre.

❐ **1. West Corner V1** ★★
The left blunt arete. Starts on a deep three-finger pocket and up the arete with a long reach to gain the top. Many variations exist to this problem.

❐ **2. V1** ★ 🌓🌗
Just right start in the pod before the blunt arete. A little scary pulling over the top.

❐ **3. South Face V3** ★★ 🌓🌗
Another pebble-pulling affair right of #2 (seven feet left of *High Step*). Difficult footwork pulling onto the slab.

❐ **4. High Step V2** ★★ 🌓🌗
To the right of #3 (left two feet of #5) is an easier version of *Direct South Face*.

❐ **5. Direct South Face V2** ★★ 🌓🌗
Just right of *High Step* (left five feet of #6) is a more demanding problem. Start off a well-beaten root and climb straight up.

❐ **6. Crystal Mantle V3** ★★
Right of *Direct South Face* is a slabby face with a large crystal four feet up. Climb up and past the pebble with a mantle if necessary. A sds adds a little spice.

❐ **7. Original Route V1** ★
Right of the small boulder forming the gap is a tricky problem that climbs good pebbles. V4 from a sds. A couple fun and steep problems tackle the nose right.

❐ **8. Over Yourself V10** ★
This is the traverse of The Pebble Wall starting right of the *Crystal Mantle* and ending before *West Corner*. One of the hardest and most disgusting (on the fingertips) problems on Flagstaff. A few other varations exist to this problem.

❐ **9. Northwest Face V0**
Start the same as *Northwest Overhang* but climb left to avoid the top-out.

❐**10. Northwest Overhang V3** ★
Left of the blunt arete and out the middle of the overhang. A hard move gains the top pebbles. A V7 climbs out the right side of the overhang via cobble underclings.

Pebble Wall

Pebble Wall

Pebble Wall

NORTH ROCKS

The two small boulders that face the slabbiest side of The Pebble Wall.

❑ 1. Left V0

Climbs up the good edges over stairs.

❑ 2. Arete V3 ★★

The beautiful arete above the stone step on the upper boulder. A fairly tenuous reach gains the ramp top-out.

❑ 3. Drill Pig V7 ★

A varation that begins with a bad left hand crimp and small right hand mono. From there, go straight for the top with the benefit of a left heelhook on the arete. Originally done sans heel!

❑ 4. Right V0 ★

Climb the middle of the face on the lower boulder.

❑ 5. Sweet Nothings V8 ★

From an inobvious sds on a left-hand sidepull and right hand crimp, move up and slightly left on small holds. A V7 starts on the same left-hand sidepull and a right-hand undercling just around the bulge and goes to a series of right hand bumps until you get the decent sidepull.

North Rocks

Red Wall Area Overview

Ampitheater Right Side

North Rocks

Red Wall

The Red Wall

THE RED WALL

The boulder behind North Rocks. Multiple edges, pockets, and jugs define this vertical face. A tree used for downclimbing sits on the right side of the wall. This boulder's problems are nearly all ultra classics. Variations and extensions can reach V10.

☐ 1. **Left Side V1**

Climb the sharp edges, pebbles and pocket to the top. Seldom done since the other problems on the wall are far better. A long traverse of Red Wall starts as a sit down below this problem and traverses right.

☐ 2. **Center Left V4** ★★★ 🌀

Starts just left of the pod (five feet off the deck) in the middle of the wall. Pull up with the right hand to a good, three-finger pocket then to a small crystal pinch and the top.

☐ 3. **Standard Route V4** ★★★ 🌀

Start with the right hand in the pod and reach with the left to the pocket on *Center Left*. A long reach gains a secure edge aptly named the Potato Chip.

☐ 4. **Direct V7**

Start with both hands in the pod and throw to the small, three-finger edge nine feet straight up, then to the Potato Chip.

☐ 5. **Eric Varney Direct V5** ★★★

Right of the pod is a viciously sloping dish at exactly 7.5 feet from the ground. Start with the right hand on this greasy hold and reach the three-finger edge on *Direct*, then use a small two-finger pocket and the Potato Chip. *The Moffat Direct* (V8) starts with both hands on the flake below and right of the pod and climbs through *Varney Direct*. Starting on *Moffat Direct*, traversing left, and finishing #1 is V7.

☐ 6. **Ooze Pig V7** ★

This problem starts the same as *Right Side* with the left hand in the sloping dish and the right hand in a shallow two-finger pocket. Reach straight up and left of *Right Side's* holds to a hard-to-see two-finger pocket with the right hand then again with the right hand to a sloping three-finger pocket. Pull all the way to the top not using any intermediates.

☐ 7. **Red Wall Route aka Right Side V4** ★★★

Left hands in the sloping pod. Right hand in a tiny two-finger hole. Pull straight up with the right hand to a crystal pinch then again with the right hand to the large pocket. This problem is considered one of the all time best on Flagstaff.

☐ 8. **Crossover V4** ★★

Start on *Right Side* and use the sloping dish on Varney then crossover to the three-finger edge (also on *Varney*) then to the Potato Chip.

☐ 9. **Far Right V4**

Behind the tree is a set of sharp crystals and edges. Pull through to the top. Not so classic.

☐ 10. **Just Another Traverse V10** ★★

Start a few feet right of the pine tree and traverse left to the high four-finger edge, then slide left to the soapdish and crimp, drop down to the rail and traverse left until you can finish up #1.

☐ 11. **Sleeper V7** ★

On the backside on the boulder's left face. Sds with both hands on the obvious low shelf. Get to the sloping lip via an intermediate crimp and pull over.

☐ 12. **Guy's Overhang V7** ★

Located to the far right side of #11. Begin from a low sds just down and left from the protruding cobble. From underclings, do an improbable-looking left-hand crossover move to the protruding cobble and top-out.

THE AMPHITHEATRE RIGHT SIDE

A tall boulder uphill from North Rocks and The Pebble Wall, defined by a large face on the right and an undercut slab on the left. This wall has classic problems stretched across its right portion.

☐ 1. **Far Left V3** ★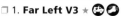

On top of the rock pedestal (directly right of the crack separating the right and left wall of The Ampitheatre) is a highball problem on fairly marginal rock. A V5 climbs closer to the crack.

☐ 2. **Overhanging Hand Traverse V1** ★★★

Climbs the good holds diagonally right to the jug complex at the top of *Gill Direct*.

☐ 3. **Gill Direct V4** ★★

In the middle of the flat face and six feet left of #4 are small edges that lead to the jug complex. Long reaches are mandatory on this problem.

☐ 4. **Sandpaper Ledge V3** ★★

Climb to the high sloping holds on the right side of the flat face. Seven feet from the SE arete are pebble holds marking the start of this problem, which climbs straight over the top. Climbing out left to the jug complex is the *Aerial Shoot* V3.

☐ 5. **South Bulge V1** ★

Right of #4 is a problem that pulls on to the upper face to the right.

☐ 6. **South Corner V1**

Just left of *Wasp Nest* is another problem.

☐ 7. **Wasp Nest V1**

On the far right side (facing Red Wall) is an easy problem that surmounts a crack in the bulge.

THE AMPHITHEATRE LEFT SIDE

☐ 1. **Mongolian Cosmonaut V8** ★★

In the small notch up and left of the Amphitheatre. A difficult problem starting on a slopey gaston and a shallow pod. One of Flagstaff's steepest problems with high quality stone. A V10 starts on the right hand pod with the left hand under the roof on a poor sidepull.

☐ 2. **High Overhang V0** ★

Starts on the boulder, which forms a squeeze to reach *Mongolian Cosmonaut*.

☐ 3. **South Face Left Side V3** ★

Climbs the seam five feet left of *Briggs*.

☐ 4. **Briggs Route V3** ★

Left of *Direct* is a left-facing dihedral and similar pebble pulling.

☐ 5. **Direct South Face V3** ★

Climb multiple pebbles on the wall above the undercut.

☐ 6. **Crystal Swing V2** ★

The problem left of the crack on the undercut wall. Climbs via a dynamic move off a pink pebble to an obvious brown pebble.

☐ 7. **V2**

On the north face (around left from *Mongolian*) is a graffitied overhang with a marginal landing. The V2 pulls straight out the roof. A V4 called *Mannboy* pulls the high overhang on the left side of the wall.

☐ 8. **V8** ★★

A difficult V8 traverse skirts the low part of the wall going from the huge jug on the left and finishing at the far right.

Amphitheatre Right Side

Amphitheatre Right Side

Amphitheatre North Side

Amphitheatre Left Side

Marmot® FOR LIFE

Unstoppable Marmot Momentum.

You can't slow down when it warms up. That's why we've created the ultimate lightweight, packable outdoor collection for summer adventures. The Marmot Momentum Collection is action-oriented clothing designed for motion with fabrics that wick moisture, dry quickly and offer terrific UPF protection - perfect for bouldering, climbing, riding, hiking, or any other activity that moves you. With Marmot Momentum you'll feel unstoppable out there. No worries, your friends will catch up.

See the collection on Marmot.com.

Athletes: Pete Takeda & Abbey Smith
Location: Boulder, CO   Photo: Ace Kvale

PEOPLE / PRODUCT / PLANET™

OVERHANG WALL

This wall is located up and left from The Ampitheatre. Walk past the Pebble Wall (the lowest tier of boulders) and skirt the fragile-looking slabs and grooves on the right. There are a couple of decent problems on this south-facing wall.

Overhang Wall

❏ 1. Cove Crack V1
The left pin-scarred crack that climbs through a small overhang.

❏ 2. Short Crack V1
The crack left of *South Undercling* and starting right of #1.

❏ 3. South Undercling V3 ★
The first problem encountered from The Ampitheatre. Climbs the south face via edges and an undercling.

❏ 4. Big Overhang V2 ★★★★ 🌀🌀
Top Three on Flag. On a miniature Flatiron just up from *Cove Crack* is a super classic 15-plus foot problem up very good holds.

❏ 5. V3 ★★
Two attached boulders with a left to right traverse. Found just below *Big Overhang*. A V3 crack climbs up the middle from a sit down start.

THE GREAT RIDGE

The long section of boulders uphill from the Overhang Wall. These walls/boulders can be reached by skirting the lowest tier of boulders leading uphill from the Red Wall Ampitheatre Area or parking at the pull-out 1.7 miles up Flagstaff Road from the kiosk and walking north to reach the middle section of The Great Ridge. This conglomeration of boulders is excellent for midwinter bouldering as they face south and are overhung.

Big Overhang

THREE OF A KIND WALL

Uphill slightly from Overhang Wall. Be sure and walk around left to reach the low tier of boulders. Three of a Kind is defined by gray-white rock with a long, chalked traverse stretching from its far right side to the middle of the wall.

❏ 1. Little Sloper Boy V3 ★ 🌀
A sit start down and left of *The Face* that either climbs into *The Face* or goes left to good edges.

❏ 2. The Face V3 ★★★ 🌀🌀
Left of the seam up a good layback and sloping dishes. A classic for Flagstaff. A V6 is just right!

❏ 3. Round Pebble V4 ★★ 🌀🌀
Left of the traverse's end is an incipient seam with an undercling start to bad edge's then it climbs right to a large pebble and ends in a wide trough/crack. A highball problem best done with a spot.

Three of a Kind

❏ 4. V5 ★★ 🌀🌀
Just left of the traverse's end is a tall face with small edges. Another highball problem with hard-to-see holds.

❏ 5. V4 ★
At the end of the traverse is an undercling problem that starts on good edges and underclings a small left hold then throws to the jug and over.

❏ 6. The Groove V0 ★
Climb the groove on the right side of the wall.

❏ 7. Bulging Slab V1 ★
A straight-up problem between the start of the traverse and *The Groove*.

❏ 8. Three of a Kind Traverse V4 ★★★
The long traverse going from right to left and finishing above the obvious jugs just past the middle of the wall.

UPPER Y TRAVERSE

Uphill from Three of a Kind is another long wall with an excellent traverse and tons of eliminates. Many problems are unlisted, as they are either nameless or too obscure.

Upper Y Traverse

❑ 1. V1 ★★

At the far left end of the wall is a small overhang that starts with tiny crimps then pulls up to ever-bigger holds. The actual end to the traverse.

❑ 2. V1 ★★ 🔵🔵

Starting above the boulder found adjacent to the wall near the big pebble is a straight-up problem on super, although fragile incuts. Another V1 is just left and finishes by climbing around a small pine tree.

❑ 3. V1 ★★ 🔵🔵

Just left of the Y crack is a fun overhanging face up good holds to incuts at the lip.

❑ 4. Y-Right V0 ★★★ 🔵

A superb warm up. Starts just right of the Y crack and climb the jugs to a sloping finish. It is an easy downclimb to get the juices flowing. A V1 climbs in from the left arete.

❑ 5. Pinch Bulge V2 ★★

On the far right side of the wall is a ten-finger edge at tongue-height. From this flake reach a pinch straight up on a blunt arete then the top. The sit start to *Pinch Bulge* V5 starts on the small crimp pockets at the base and then throws to the flake and finishes the problem. Multiple direct starts in this area have problems ranging from V2 to V8.

❑ 6. Traverse V4 - V6 ★★

The entire traverse of the wall starting from the right side and ending at the far left side. A thousand variations exist to this problem.

LITTLE FLATIRON

The spire just right of King Conquer (facing the boulder) and uphill from Upper Y. Two good problems climb the overhanging aretes.

❑ 1. Left Face V1 ★

The left arete on Little Flatiron. Good holds up to a sloping top-out.

❑ 2. Right Arete V3 ★

The right arete using the face holds in the overhang.

SHARK'S ROCK AREA

Uphill from the Upper Y is a small spire halfway to King Conquer boulder.

❑ 3. Northern Arete V1 ★ 🔵

Just left of *Leap of Faith*.

❑ 4. Leap of Faith V2 ★★ 🔵

A dynamic problem found on the boulder just north of Shark's Rock. A tad on the scary side. A V3 is on the right arete from a sit start.

❑ 5. The Arete V3 ★★ 🔵

The problem on the right arete of the block between Shark's Rock and the Upper Y Traverse.

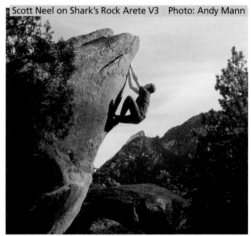

Scott Neel on Shark's Rock Arete V3   Photo: Andy Mann

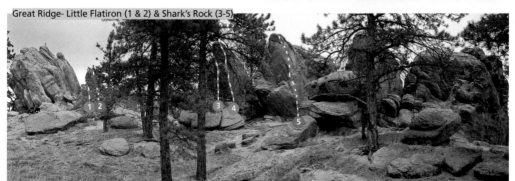

Great Ridge- Little Flatiron (1 & 2) & Shark's Rock (3-5)

Johnny Goicochea on Mongolian Cosmonaut V8   Photo: Brian Solano

KING CONQUER ROCK

The westernmost boulder on The Great Ridge. A lightning rod sticks out of the top and an obvious splitter crack breaks the boulder in two. One of the classic boulders on Flagstaff with many variations to the main themes.

❒ 1. Direct Left Slot V1
The small overhanging face left of *Left Slot*.

❒ 2. Conquer Traverse V7 ★★
Start on the far left of the boulder and traverse across then up through *Face Out*. Finish on *Reverse Face Out* for a V8.

❒ 3. Right and Left Slot V1 ★
Left of *King Conquer Overhang* are two wide cracks.

❒ 4. Lowdown No Good Arete V4 ★★
The arete below the slots. Starts pinching with the left hand, the right hand crimped down low and slaps up the arete to the jug at the top of the small triangular block.

❒ 5. King Conquer Overhang V3 ★★★
This climbs the beautiful crack in the middle of the boulder via jams and edges. An upper finger jam has broken out making the problem more difficult. Many variations climb out the crack after the bomber hand jams. Another V3 climbs the middle of the wall.

❒ 6. Face Out V5 ★★★
The ultra-thin crimps just left of *Layback*. A reverse sequence (V6) to this problem begins on the same starting holds and reaches with the left hand to the flat edge then up.

❒ 7. Layback V1 ★
The flake leading up the right side of the boulder to good jugs.

King Conquer Rock

FIRST OVERHANG

This is the first boulder seen looking north after parking in the pull-out 1.7 miles up Flagstaff Road from the kiosk. A classic, although very thin problem faces the pull-out. Five other boulders line the hillside to the left of First Overhang.

❒ 1. Masochism Tango V6
Left of *First Overhang*, almost inside the gap is a difficult problem that climbs the overhanging face. The starting moves are atrocious then it eases up for the top-out. Bypassing the starting moves is a fun V1.

❒ 2. First Overhang V5 ★★★
The classic that recently broke and got reglued. Climbs the thin crimps to a lunge at the top. More ankles have been broken here than any other boulder. Use a spot! *French Trumpeter* V6 begins on *First Overhang* and moves left and up before *Masochism Tango*. A V6 traverse starting on the far right ends on *First Overhang*.

First Overhang

PINNACLE COLADA

The first prominent boulder left of First Overhang.

❒ 1. Colada Traverse V5 ★★
A low traverse from left to right. Difficult moves include getting to the jug and standing up on the south face.

❒ 2. Standard Route V0 ★★
Up the middle of the face and exit out left. A V4 continues straight up the face just left of the white pebble.

❒ 3. Loman's Highball V5 ★★★
Start as for #2 but head straight up the face. Dyno for a jug just below the lip from a slick pebble and a bad crimp. Missing the final move has claimed at least three ankles!

❒ 4. Pebble Reach V3 ★★
On the right side is a pink/white pebble near the top. Pull on this pebble and pray it does not bust.

❒ 5. Southwest Corner V3 ★★
Hard pulls off pockets. Exit out right.

❒ 6. South Face V0 ★★
Good edges lead to flakes and the top. This also serves as the downclimb.

Pinnacle Colada

TOMBSTONE SPIRE

Just left from Pinnacle Colada boulder. Problems are listed left to right.

☐ 1. North Face Slab V1

Best described as dirty and fragile and not worth the time.

☐ 2. Triple Bulge V3 ★★

On the north face. Long reaches from solid edges and pebbles ending in a massive hueco over the top. A low sds from the right adds a solid grade.

☐ 3. West Side V0 ★★

An even easier version of *Southwest Bulge*.

☐ 4. Southwest Bulge V1 ★★

An excellent jug haul.

LOOSE FLAKE SPIRE

Left of Tombstone Spire is a smaller boulder with one problem. Loose Flake Spire is not pictured.

☐ South Face V2

Climb the face on the south wall up to a loose flake and up. A bad landing is the price to pay if you end up trusting the flake then it explodes.

FACE WALL

Left again is a tall boulder with excellent pebble problems. A few trees grow against the boulder.

☐ 1. West Roof V1 ★

Pull over the small roof.

☐ 2. Left Side V2 ★★

Left of *Center*, climb numerous pebbles up and left, ending at an obvious white pebble.

☐ 3. Center V4 ★★★

A classic highball problem that climbs up the middle of the vertical face. An absolute must do!

☐ 4. Right Side V0 ★

Good edges at the start lead up to lichen-covered rock way off the deck.

☐ 5. Mateus Highstep V7 ★

Traverse the vertical wall from right to left and finish on *West Roof*. Extend all the way across the west face for V8.

HIGH BOULDER

A small boulder left of Face Wall with a tiny right-facing dihedral that faces south.

☐ 1. V2

A low start in the dihedral that climbs through sloping sidepulls.

☐ 2. The Block V2

The face right of the dihedral a few feet. Try not to climb into the right slot, although the holds take one there.

LAST OVERHANG

☐ Last Overhang V7

Drop down the hillside another 50 yards and hidden in the hillside is a steep problem on questionable stone.

Tombstone Spire

Face Wall

High Boulder

Phillip Benningfield on Conundrum V8   Photo: Andy Mann

GROSS RESERVOIR

Opinions on this area vary, but the rock is solid granite well above the sweltering plains. Three different zones constitute the Gross experience. Differences are stark: the oldest and newest developed areas are located in a fire destruction zone; the other by railroad tracks. Whichever area you visit be assured the challenges are substantial with sick problems. Gross' finest area, The Damnation Boulders, host some of the state's best granite testpieces, are now closed due to terrorist threats. Lame.

Directions: *From Boulder drive up Baseline Road to Flagstaff Mountain. Continue 8.9 miles from the base of Flagstaff over the summit and past Walker Ranch to Gross Dam Road. Take a left on Gross Dam Road (a dirt road).*

To reach Hazard County *drive 0.5 mile down Gross Dam Road and park on the right at the Scenic Overlook. Walk south on a trail past a fence then veer left (SE) for approximately 310 yards under a powerline to the Corridor Boulder. Continue west and south from the Corridor Boulder to the ridgeline (65 yards) then go due west (right) under the cliffband and skirt ledges to a small boulderfield (80 yards). Weave down through the boulders to south-facing problems.*

The Burn *and* **Natural Apparatus Area** *are located at 1.2 miles down the Gross Dam Road. Parking is on the right at 0.9 and 1.1 miles. Further directions are found in the text with The Burn. This area may fall into a temporary dead fall closure, although isn't technically in a "burned zone."*

The Freight Train *parking is located 4.2 miles on the left in a large lot. Park and hop the wooden fence (do not take the Crescent Meadow Trail) and walk across the meadow to the south (a wooded hillside is on the far end of the meadow). Hit the woods and an old roadbed then go left and walk 200 yards. A small cliff band faces due south near the railroad tracks.*

Chip Phillips on Avante Guardian V7   Photo: Andy Mann

HAZARD COUNTY

Fairly tall boulders of the same quality as the Damnation Boulders with mostly overhanging problems make this a great winter area. This was recently developed by Kevin Murphy, Ryan Fields and other locals.

CORRIDOR BOULDER

A gorgeous northeast face within a corridor with plenty of sloping features to tantalize the skin.

□ **1. V4** ★ 🔘
Start left of the gray patch and move up and right to sloping seams.

□ **2. V3** ★ 🔘
Start on the right side of the face and move up to nice slopers.

THANKLES CLIFF

The north end of a cliff band past a pine tree where the cliff shortens to "boulder size." Not pictured.

□ **1. The Shield V5** ★★ 🔘
Thin climbing. Stay direct for the true V5 experience.

□ **2. Thankles Traverse V4** 🔘
Follow pockets to end of bulge and top out. A pad won't help the landing.

WAYLON JENNINGS BOULDER

Located 15 yards below Thankles.

□ **3. What About Waylon? V2** ★
Climb the face using broken cracks.

□ **4. Waylon Jennings Memorial Arête V3** ★★★ 🔘🔘
Left of #3.

*** Three lowball problems on a nearby block are good for warming up.

THE BOAR'S NEST BLOCK

Fifteen feet west of the Waylon Jennings Boulder.

□ **5. V2** ★★
An excellent warm-up.

□ **6. Boar's Nest V5** ★★★ 🔘
A tricky sds leads to great crimps to slopers and a jug top-out. Absolutely incredible problem.

CRAZY COOTER BLOCK

Drop down to the north 30-40 feet and look for a nice overhang above you.

□ **7. Crazy Cooter V2** ★★ 🔘
A sds to a left-angling crack to a reasonable top-out.

DAISY DUKE BOULDER

Drop down 50 feet to the southwest and look for an obvious boulder on the left.

□ **8. Daisy Duke V5** ★★★
Start sitting with the right hand on a big slopey side-pull and left hand on a low crimp on the left arête. Excellent dyno move.

Corridor

Boar's Nest and Waylon Jennings

Daisy Duke

GROTTO AREA

Continue south to a large grouping of boulders.

Grotto

BOULDER #9

☐ **9. The Frangilator V8** ★★

Slightly contrived at the start. Begin with both hands down and left on the sloping rail. Continue right, utilizing knee-bars, and top out straight up once you reach the right arête. Originally done much more direct from under the roof near the start of #10.

☐ **10. Head and Shoulders V6** ★★

A sds to a big undercling. Look out for the Boss Hog boulder behind your head.

BOSS HOG BOULDER

☐ **11. DVY V6** ★★★

The obvious arête. Great slopers to a tricky crux top-out. As low as you can go sds adds spice and boosts the grade.

PROJECT WALL

Great futuristic lines to the right of the Boss Hog Boulder. The obvious left face has seen attempts but no ascents. There is the possibility for two more lines to the right.

Chris Schulte on The Fragilator (left varation) V8 Photo: Andy Mann

Dead Tree Boulder

Head back up to Crazy Cooter and drop down to the south looking for a fallen dead tree. Follow the tree to the boulder. The Dead Tree Boulder is not pictured.

❏ **12. Scott's Dyno V3** ★★★

A few pads are recommended if you plan on falling.

The Burn

This zone has variety; there are long traverses, gorgeous tall slabs and, sadly, chipped pockets. One idiot climber's near-sighted vision spoiled many lines by drilling over 30 holes. Luckily the destruction is contained on mostly one block. The natural lines offer a handful of entertaining problems. This area is closed temporarily for revegetation. Consult with Boulder OSMP for further information.

The Warm-up Traverse Boulder

This long wall is located just before the parking at 0.9 miles. Walk back the way you came on Gross Dam Road to an Open Space boundary sign (50 yards). The boulder is visible 50 yards to the north.

❏ **Warm-up Variations V0-V4** ★★

A smorgasbord of problems can be done across the boulder's southeast face. A few hard mantles are on the left side with casual jug hauls from low starts in the middle.

❏ **Warm-up Traverse V5** ★★

From the far left side climb across the entire face to an exit on the far right.

Natural Apparatus Area (Main Burn Zone)

The name is not befitting; a mindless chipper abused the rock with only his self-serving interests in sight. I could go on and on about how stupid the chipping is, but the twit who did it should feel some shame now that boulderers climb V15. The unchipped lines vary from casual slabs to a couple of super fine problems that will challenge even the bouldering metaphysical guru.

Directions: From the parking at 1.1 miles, on the right of Gross Dam Road, walk down the road past the power line pole #221. Continue 25 yards to a blocked two-car parking spot then head north (left off the road towards the big dome). The first block is 40-odd yards down a faint trail (under the powerline).

Green Slab Block

Power Boulder

Probably not the name the first climbers gave it—but big deal. The block is located on the south end of a boulderfield consisting of a handful of boulders. A distinct left-angling crack is on the south face.

❏ **1. V4** ★★

Climb the very left side of the west face starting on the very low jug and moving slightly left to a balancy top-out.

❏ **2. V2** ★★

Climb up and right from the same start as #1.

❏ **3. V2** ★

A traverse can be done either way on the west face.

❏ **4. V1** ★

Climb the southwest arête from a stand up and finish left. A V4 can be done, starting low on the arête, to bad slopers and a thin seam, then finishing up the black face.

❏ **5. Avante Guardian V7** ★★

Climb the south face bulge starting on a left-hand undercling and right-hand finger jam. Finish straight up to a hidden seam over the lip or continue left for more moves.

❏ **6. V3** ★

Climb the right side of the south face, off an undercling, to bad slopers.

Power Boulder

Green Slab Block

Twenty yards closer to the dome is a low-angle bulbous boulder.

❏ **1. V2** ★★

This one doesn't have a bad landing but you will want a spot. Climbs the west face bulge to a huge hidden hueco. A massive V5 dyno fires directly out the overhang just left.

❏ **2. V0**

A selection of slabby V0 lines can be done on the lichen-covered south face.

❏ **3. V0**

Climb the east face just left of the pine tree.

*** Uphill from the Green Slab Block are two small boulders. The first encountered has one-move problems. The block approximately 50 yards west has a V2 on the southwest face. More blocks are near the dome but require serious gumption, many pads, and excellent spotters.

NATURAL APPARATUS BOULDER

Downhill and east a mere 25 yards from the Green Slab Block. A trail weaves through the trees.

☐ **1. V0** ★★
Climb the left arête on the west face. Also used as the downclimb.

☐ **2. V2** ★
Climb straight up just right of #1, not using big holds until up high.

☐ **3. V0** ★★
Climb the middle of the west face trending right on the best holds. Also a good downclimb.

☐ **4. V3** ★
A sds just right of #3 moving up to a natural pocket. Easy finish.

☐ **5. V5** ★
A sds that stays true to the southwest arête. Sloping holds and a sharp crimp keep the problem from garnishing more stars. Bailing left two moves can be V4.

*** The first chipped problem in the area is on the south face with old bolts rusting away on the fine granite. It's not too hard to climb but a f*%#ing shame. V4 just right.

☐ **6. Party Trick V4** ★★
On the north side is a clean face with tiny crimps to a big throw and a jug. This problem attracts many suitors; it's fun to watch your friends flail and moan. A tall V0 starts the same as #6 but climbs the arête behind the pine tree.

☐ **7. V0** ★★★
A stunning low-angle slab on the west face. Slabs don't get more enjoyable than this.

*** A couple of sporadic V0-V1 problems are west and north on the smaller blocks 10-20 yards away.

CHIPPED BOULDER

The block is located 20 yards east of Natural Apparatus. Most lines are chipped. The destruction of the boulder is the saddest accomplishment ever achieved by a nefarious climber too self-absorbed to see beyond his own petty goals. Chipped problems are not pictured or described.

☐ **1. The Conundrum V8** ★★
On the north face is a beautiful lichen-covered seam. Climb the seam using thin edges and finish in the wide groove up and left. A sds goes at about the same grade.

☐ **2. V0**
On the west face are casual V0 up-climbs and the downclimb. A butt-dragging traverse skirts the lowest flanks.

☐ **3. V4**
Climb over the mini-roof just left of the seam on the southwest face to terrible pebbles.

☐ **4. V0**
Climb up broken seams on the right side of the southwest face.

Natural Apparatus

Chipped Boulder

Krong sends Party Trick V4

Freight Train

FREIGHT TRAIN

The Train is a petite cliff band that is great to climb on in the winter. The south face offers more double-scoop problems than most boulders in the Boulder area.

*** Problems are listed left to right. Only the main problems are listed (rest assured there are a few additional squeeze jobs).

☐ 1. The Prancing Cow V4 ★
A sds on the cliff's left side starts off a low under-cling to the seam then busts right to a flat edge and then a jug.

☐ 2. Chubby Bunny V7 ★★★
Start low at the base of the crystal band then move left on bad edges and a perfect left-hand pinch. A throw is next to a finger-ripping edge and reasonable top-out.

☐ 3. V2 ★★★
Start just right of the crystal band and climb straight up on excellent holds.

☐ 4. V3 ★
Start just right of #3 then move behind the pine tree and continue up the right-trending break. Your basic terrifying boulder problem.

☐ 5. V0 ★★★
Start right of the pine tree and follow fantastic edges and jugs and flakes to the top.

☐ 6. V4 ★★
Start on right of V-slot and climb straight up. Hard after the initial bulge.

☐ 7. V2 ★★
Start off a rock pedestal and trend right along a diagonal break.

☐ 8. Buddha's Belly V3 ★★★
Start in the middle of the right bulge (eight feet right of #7), move up to a sloping shelf then the horizontal break to top out moving right.

☐ 9. V1 ★
Climb the left-angling crack just right of #8.

☐ 10. The Muckler V1 ★
Climb the slab just right of the crack utilizing an undercling. at 10 feet.

Andy Mann sends Chubby Bunny V7   Photo: Sheyna Button

Cameron Cross on Gigantor Boulder Roof V5 Photo: Andy Mann

GREEN MOUNTAIN BOULDERS

This extensive area with lots of completed problems on good stone and plenty of potential lies on the peaceful west side of Green Mountain, facing away from the heinous froo-fraa of yuppie-packed Boulder. Though the blocks are somewhat scattered and hard to find due to the thick pine forest blanketing the mountain's slopes, many of them sit in convenient fall-lines in the gullies below the Sacred Cliffs. The ambience is unbeatable: forests, meadows, and unimpeded views of the striking Indian Peaks to the west. Seasonal bird closures (Feb 1- July 31) at the Sacred Cliffs block access to many of the boulders higher on the ridge. Here's a tip: Respect all closure signs and call Boulder Mountain Parks (303-441-3408) if you're unsure as to where you can or can't climb during the closure. Expect much walking and exploration, as it is difficult to readily locate many of the boulders your first time out. Permits are needed certain times of the year for many of the blocks. A downloadable PDF of closures and permits needed is available throught the Boulder Mountain Parks website.

Directions: From the intersection of Broadway and Baseline in Boulder drive 6.1 miles west up Baseline (soon Flagstaff) road, reaching a shoulder where the road flattens out after the last hairpin turn on the ascent. Park in a pullout on the right and head for the Green Mountain West Ridge trailhead on the south side of the road. This trail follows the expansive ridge west for about a mile to the summit of Green Mountain, coming to a four-way intersection (at 20-25 minutes) with the Ranger Trail and the Green-Bear Trail (well below the summit pyramid).

Green Mountain North: While all the boulders on this section of the mountain sit more or less in the same gully, there are two different approaches for the upper and lower areas.

For the upper area (Ramp Rock, The Sacred Corner, The Sugar Cube, The Highlander Block): Stay on the Green Mountain West Ridge Trail heading east from the intersection, reaching Ramp Rock after five very steep minutes of hiking. The other boulders are slightly south and down from here.

For the lower area (The Butter Maroon): Follow the Green-Bear Trail downhill and south for about five minutes from the intersection, crossing a large open area before hitting a ridge. Immediately upon hitting the ridge drop left into the grassy gully (the northernmost fall-line from the Sacred Cliffs) to find the boulder. Alternately, drop 50 yards straight down the gully from The Sugar Cube to reach the Butter Maroon.

Green Mountain South: The bulk of the bouldering sits below the southern spine of the Sacred Cliffs. Continue east on the Green Mountain West Ridge Trail past a couple of switchbacks until you reach the obvious Ramp Rock, a green slab with multiple overlaps right on the trail. A faintly-marked game trail takes off 150 feet south of here, just past a "Closed for revegetation" sign and a pile of logs. Avoid the closed area by hiking high or low to pick up the trail further along. Do your best to stay on the trail and tread lightly.

This trail then winds its way south, passing numerous areas (such as the impressive Teton, a gigantic pyramid-shaped boulder west of the trail and surrounded by many other worthy boulders) on its way to the Standard Block.

The Standard Block: This boulder sits just south and west of the sandy saddle between the two spines of the Sacred Cliffs, about ten minutes off the Green Mountain trail. The Platinum Block is six minutes further south and sits about 60 yards downhill from the prominent box-car shaped cliff on the northern tip of the Southern Spine of the Sacred Cliffs. The Gigantor Boulder is obscured by trees in the big gully down and vaguely west-northwest from here, about five minutes away.

Areas have been developed further south and west of here. Please be aware that this is a sensitive erosion-prone area that might be better left unvisited.

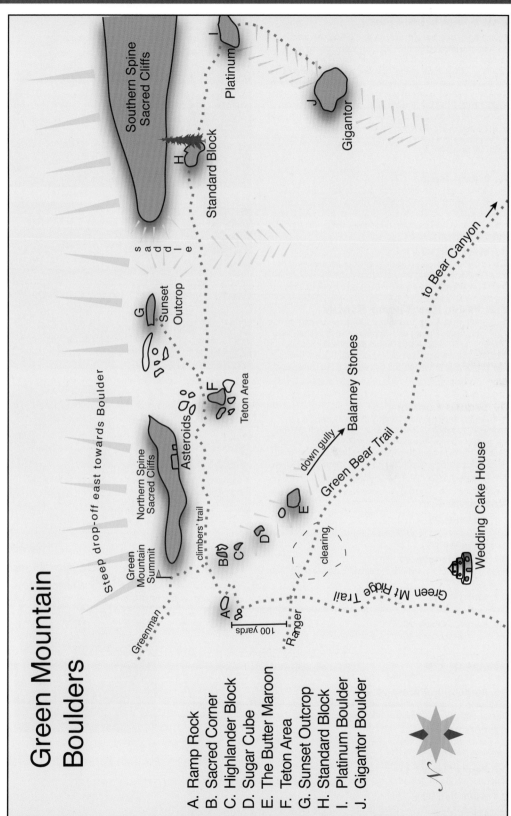

Green Mountain Boulders

A. Ramp Rock
B. Sacred Corner
C. Highlander Block
D. Sugar Cube
E. The Butter Maroon
F. Teton Area
G. Sunset Outcrop
H. Standard Block
I. Platinum Boulder
J. Gigantor Boulder

Southern Spine Sacred Cliffs

Platinum

Standard Block

Gigantor

to Bear Canyon

s a d d l e

Sunset Outcrop

Balarney Stones

Asteroids

Teton Area

down gully

Green Bear Trail

Northern Spine Sacred Cliffs

Wedding Cake House

steep drop-off east towards Boulder

Green Mountain Summit

climbers' trail

clearing

Green Mt Ridge Trail

Greenman

100 yards

Ranger

N

GREEN MOUNTAIN NORTH

If your bandy little legs are quaking by the time you reach the four-way intersection then you may want to stop and boulder here, as the areas further south require a bit more slogging. Though most of the rocks are a ways off the trail, use discretion and mind your Ps and Qs while bouldering here. The Butter Maroon is one of the finest sandstone blocks in the Boulder area, while the other boulders offer a host of good problems on varied, solid rock. The first boulders encountered on the way to Ramp Rock are the Blob Boulders. These fine blocks offer several great problems right off the trail, a few of which are very difficult.

Blob Boulders

A. RAMP ROCK

This slabby, green wall just off the trail provides a good warm-up and a useful landmark for finding the game trail, a faint track which takes you to the southerly areas. Ramp Rock sits five minutes up the Green Mountain West Ridge Trail from the four-way intersection below.

❏ **1. West Slab V0-V1** ★

Many variations possible. The most obvious line moves right to left along the undercling flake and tops out in the groove on the left. A fun and easy double arête is on a block just left.

Ramp Rock

THE WAVE AND THUMB BLOCKS

Head South from Ramp Rock about 150 yards staying near the ridge, pass Sacred Corner, and drop downhill slightly to find this amazing little area. With Thumb Block's bullet moderates, and The Wave's steep power problems, this is a great area to spend an afternoon and take in the sunset. Individual problems are not described here.

B. SACRED CORNER

With decent landings and a handful of fun moderates on Flagstaff-like, pebbled stone, this little grotto just off the trail is a great place to warm up. From Ramp Rock walk 150 feet south on the main trail, then follow the faint trail another 80 feet south, passing a seasonal closure sign. Drop 20 feet west down the steep slope into this south-facing alcove.

Wave Block

NORTHERN FIN

❏ **1. Riff-Raff V3** ★

Climb the center of the south face of the alcove's northern fin via diagonaling edges.

❏ **2. Love Triangles V1**

Seven feet right of #1, layback the offwidth then lean left into the groove system.

❏ **3. Sinister V2**

Layback up the left side of the offwidth. Easier if you use holds back in the crack.

❏ **4. Karen's Crack V0**

The cruiser hand crack in the back (east) end of the alcove. No chimneying!

SOUTHERN FIN

The Southern Fin is not pictured.

❏ **5. Pathological Arête V0** ★

This problem is on the north face of the alcove's southern fin. Climb the shady red wall via a right-trending flake system which leads you to the arête.

Thumb Block

❏ **6. Cola V1** ★

The fun excursion climbs the west side of the arête around from #5. Start on a small seam studded with large crystals and move left to the arête to finish.

❏ **7. Peppy Slab V3** ★★

Start on the good crystals on #6 but stay right, climbing into the faint black streak on tiny pebbles to finish.

❏ **8. Addictive V3** ★

Start six feet right of #6 and climb straight into the scoop above. Shares some holds with #7.

❏ 9. Princess of Darkness V1
The pleasant line on incut pebbles up the south face, just uphill from the arête.

❏ 10. Three Strikes V0
Master the center of the south face via the ramp and reach good holds above.

C. HIGHLANDER BLOCK

This appealing cube of sandstone sits due west and downhill 100 feet from Sacred Corner. It has a distinctive northwest face, which sports two high, clean arêtes.

❏ 1. Northeast Flakes V0 ★
Sds on good flakes, then traverse up and left along the flake system on killer jugs.

❏ 2. Highlander V2 ★★
Start above the embedded block then move past crimps to the left-trending flake, which you follow up and left to the lip near the left arête.

❏ 3. Highlander Arête V3 ★★
A slightly gripping excursion up the right arête of the wall. Fortunately the crux comes at mid-height, before the mossy top-out.

Highlander Block

D. THE SUGAR CUBE

Yee-haw! A smaller replica of the Butter Maroon with fewer problems, this unique blob of solid, overhanging maroon stone in a quiet meadow is well worth a visit. Walk downhill and west 50 yards from the Highlander Block, passing through a pine grove littered with smallish boulders that offer congenial problems in the V0-V1 range.

❏ 1. Middleman V4 ★★
Long moves to hidden incuts define this powerful line, which starts on a good left-facing layback toward the right side of the west face. Really good.

❏ 2. The Flying Overhang V3 ★★★
The obvious line up the flake system on the arête. Save some gumption for the awkward, thrutchy top-out.

❏ 3. Mat Mover V1
This uninspiring line is located just behind the tree on the right side of the south face. A low sds ups it to V4.

The Sugar Cube

E. THE BUTTER MAROON

This dreamy boulder sits in a nice, grassy gully just off the Green-Bear Trail and offers a handful of stellar highballs in the middle V-grades. Expect engaging moves on colorful, swirly rock featuring sharpish crimpers. Nearby boulders worth checking out, but not described here, include the Power Boulder (a little ways uphill) and Walrus Boulder (50 yards down gully). They both offer thin climbing on bulging stone.

❏ 1. Land O' Boulders V5 ★★
This sustained, crimpy line climbs into a small, right-facing corner on the left side of the northwest face. Much harder from a sds.

❏ 2. Sweet Arête V5 ★★★★
A perfect line up the nose of the boulder, finishing in a funky finger crack feature. An eliminate, *Peregrine* V7, climbs the seams on the left sans the arête.

❏ 3. Buffalo Gold V4 ★★★
Oh yeah, baby! Climb the flake feature just right of the arête to a puzzling top-out.

❏ 4. Parkay V5 ★★★
Looks to be much harder. Climb the proud black streak right of the flake.

❏ 5. Butter Rum V3
An also-ran. Climb friable flakes into a bathtub jug by the small tree. Some holds have broken.

Butter Maroon

GREEN MOUNTAIN SOUTH

With a remote feel and beautiful views both to the east and west, the boulders south of Green Mountain's summit make for a rewardingly obscure experience. Both spines of the Sacred Cliffs offer a labyrinth of walls and boulders along the summit ridge, with many interesting blocks hidden in the trees down below. Take your time, explore, and tread lightly. This is a beautiful, seldom-visited zone which we should do our best to keep pristine and impact-free.

F. THE TETON AREA

This is the next good concentration of blocks south of Sacred Corner. Walk south along the Maroon Trail for five minutes past Sacred Corner, passing along the base of the Northern Spine of the Sacred Cliffs and many other bouldering possibilities. The Teton itself is hard to miss—it's a 30- to 50-foot-tall, crystal-studded pyramid poking out of a jumble of blocks just west of the game trail.

THE TETON

When does a highball become a solo? Sample the tall, committing lines up small crystals on this one-of-a-kind spire and you'll soon find out. Use caution with the more protruding pebbles and crystals—they have been known to break!

☐ **1. Mangy Moose V3** ★
A huge dead tree leans against the right side of the west face. Start left of this and climb the steep, pebbly groove then amble left up the high, crystal-studded slab to the summit (5.7).

☐ **2. Grande V2** ★★★
Start from the good-landing tier under the southeast face and climb the sustained wall via tiny nubbins and crystals.

☐ **3. Tits Ville V0**
Also the downclimb. The obvious crack/flare line up the east face.

☐ **4. The Hostel V3** ★
Climb the slabby northeast arête of the boulder, moving slightly right at the finishing bulge to top out at a hangerless bolt. Dirty.

THE ASTEROIDS AND OTHER BOULDERS

This is the pleasant grouping of boulders surrounding the Teton on its north and east sides. These varied rocks offer good moderates, as well as a few thin desperates on some of the steeper walls. Some problems are still crumbly, but this area should clean up well with traffic.

G. SUNSET OUTCROP

This radically overhanging west-facing wall makes a useful landmark for finding other blocks in the area and provides breathtaking views to the east and the west. It sits at the southern tip of the Northern Spine of the Sacred Cliffs on the northern end of the open, gravelly saddle between the two Spines. Plenty of existing problems and potential desperates grace the walls and boulders just north of here along the ridge.

☐ **1. Arêtes Away V2** ★★
The thuggy, scenic arête on the far left side of the wall.

☐ **2. Cracking Up V2** ★★
This is the overhanging crack just right of the arête. The top-out is awkward.

☐ **3. Crystal Dyno V8** ★★★
A difficult line near the center of the wall, starting on a large, white crystal and cranking sick moves to the lip.

☐ **4. Sunscreen V1**
The somewhat uninspiring little line on the right side of the wall.

The Teton Area

The Asteroids

Sunset Outcrop

Sheyna Button on The Sweet Arête V5   Photo: Andy Mann

H. Standard Block

With four splitter lines on its multicolored, highball south face, this exemplary block personifies what all other choss in the Flatirons aspires—yet fails—to be. Killer views of Walker Ranch and the Indian Peaks sweeten the deal. The block sits just below the cliff line on the northern end of the Southern Spine.

❏ 1. Wavey V2 ★★ 😎
The highball southwest arête. Climb vertical slots and pinches to a slightly grubby top-out.

❏ 2. The Groove V3 ★★★★
The superlative central line up huecos in the tan streak.

❏ 3. Standard Shield V2 ★★
Layback on dishes in the maroon streak, heading for a good hueco in the maroon-colored rib.

❏ 4. Crystal Scoop V4 ★★★
Sds on the east end of the south face and climb the orange-streaked scoop via small but positive crystals. Kinaesthetically pleasing.

❏ 5. Crystal Arête V3 ★
Sds as for #4 but crank right around the arête and head up to good holds. V0 from the stand-up.

❏ 6. Short Crystal V0
The downclimb. Start on jugs at chest-height in the middle of the east face and climb the cobbles.

I. Platinum Boulder

Steep, remote and punishing. The long, overhanging west/ southwest wall of this boulder offers a number of killer over-hangs on positive holds reminiscent of Hueco Tanks. A couple of undone lines promise to be very hard. Near-perfect landings more than make up for the flakiness of a few holds.

❏ 1. Plato's Arête V7 ★★★ 😎
Sds with your hands on good horizontal holds at chest-height then move left to the severely overhanging arête. Superb.

❏ 2. Socrate's Overhang V5 ★★★
Start on #1 but trend right on small incuts to a horn at the lip. Powerful and crimpy.

❏ 3. Pop Overhangs V3 ★
Throw from a horn at arm's reach to the juggy lip 13 feet right of #2. Finish via a classic mantle.

❏ 4. Main Hang V7 ★★
Big moves out a big roof. Start on the incut and move left, eventually throwing for a slopey cobble high and left at the lip.

❏ 5. Platinum Overhang V8 ★★★
Harder since holds have broken. The incredible line leading out the steep maroon face to a shaky-looking horn/flake below the lip.

J. Gigantor Boulder

One of largest single boulders in the Flatirons, this hidden behemoth doesn't reveal its true size until you stumble onto it amidst a thick grove of trees. Aaah, if only we could still bolt. The entire Gigantor Boulder is not pictured.

❏ 1. Tobar V? 😎
Way harder since holds have broken. Climb the heinous-sick looking line on the left side of the bulging alcove on the south face. Was this really done?

❏ 2. The Surf V7 ★★★ 😎
Big, bad, bold and butch. Punch your way straight out the alcove via layaways and sloping edges. A jug flake at mid-height lets you either psyche up for the dicey exit in the bowl out left or cop out and jump to the pads.

Standard Block

Platinum Boulder Left Side

Gigantor Roof

❏ 3. Gigantor Roof V5 ★★★★ 😎
Yep, climb the roof/flake past old pitons and top-out. The sickest roof in The Flatirons! The amazing sds is undone (and a bit chossy) but promises to be the boldest hard line around. At least one person has broken their ankle rocking the lip. Sketchy! Start on cheater stones.

Daniel Woods sends Free Range V13 at Castle Rock   Photo: Andy Mann

BOULDER CANYON

Many bouldering possibilities exist on the granite roadcuts, cliff bases and fine boulders lining the canyon. Problems spread across the scale from V0 to V15—from the casual problems found on the roadcut below The Dome to the industrialized Barrio just past Nip and Tuck cliff to Castle Rocks double-digit classics. Most of the granite is solid, and, if not, has been reinforced with glue.

Directions: All the areas with problems are all reached by driving on Canyon Boulevard (State Route 119) toward Nederland. Mileage for the areas is given from the intersection of Canyon and Arapahoe Road.

The Dome: Bouldering is 0.8 mile up the canyon on the right. Park and walk toward the creek on the left side of the massive roadcut. The problems face the creek.

Road Warrior Area: 1.3 miles upcanyon on the left behind a guardrail. Park in the right pullout.

Cobb Rock: 6.7 miles upcanyon on the left. Park and cross the creek. The talus and boulders are visible from the eastermost (downriver) parking.

Graham Boulder: 7.4 miles upcanyon on the left (across the creek) just before the Boulder Falls 1000 feet sign. Park on the left at the sign and cross the creek. The GB is a single block visible from the highway.

The Patio: is located at 8.1 miles across the creek and below Bell Buttress. Park on the right pullout and cross the creek if the water allows it.

Nip and Tuck: 10.8 miles upcanyon on the right. Park directly in front of the cliff.

The Barrio and Nursing Home: 10.9 miles upcanyon on the right. The Barrio is located directly behind the guardrail. Parking is just up on the left from the guardrail. WTMS is located across the highway from the westernmost (up creek) parking.

Castle Rock: 11.7 miles up canyon on the left. Turn left on the dirt road and park as close as possible to the bridge below Country Club Crack.

THE DOME
The bouldering on this roadcut consists of easy straight-up problems that escape before going high into the lesser quality rock. A toprope is recommended for problems reaching the top. Problems range from V0 to V3. A good area to get a feel for granite skills.

ROAD WARRIOR AREA
AKA SPEED BUMP BOULDER
Probably the closest problems to the persistent traffic in the canyon. Located within spitting distance of the highway.

❒ 1. **V3** ★
Climb left of the arete and finish up a corner.

❒ 2. **The Feral Kid V6** ★
Climb the arete left of the crack.

❒ 3. **Road Warrior V8** ★★
Climb the obvious crack through the overhang. Do not stem the face to the right.

❒ 4. **V1** ★
The two-move dihedral right of *Road Warrior*.

The Dome

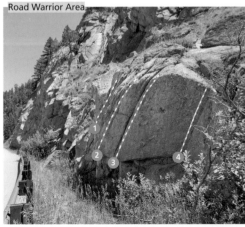
Road Warrior Area

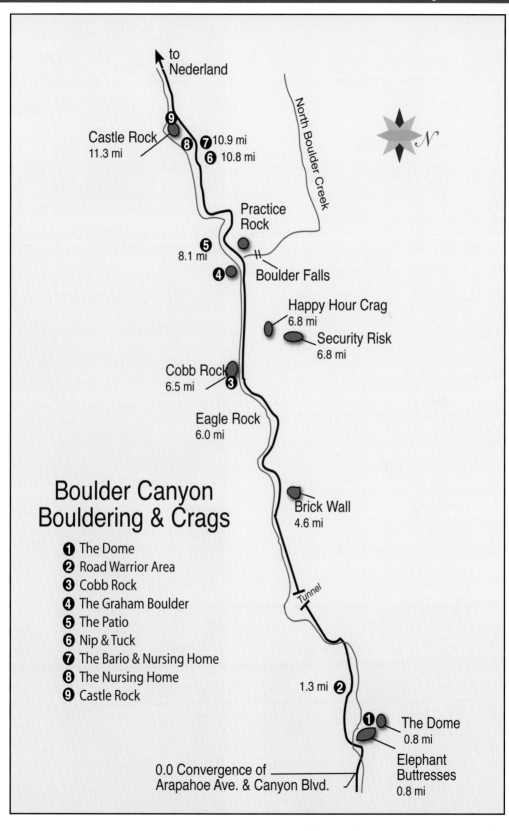

to
Nederland

Castle Rock
11.3 mi

⑨
⑧ ⑦ 10.9 mi
⑥ 10.8 mi

North Boulder Creek

Practice
Rock

⑤
8.1 mi

④

Boulder Falls

Happy Hour Crag
6.8 mi

Security Risk
6.8 mi

Cobb Rock
6.5 mi
③

Eagle Rock
6.0 mi

Brick Wall
4.6 mi

Boulder Canyon
Bouldering & Crags

❶ The Dome
❷ Road Warrior Area
❸ Cobb Rock
❹ The Graham Boulder
❺ The Patio
❻ Nip & Tuck
❼ The Bario & Nursing Home
❽ The Nursing Home
❾ Castle Rock

Tunnel

1.3 mi ②

① The Dome
0.8 mi

Elephant
Buttresses
0.8 mi

0.0 Convergence of
Arapahoe Ave. & Canyon Blvd.

𝒩

COBB ROCK

A large talus field of bullet granite chaotically jumbled from the base of the cliff down to the river. There are a few, albeit lowball, difficult problems to be found here. Only a few problems are listed, a creative mind will find other nice aretes and two movers throughout the talus. Park at the Cobb Rock pulloff, cross the river and head east along the bottom edge of the talus to locate the first boulders.

THE GAME BOULDER

❏ **1. The Game V15** ★★★ 🔺🏃

Jutting out from the middle of the talus field is an obvious massive roof. Start matched on a good hold at the bottom of the seam. Daniel Woods did the first ascent of this extreme problem.

BOULDER 1

The first boulder encountered when skirting the creekside heading downriver.

❏ **2. V9** ★ 🏃

Start on double underclings and fight out the short right-trending arete. A V7 dyno can be found to the right

❏ **2. V9** ★ 🏃
BOULDER 2

The next little boulder downstream.

❏ **3. V3** ★★ 🏃

Sit start on edges and work into the face. Finish through the sharp arete out right and up. Devious.

BOULDERS 3 & 4

A nice little cluster another 20 yards downstream.

❏ **4. V5** ★★ 🏃

Sit start on sidepulls and pull a few powerful moves to the lip.

❏ **5. V4** ★ 🏃

Climb the left side of the face to a sloping lip and up through the dihedral.

❏ **6. Project V?** ★★ 🏃

Undone since a key crystal broke. Start way down in the hole sitting on a boulder and climb up the center of the wall.

❏ **7. Arete V2** ★ 🏃

Start low on the right arete and surf it all the way.

Game Boulder

Boulder 1

Boulder 2

Boulders 3 and 4

THE HUG BOULDER

Located just uphill from Boulders 3 & 4.

☐ 1. **The Hug V10** ★★

Sit down low in the small cave and move right to poor pinches and slopers and do the heinous mantle.

☐ 2. **The Hug Left V8** ★

Start the same for the previous but trend left and up the slab.

☐ 3. **The Hug Right V11** ★

Start the same for the previous but trend right and up the arete.

THE HALLOWEEN BOULDER

Follow the talus field all the way up and find this nice boulder leaning against the base of the cliff.

☐ 3. **Sleepy Hollow V9** ★★★

Sit start way down low as far as you can go, pull the crux moves with a boulder right at your back and continue up and out the face through a neat pocket to the lip.

☐ 4. **The Headless Horseman V10** ★★

Start as for the previous problem, but bust right onto the slopey arete and top out on the eastern side of the boulder.

Hug Boulder

Halloween Boulder

Chris Shulte on the FA of Sleepy Hollow V9   Photo: Andy Mann

THE GRAHAM BOULDER

Park at a pull off on the left side of the road at the *Boulder Falls 1000 feet* sign. This fine little block is downstream a hundred feet and across the river.

❑ 1. The Left Graham Arete V11 ★★
Sit start down and right and power your way to the lip. A nice V5 can be done from a stand start.

❑ 2. The Rail V1 ★
Traverse the rail right and top out.

❑ 3. The Fields Face V6 ★★
Pull a couple sharp crimpers and make a big move to the rail.

❑ 4. The Little Sloper that Could V9 ★★
Start low and sqeeze your way up slightly left to the top.

❑ 5. Dihedral V4
Climb the dihedral around back from a sit down start. A few variations can be done to this line. Ouch!

THE PATIO

On the bottom right section of Bell Buttress is a flat area with a cave. This area can be climbed in a torrential rainstorm, but only reached during low water.

❑ Godzilla V3 ★★
A fun lowball outing. Traverse either way across the slopers, incuts, and water-worn holds.

NIP AND TUCK

Two highball problems are found on these cliff bands and next to bolted climbs. Some boulderng can be found just west around the corner, although the problems do not top-out.

❑ 7. Caddis V10 ★★ 🌐🌀
Located just left of *Gyro Captain* overhang on Tuck. The problem was bolted, but not climbed, before it was bouldered out. Climb up the left-facing dihedral and escape left after reaching the ledge approximately 15 feet up.

❑ 8. Gyro Captain V8 ★★ 🌐🌀
A bolted sport route at a reasonable highball's height, probably twice as hard with rope management. Climb through finger locks and sidepulls to a slopey lip encounter. A harder variation, *Mr. Spiffy* (5.13a), heads past bolts trending right instead of finishing left.

❑ 9. Warm Up Traverse V0
Traverse and contrive your way along the little wall right of *Gyro Captain*.

THE BARRIO AKA 12 CANS

A true testament to the will of man. This area was dug out then glued into existence. The use of 12 cans of industrial glue were necessary to secure the holds and create a superb traverse. Many variations pull out the lowest section of the overhang and are rated up to V10 and 5.14. The easiest line moves left from the beginning of the overhang as a warm up at V1. The lower cave offers other great steep beginner variants.

❑ 1. The Barrio Traverse V8-V10 ★★ 🌐🌀
Begin far left and traverse butt-draggingly low through the lower cave and up the entire overhang reaching a slab with an easy vertical ending. Using the skirt near the ground for your feet ease the difficulty. *Choss Boss* (V9) starts the same but stays high on the lip of the lower cave and traverses the entire slot staying high in the black rock as well.

❑ 2. V10 🌐🌀
Halfway through the traverse (before the spot where the traverse comes closest to the cliff drop-off) a problem moves back and left up the overhang.

Graham Boulder

Nip & Tuck Boulder

The Barrio

THE NURSING HOME

Park as for The Barrio and this wall is located across the street from the western most tip of the gravel pull-off just up the hill. Many problems in the V0-V5 range grace the extent of this wall.

❒ 1. **Where the Monkey Sleeps V10** ★★
Pull into slopey crimps and make some big lock-offs directly up the black rock.

❒ 2. **Freak Accident V12** ★★
Start from the set of holds immediately right and do some hard shoulder moves into the start of the previous problem adding some spice.

CASTLE ROCK

Known for its steller traditional routes and quality sport lines, this little island of a pull-out has recently been a hotspot for hard development in the canyon. Bullet rock, a beautiful river, and some separation from the road make it a choice spot for a desperate session.

CASTLE ROCK BOULDER

❒ 1. **Standard Bulge V5** ★★★
Pull on to the slab and work your way out the double bulge on slopers to a big move to gain the summit. Classic.

❒ 2. **The Citadel V8** ★★
Sit start under the bulge and pimp your way up the tiny crimpers and slopers on the prow.

❒ 3. **Free Range V13** ★★★
Sit start on the low left side of the north face and work right into the start of *Cage Free*.

❒ 4. **Cage Free V10** ★★ ★★
Start standing, matched on an undercling, make a move to set-up, and dyno to the lip.

❒ 5. **Project V?** ★★
Start matched on the good incut edge of *Surface Tension* and traverse left into *Cage Free*.

❒ 6. **Surface Tension V10** ★★
Start matched on a good incut edge and pull around right of the bluge. Unclimbable when the water is high.

❒ 7. **Hit Hard Tactics V7** ★★
The original stand start to #6 starting with a horizontal left crimp on arete and a crystal feature lower and right.

The Nursing Home

Castle Rock Boulder

Chris Schulte bouldering *Gyro Captain* V8   Photo: Andy Mann

MIDNIGHT EXPRESS BOULDER

On the opposite side of the creek, head up into the woods and uphill 50 yds.

❐ 1. Trainspotting V12 ★

Start sitting on very low holds left of *Midnight Express* and bust left, gain the crack, and top out.

❐ 2. Midnight Express V14 ★★★

Done first as a stand start in the V8 range, young Brit, Tyler Landman, opended the full line from the sit. Start with a left hand on an incut crimp and right hand on a sloping crimp at the bottom of a bulbous feature. Heady topout.

HARDBOILED BOULDER

Park at Castle Rock and walk about 75 yards upstream, the boulder lies in a small talus jumble across the creek.

❐ 1. Hardboiled V11 ★★

Sit start under the little roof, and gain the face where the crux comes getting established on the upper face.

❐ 2. The Replacement Killers V11 ★★★

Same start as previous problem, but follow the arete left to finish. Slightly less awkward.

❐ 3. Ninetendo V4

Immediately above *Hardboiled* is a small A-frame block. Sit start and ascend the double arête to a six foot top-out.

KOYAANISQATSI BOULDER

Park just past the bridge near Cage Free. Hike away from Castle Rock, steeply up the hill for 5 minutes and look left.

❐ 1. Koyaanisqatsi V11 ★★

Sit start under the little roof on a good hold, and climb the compression feature, up and left.

❐ 2. Things Done Changed V12 ★★

Walk over the hill to the left 100 ft to a small dark cliff band. Start on a good incut and climb straight up. Drop off.

Midnight Express Boulder

Hardboiled Boulder

Daniel Woods Midnight Expresss V14 Photo: Andy Mann

BOULDER CANYON ALSO-RANS

★★★ Boulder Falls Bouldering - Fine bouldering can also be found 200 yards directly above Boulder Falls, right on the creek, on a massive and obvious boulder. This is home to the south-facing V9 *Freedom*, its classic V11 variant *The Amendment*, and a terrifyingly tall V7 arete on its northwest face. The Right V13, starts on The Amendment and heads right and up the compression feature. The landing is very poor. Although climbers have been approaching this boulder from Boulder Falls parking for years without trouble, signs suggest you do otherwise. Please use caution. Another also-ran is *Velvet Revolver,* a V8 right at the top of Boulder Falls next to the water. Start sitting far right and climb up and left. At press time the falls area was closed due to rockfall.

★★★ Coney Island Bouldering - Drive up Boulder Canyon approximately nine miles and watch for a large rock crag on the north side that sits 30 feet above the road on a steep hillside. This crag is actully much easier to identify when driving down the canyon. Parking may be found on either side of the road, though the pullouts are very thin. To find the problems, ascend the obvious trail on the up-canyon side of the formation, cross in front of the first stage of sport climbs (walking down-canyon along the cliff line) and continue uphill with the trail on the down-canyon side of the formation. On the top of the first tier of sport climbs sits a lone boulder, home to the V7 *Angry Dragon,* a dihedral/roof system facing the road that starts almost laying down. Other moderates exist on this fun boulder.

Jonathan Siegrist sending Fleshfest (variation) V9 in the Satellite Boulders   Photo: Andy Mann

THE FLATIRONS

Throughout the expanse of The Flatirons lie hundreds of old and new boulder problems. From the problems near Fern Canyon on The Negatron and Burgundy Boulders to The Cube and the nearby *Slapshot*, quality bouldering abounds. Further north, on the Third Flatiron, is The Ghetto—a well-developed area with classic problems all along its expanse. And lastly to finish out the tour visit the newer problems found in the Satellite Boulders. With the multitude of areas, some closed to climbing during raptor nesting season, a good change of pace can be found from the more frequented areas like Flagstaff.

Mesa Trail South Boulder *is located by driving west on State Route 170 off State Route 93 (just south of Boulder) for 1.7 miles to a right parking area for the Mesa Trail South Trailhead. Walk north on the Mesa Trail (the right hand trail–not Towhee or Homestead) for approximately 10 minutes to the boulders. The boulders are easily visible from the stone house just after crossing South Boulder Creek. The Mesa Trail South Boulder is the largest block in the boulderfield.*

Fern Canyon *is reached from the end of Cragmoor Road. Walk west until reaching a gravel road (Shanahan Trail). Continue west taking the North Fork Shanahan Trail past the Mesa Trail until close to the slabs forming the two sides of Fern Canyon. The Go-Go Traverse is at the base of the slab approximately 100 yards left on a faint trail/drainage. The Negatron Boulder, Burgundy Boulder and Resin Wall are right (north). Go past the Fern Canyon Trail sign headed north along the right slabs of Fern Canyon to reach The Resin Wall. It is a hard find, but go past the first break in the slab following a trail to a broken slab section (approximately 200 yards north of the Fern Canyon sign). Go up the slabs to the first flat tier and a trail leads back to the south. Go south until reaching an amphitheater (a bolted line goes up the large overhang to the left and the Resin Wall is on a small tier to the right and easily seen from the trail. The Negatron and Burgundy Boulders are 175 yards north (staying on the path) from the Fern Canyon sign. The Burgundy and Mound Boulder (just below the Negatron Boulder) are visible from the trail. Negatron is above the Fern Canyon Trail west approximately 100 yards and the Burgundy is below the trail east approximately 80 yards. The boulders are almost dead even across the Fern Canyon Trail from one another.*

Bear Canyon (Bongo Boulder) *is reached by parking at NCAR (The National Center for Atmospheric Research) and hiking west on the Walter Orr Trail to the Mesa Trail. Walk south on the Mesa Trail until crossing a creek (the trail becomes a wide dirt road). The trail opens in a large meadow a short distance past the creek. The Bongo Boulder sits within this meadow on the right and is easily seen.*

The Cube/Slapshot Area *is reached by taking Table Mesa Road west and parking at NCAR (The National Center for Atmospheric Research). From NCAR walk west on the Walter Orr Roberts Trail to the Mesa Trail. Go past the water tower and take the south fork to reach the Mesa. The trail eventually dissects the Mesa Trail. From the Mesa take the Mallory Cave Trail up two steep hillsides until it flattens out. The Cube is the well-chalked boulder on the left side of the trail just past the flat section. Slapshot can be found by walking past The Cube on the Mallory Cave Trail until the trail goes between a separate boulder on the left (Slapshot) and a ridge on the right.*

Second Flatiron Areas—Satellite Boulders, The Gutter, The Compound: *From Chatauqua Park walk south up the old paved road (Bluebell Road) that begins behind the Ranger Station. Walk past the toilet and covered picnic area staying on the road. This leads to the Third Flatiron Trail. Follow the trail past the turn to Royal Arches (access to The Ghetto) and continue across a large talus slope. The Satellite Boulders are located in the woods after crossing the talus and appear trailside. Continue uphill past the Sputnik Boulder to reach the main set of blocks.*

To reach The Gutter and The Compound simply walk around the BBC Boulder (Satellite Boulders) up a faint trail to the northwest for approximately 100 yards. The Gutter is directly below a large, wide shield of rock above the slabs. The Compound is reached by walking directly above The Gutter (it can be seen from on top of The Gutter-a long, continuous overhang with a dead tree at the far left edge). Continue west past The Gutter and drop down into the next gully. Across the gully is The Compound.

The Ghetto *is reached by following the the Royal Arch Trail which skirts the southern base of the Third Flatiron. Walk along the flat trail until it reaches a small drainage crossing (the trail becomes quite steep here). A couple hundred yards up (approximately 30 yards past a large overhanging block on the left of the trail) is a faint trail diving down and right. As of the printing of this book, Boulder's OSMP has strung a cable across this trail with a seasonal wildlife closure sign attached to it. (If the sign isn't there and you encounter switchbacks, you have gone too far). Follow the spur trail along the south face of the Third Flatiron past a couple of bolted routes. Forty yards past these routes, a short climb must be done (5.4–if you can't do this The Ghetto is not for you) to gain a hidden upper level. A well-worn pine tree is just left of the climb (a good downclimb). Climb up and The Ghetto is right in front of your nose.*

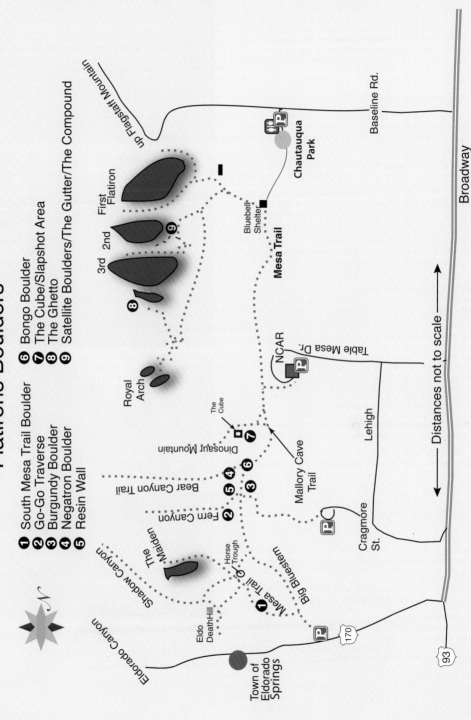

Flatirons Boulders

❶ South Mesa Trail Boulder
❷ Go-Go Traverse
❸ Burgundy Boulder
❹ Negatron Boulder
❺ Resin Wall
❻ Bongo Boulder
❼ The Cube/Slapshot Area
❽ The Ghetto
❾ Satellite Boulders/The Gutter/The Compound

Distances not to scale

First Flatiron

3rd 2nd

up Flagstaff Mountain

Chautauqua Park

Bluebell Shelter

Mesa Trail

Royal Arch

NCAR

Table Mesa Dr.

Baseline Rd.

Broadway

The Cube

Dinosaur Mountain

Bear Canyon Trail

Fern Canyon

The "Maiden"

Shadow Canyon

Eldorado Canyon

Mallory Cave Trail

Lehigh

Cragmore St.

Horse Trough

Mesa Trail

Big Bluestem

Eldo DeathHill

Town of Eldorado Springs

170

93

South Mesa Trail Boulders

These high quality boulders have certainly seen ascents through the years but do not show active signs of high traffic. It is certainly a good place for beginners as well as for a change of pace from the crowded areas like Flagstaff. Where the Fern Canyon talus field empties from the gully onto the trail, five mintues south from the entrance of the canyon, look up and west to see a nice overhanging boulder with a rising traverse called *Fire Dance* V10.

Fern Canyon

The southern end of The Flatirons with scattered blocks before and after entering Fern Canyon proper. As well, many nice short problems can be found off the inner canyon trail on the way up to #2.

❒ 1. **Go-Go Traverse V6**
A right to left traverse on the steep part of the left slab that makes up the south end of Fern Canyon.

❒ 2. **Black Ice V10** ★★★
Follow the trail uphill a quarter mile until you hit an obvious overhanging arête sport climb in the trail. The boulder sits immediately off to the left. The best stone in the Flatirons! This Lemaire classic climbs the roof on amazing holds to a scary topout. A sit start makes it V11.

Burgundy Boulder

A nice 11-foot tall block set below the trail and across from The Negatron as one heads north from Fern Canyon. The problems on the left (east) face are very worthwhile. The right (north) face has problems but they are extremely thin and fragile.

❒ 1. **V6** ★★★
The east face 19-foot long traverse going right and ending on a high rail past the pine tree. The footholds are disintegrating at the start. A V1 is on the furthest left side and goes up from the start of #1.

❒ 2. **V4** ★★
Just left of the huge low jug is a set of sloping edges. Move left to a hold in the traverse then dyno to the lip and muckle over.

❒ 3. **V4** ★★★
Start on the huge jug left of the pine and climb straight up. A difficult and sharp V6 crimping problem is 30 feet right on the northwest face which exits right or left (slightly easier).

Negatron Boulder

A quiet block to spend time on. Located approximately 40 yards uphill from the huge Mound Boulder. A number of problems grace the sides from solid edges to questionable flakes. The downclimb for this boulder is a down-jump or tree climb.

❒ 1. **V2 - V3** ★★
On the far left of the north face are a couple of decent problems on incut edges out the bulge.

❒ 2. **V5's** ★★ 😊
Up the steep left and right sides of the north face are a couple of problems. The rock looks quite questionable in the middle of the face. Both problems ascend just on the outskirts of the loose flakes.

❒ 3. **V2** ★★
Traverse the west face from left to right starting below the large overhang on the north face. A complete traverse across the north face through the west face is substantially harder.

❒ 4. **Absolute Surrender V5** ★★★★ 😊
Just left of the pine on the west face is a tall problem on perfect incut flakes. The crux comes with a big move to a crimpy rail about 15 feet up. A must do! All superlatives apply!!!

Black Ice

Burgundy Boulder

Negatron Boulder

❒ 5. **Absolute Control V3** ★★★ 😊
Just right of the pine on the west face is a tall problem on good edges. One of the best problems around.

❒ 6. **V1** ★
Just right of the V2 with the same start but move up and right to finish.

❒ 7. **V2** ★
Climb the southwest bulge on sloping edges. Also the best place to down-jump the boulder.

*** The Mound Boulder, 40 yards east of Negatron, hosts many proud undone highballs.*

BEAR CANYON / BONGO BOULDER

The lone boulder sitting in a meadow next to the Mesa Trail. This overhanging block has fire-blackened stripes on burnt orange rock. The far left side is gritty and not worth a moment's notice.

☐ 1. **V2** ★★ 🔵
Start off the adjacent block and climb up and right on huge huecos and holes. A tad licheny on the top-out moves.

☐ 2. **Bongo Boulder Traverse V6** ★★★
One of the nicest traverses in the Boulder area. Traverse the block beginning from the broken glass sds on the right and finishing on the V2 on the far left.

The Cube

THE CUBE / SLAPSHOT AREA

Also known as Dinosaur Mountain, this area of boulders is best known for the unrepeated *Slapshot* done by Jim Holloway.

THE CUBE
A tall toprope boulder with excellent high problems on the shorter west face.

☐ 1. **V1** ★ 🔵
Just right of the tree is a problem on good holds.

☐ 2. **Merest Excrescences V5** ★★★ 🔵
The tall vertical face right of the V1. Climbs up to a left-hand pocket then up the prow.

☐ 3. **The Holy One V8** ★★ 🔵
Climb the shallow pocketed face 10 feet right of #2.

☐ 4. **V3** 🔵
Around the corner on the left side of the south face.

THE JIM AND I BOULDER
The boulder 20 feet west of The Cube has a few nice lines.

☐ 1. **Gemini Traverse V4** ★
Sds the north face and make the long lip traverse topping out left of #2.

☐ 2. **Gemini V3** ★★ 🔵
Sds and ascend the arête on the right side of the north face.

☐ 1. **Bolt Slab V0** ★ 🔵
An excellent highball slab on the boulder's west face.

Melissa Lacasse cruising the classic Merest Excrescences V5   Photo: Andy Mann

ELEVATED ROCK

Just uphill (west) approximately 80 yards from The Cube is a boulder with severely overhung eastern face.

☐ 1. **Edging Edgio V8** ★★

Climb the roof heading right to a small crimp in the face to attain the top. Lowest lowball start undone V?.

☐ 2. **Slapshot V?**

Unrepeated Holloway problem that will stay that way as the glued hold doesn't allow any gripage.

☐ 3. **Elevated V8** ★

Start pinching the arête with right and the left on a small chip. Long move to a crimp and muckel the sloping arête. V4 jump start.

☐ 4. **Locked and Loaded V8** ★

On the left side of the west face just off the trail is a glorious sharp problem. Even further left is a hard one-move wonder.

☐ 5. **Spring Loaded V7** ★★★

Located in the middle of the west face, this problem starts low on good crimps. Move to decent edges and then a monster throw to a good incut.

Elevated Rock East Face

TRAILSIDE BOULDER

Just past Elevated Boulder on the left side of the trail.

☐ 1. **Jerome Bettis V5** ★

Ascend the left arête of the south face. A few V0 slabby warm-ups can be done left of this problem.

☐ 2. **The Common Front Range Flying Squirrel V4** ★★★

Classic line that climbs the middle of the south face and moves right to the arête.

Fred Nicole sets up for the crux jump of Spring Loaded V7   Photo: Andy Mann

Trailside Boulder

Quixote's Boulder

Lowball Zone

Medicine Boulder

QUIXOTE'S BOULDER

This unique block is located off the trail to the right about about 50 yards up trail from the Trailside Bolder.

☐ 1. **Dulcinea V7** ★★★
Sit start on an obvious matched hold under the roof, surf out and right up the grooves and slopers to an engaging top-out.

☐ 2. **Project** ★★
Climb the arête to the right of the previous problem. Needs lots of cleaning.

LOWBALL ZONE

Just off the trail on your right immediately after *Dulcinea*.

☐ 1. **Rennak's Delight V8** ★★
A suprisingly cool and difficult problem for being the lowest of all lowballs. Pull on under the roof and make a huge move to a sloping lip and desperately exit up and left.

☐ 2. **Mini Victory V6** ★
Start down and right and traverse across the face to a frustratingly slopey arête top-out.

☐ 3. **It Ain't No Layup V7** ★
Start as for the previous problem, get established on the face, and dyno for the lip.

MEDICINE BOULDER

Just off the trail on the way to the Avs Wall and directly across from the Trailside Boulder. A few boulders can be found directly uphill three minutes from this boulder and south of Avs Wall.

☐ 1. **Flash in the Pan V11** ★★
Left to right traverse across entire east face finishing around and up *Its Spicy*.

☐ 2. **Its Spicy V8** ★
Climbs the left side of the north face from a low start.

☐ 3. **The Schnaz V8** ★
Climbs up the middle of the east face.

☐ 4. **Invasion of the Body Scratchers V7** ★
The left arête of the east face. Watch that tree!

*** *Further up the main trail towards Mallory's Cave another 10 minutes is a Hueco-esque boulder that sits right off the trail at the final switch back. The trail actually cuts through the left side of this boulder. Many fine problems on brilliant fountain sandstone can be found here and on a couple boulders below. The landings here can be horrendous.*

Avs Wall

Sputnik Boulder

Avs Wall

Above and southwest (more west than south) approximately 65 yards from Elevated Rock is a long steep wall with a V12 traverse (*The Long Shot*) and straight up V1 to V10 problems across its expanse. Follow a trail heading northwest from the Medicine Boulder. Head northwest for more obscure blocks!

Second Flatiron Area

The Satellite Boulders

These sporadic boulders are quite similar to Flagstaff in texture, but have more varied aspects like blunt sloping arêtes, steep one-move problems, and solitude. Many more problems not covered in this guide can be found in this fine area.

Sputnik Boulder

The first boulder in the Satellites that is developed. It sits on the left side of the trail immediately after crossing the talus field. Directly above Sputnik left of the trail are a couple of recent problems. Grades are unknown.

❏ 1. The Bleep Traverse V4 ★
A left to right traverse across the entire face.

❏ 2. V2 ★
Climb the left side of the offset crack from a low start.

❏ 3. Sputnik One V1 ★★
Just right of the offset crack up the green lichen face.

❏ 4. Sputnik Two V0 ★
Ascend the low-angle slab right of #2.

The Wave

Stardust Boulder

An obvious long boulder just left of the trail above Sputnik approximately 25 yards. The slab has a few good lines as does the south face from a low start.

The Wave

Stardust Boulder

The first developed block on the right side of the trail after The Wave. A superb traverse skirts the north face.

❏ 1. Aerogel V5 ★★★
Start low and left and traverse to the matched sloping hold. Pull straight up to a small right-hand crimp then all the way up to the top. An easier pull grabs the low arête hold. A few variations exist to this problem.

❏ 2. The Hard Traverse V5 ★★ ⬤
The same as #1 but continue right around the corner on a huge layback. Get situated around the corner then punch to the neighboring block and finish on that boulder.

G-Friend Boulder

G-Friend Boulder

This short block faces uphill and is on the left side of the trail approximately 15 yards from Stardust Boulder.

❏ 1. The Girlfriend Traverse V4 ★★
Start left of the vertical face in a layback. Traverse left to right across the entire southwest face. And don't use the lip!

❏ 2. V1 ★★
On the backside of the G-Friend is a problem starting off a bomber incut and climbing through the undercling. The sds is V7 and adds a big move.

A-7 Boulder

Just past the G-Friend on the left is a short block with a small undercut section on the left side.

❑ **1. V1** ★★★
Climbs from a low start on the flat rail and tops out.

❑ **2. Captain Hook V9** ★
Start matched on the jug flake and climb directly out the roof.

❑ **3. Face Full of Brian V8** ★★
On the back of this block is a sds problem off a good undercling to bad slopes, sidepulls, and a painful fingerlock.

Zero Boulder

A small block just downhill from BBC and across the trail from A-7 and slightly downhill.

❑ **4. Zero V5** ★★
An excellent sloping arête problem from a low right start. A good warm-up starts fom the good edge in the face left and shares the arête holds.

Warm Up Boulder

A small block just left from the Zero Boulder that leans against the southwest side of the BBC Boulder.

Warm Up Boulder

❑ **1. Warm-Ups V0** ★★
Excellent face problems on cobbles and crimpers offer the best warm-ups to the hard problems that surround it. The best boulder in this area for beginners.

A-7 Boulder

Zero Boulder

David Lama flashing Captain Hook V9 on a cold winter's day   Photo: Andy Mann

BBC Boulder

This huge boulder is beautiful with a number of fine, albeit sharp problems skirting nearly all its sides. It is located up and right from A-7 approximately 25 yards and has a flat, easy-to-gain top. A massive overhanging boulder rests over its west face. Good, slabby warm-ups are on the block just southeast of BBC.

BBC Boulder

❑ 1. Fleshfest V10 ★★★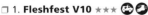

The amazing south arête. Start low and power out the arête staying true to the feature. The original method uses a miserable pebble pinch with the left hand (crux). A slightly easier variant (V9) pulls through crimps just right of the arête at the crux and gains the same finish. Stand start this fine line off an adjacent block for an amazing V5!

❑ 2. Lawn Dart V1 ★

A low start on the northeast face that climbs past a fragile left-hand edge.

❑ 3. Major Tom V4 ★★

On the far left side of the west face is a low start problem that trends right on crimps in the face to a big move to the lip.

❑ 4. Balance in Nature V6 ★★

Climb the left-facing dihedral starting from a low undercling then moving slightly left to finish. A direct finish is a little harder.

❑ 5. Re-Entry Burn V6 ★

Pain! This is one hell of a sharp problem but worth doing. That doesn't make a bit of sense but then again consider the amount of flappers your fingers have dealt with. Start on underclings and climb through the sharp edges and atrocious footholds. A V5 is just left from two small crimps; throw from a terrible sloper to gain the lip.

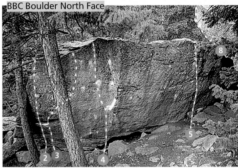
BBC Boulder North Face

❑ 6. The Grundel City Boy V10 ★★

Located on the left side of the south roof. Start low on an obvious matched hold and power past slopers to a difficult finish. A version recently done by Fred Nicole off-routes the left arête and goes at V12.

❑ 7. Original Grapple V4 ★★

On the south face is a roof. Start low on a bomber incut and continue up past some small edges to huge top-out jugs. A V5 starts the same as *Original* but finishes further left.

Turning Point Boulder

❑ 8. The Turning Point V8 ★★★

On top of the BBC is an overhanging arête problem that starts almost laying down. The most photographed line in the Flatirons.

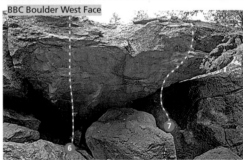
BBC Boulder West Face

Toe to Toe Boulder

❑ 9. Toe to Toe V7 ★★

Just 20 yards uphill from BBC block. Start on a flat shelf and climb out the short but tension-rich roof. *Blowing the Hatch* V3 goes straight up from the same start.

Vanessa Compton on Turning Point V8   Photo: Andy Mann

Toe to Toe Boulder

Rocky Balboas / Upper Satellites

The Rocky Balboas are a short, albeit strenuous, five-minute hike uphill. Lines in The Rockies are good quality and often entail tall slabs, or else short power problems. If the lower Satellite Boulders are not to your liking, or are crowded, The Rockies are a quiet change. Not pictured.

Additional boulders:

These three boulders are found in the drainage just north between the Upper and Lower Satellites.

Richter Scale

Climb a steep southeast arête from a low start V10 and finish up the slab or traverse right for bonus pump. A V7 stand start is called *Haley's Comet*.

Hobo Boulder

This distinct boulder is downhill from the arête to the north (approximately 60 yards) and sits next to the Second Flatiron. The selection of (somewhat contrived) problems range from V2 to V6 and face east (down the drainage).

Vertical Boulder

Problems on this gorgeous east face range from the easiest on the far left to excruciatingly thin problems on the right.

The following area directions are in the chapter intro, pg 156:

The Gutter

One of the many obscure, long traverses in The Flatirons. The Gutter is not pictured.

❏ **V7** ★★★
Climb the 87-foot traverse from the low right all the way to the far left side. A few variations come out of The Gutter.

The Utter

Directly left of The Gutter (hidden in a small chasm) is another similar problem on a much shorter overhang. The Utter is not pictured.

The Compound

This is the never-ending traverse west of The Gutter. Not pictured.

❏ **V6** ★★★
Climb the 202-foot traverse from the low right all the way left to the dead tree. At a mere 145 feet, a mantle must be done to reach the remaining overhang. A number of problems climb through the multitude of overhangs.

Sarah Durkee on Lip Traverse V4, The Ghetto   Photo: Fred Knapp

THE GHETTO

This is the creme-de-la creme of Flatiron areas thanks to the industrious efforts of motivated boulderers. The number of superb contrived and independent lines is staggering for such a small area. The Ghetto is basically broken into three main sections by chockstones and uneventful sections. The bottom section has excellent contrived problems and a clean landing. The middle section has possible back-slapping falls on a hard slab. The upper section is a large chasm with the best problems and requires a real go-for-it attitude due to the possible consequence of a 30-foot slide down the chasm (a rarity, but it has happened).

Note: This area is closed for raptor nesting every year from Feb.1 to July 31. Respect this closure to protect raptors and access (i.e., don't be an idiot and get it closed indefinitely because your project has to be sent). For more information visit www.ci.boulder.co.us.com.

ANACOSTIA WALL - BOTTOM SECTION

On the bottom right is a flat dirt area with a huecoed wall. It holds many fine contrived problems from V1 to V8.

❒ 1. **Anacostia V3** ★★
A low right to left traverse that can finish in a myriad of places.

❒ 2. **Dope Fiend V5** ★★
Start on the lowest dish left of the left seam. Move the right hand to a horn, and the left hand to the dope dish (a shallow edge/pocket just under the lip). Move up to the vertical section. Climb over the lip using not the slopers but rather edges on the upper face (one in the tan stone and the other on top of the green lichen streak). A V6 variation called *Anacostia Street* traverses into *Dope Fiend* from the far right.

Bottom Section

HUNTING HUMANS - MIDDLE SECTION

This part of The Ghetto is just left of the Bottom Section. A small chockstone separates the two sides that make up this section.

❒ 1. **Underdog V5** ★★ 🌢
Same start as *Doctor Slutpants* but all holds are on, including the top jugs.

❒ 2. **Doctor Slutpants V7** ★★★ 🌢
Climb straight out the chasm from a low start on the layback rail left of the chockstone. Stay on the leftmost holds and do not use the pebble midway up the problem. The top lip jugs are off. Use the crimper and tooth to bypass the jugs (same finish as *Trolling*).

❒ 3. **Ears V3** ★★ 🌢
The end of *Hunting Humans*. Starts on the ear-like holds above the large sloping hueco.

❒ 4. **Hunting Humans V8** ★★★ 🌢
Same start as *Trolling* but go straight up before crossing above the chockstone and top out on the ear-like holds (*Ears*) to the built-in pipe hold.

❒ 5. **Trolling for Skank V10** ★★★ 🌢
A long traverse that incorporates the holds of *Hunting Humans, Ears* and *Doctor Slutpants*. Start low and right of the chockstone on a right-facing broken layback. Climb left to the mini huecos and continue left to a large sloping hueco then out on thin, ear-like holds. Continue left above the chockstone and below the obvious pebble (*Underdog*) and finish out #2. Do not use the large jugs on the lip but a good left-hand crimp and sharp tooth immediately right of the huge lip jug. Pull onto the slab to a right-hand sloping edge then a higher incut edge and the end.

❒ 6. **Tabula Rasa V9** ★★
The rightmost problem, which begins right of the chockstone on the lowest incuts. Climb straight up using right-hand sidepulls and underclings and left-hand sloping dishes to high edges.

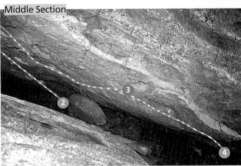
Middle Section

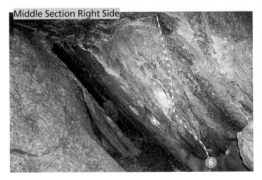
Middle Section Right Side

UPPER SECTION

The chasm on the left side of The Ghetto, with landscaped stones across the base. A distinct hueco/crack is on the bottom right side. Problems listed left to right.

❑ 1. S & M V4 ★★★
Stays below the lip and begins at the end of *Hueco Simulator*, finishing at the far left holds.

❑ 2. Inner Space V6 ★★★
Begin on the glued flake and climb up and out of the chasm.

❑ 3. Guanophobia V6 ★★★
Start left of *Spinalbifida* on left-traversing underclings. End on a large undercling below a huge glued flake with the feet on an orange bulb of rock, or link into #2 for a V8.

❑ 4. Hueco Simulator V4 ★★★
Starts on the huge dinner plate on *Lip Traverse* (left of the top-out to *Ghetto Boys*) and traverse left below the jugs of *Lip Traverse*. Ends where *S&M* begins (roughly at the point where the traverse is no longer above the chasm of *Inner Space*).

❑ 5. Ghetto Boys V9 ★★
Starts on the low start to *Spinabifida* and climbs straight up following the high seam on pockets and laybacks, an eliminate if done right.

❑ 6. Spinabifada V5 ★★★
Starts on the large hueco left of *Skin Poppin* and moves up and right on the lowest set of slopers and edges. The finish is just up and left of *Skin Poppin's* finish. A sds is V8 off a small pebble.

❑ 7. Ghetto Homos V3 ★★★
The same start as *Spinabifida* but climb straight up to the upper set of right angling huecos and slopers and finish the same as *Spinabifida*.

❑ 8. Skin Poppin Sluts V3 ★★★
The obvious huecoed crack left of *Violent Opposition*.

❑ 9. Lip Traverse V4 ★★★
Start above *Violent Opposition* and traverse the entire lip headed left.

❑ 10. Violent Opposition V5 ★★★
Start low and right and traverse left across the pinched arête and thin edges to the seam then up on jugs. A couple of contrived V7s climb straight up the middle of *Violent Opposition*. *Fear in Haiti* V9 does *Violent Opposition* and continues left past the seam (not using the jugs) to a mono and ends at *Skin Poppin Sluts*.

Upper Section

Upper Section

HOUSE PARTY BOULDER

This enormous chunk of solid, featured Fountain Sandstone high on the east face of Green Mountain (directly behind the summit of the Third Flatiron) is a great, out-of-the-way venue for highball and traverse aficionados. The long (65-foot) traverse of the north and west faces of the boulder is an ultra-classic voyage on fluted sandstone reminiscent of the Red River Gorge. The House Party Boulder is not pictured.

Directions: From the Bluebell Shelter hike 10-15 minutes up the road. Then follow the Third Flatiron Trail, which branches right off the Royal Arch Trail about five minutes up. Walk another 15-20 minutes, passing the Lower Satellite Boulders and emerging onto a large talus field below the north face of the Third. A trail leads uphill (west) from the middle of this talus field and is signed with "3rd Flatiron Descent Trail." Follow this steep, rugged trail uphill another 10-15 minutes until it hits the ridge behind the Third's summit. The north face of the boulder is right on the trail. Approach time: 40-50 minutes.

❑ 1. Sod It! V3 ★
This 30-foot high problem is a three-star problem buried under two star's worth of lichen. Start just right of the northeast arête and climb the scooped, slabby wall above.

❑ 2. Traverse V6 ★★★
Traversing doesn't really get any better than this. Start below #1 and punch right, eventually turning the northwest arête of the boulder to finish low across huecos and pods at the lip of a roof.

❑ 3. Scenic Traverse V1 ★★
On the upper tier of the west face, just above the finish to the traverse, find this huecoed wall. Go right to left. A fall off this one would be ugly.

❑ 4. House Party V2 ★★★
Start on edges near the left (west) end of the huge southern chasm and fire up for a ledge. Reach high for another horizontal then crimp your way through the crux exit moves, 25 feet above a blocky pit. Aesthetic.

BOULDERING BY PETER BEAL

When I think of bouldering I imagine Flagstaff and its steep slopes of scented pine forests or Rocky Mountain National Park and its remote alpine boulders, their surfaces scoured by the relentless winter snow and summer rain and hail. I imagine the Flatirons and their shadowy canyons and open mesas. These are just a few of the environments that draw me back again and again to bouldering. If bouldering is, as Ben Moon said, "the essence of climbing," these places and their particular characteristics draw me back again and again. So too with the textures and colors of the boulders. The smooth creases and crimps of the Park are etched into a twisted and fantastic swirl of metamorphic gneiss and schist. The various sandstones of the Front Range are shaped by water and frost in an endless variety of shapes and textures.

Bouldering is also about movement and difficulty. Early mornings in summer I find myself trying to catch just a hint of cool air and friction to stick just one move. Late fall and winter I spent huddled beneath some bleak cold wall, hoping I can figure out how to top out before my fingertips go numb. Shredded skin, strained muscles and tendons, deep mental frustration as so much effort is expended on the rock. Stabbing to a bad pocket, a small crimp, holding a terrible pinch, praying that a foot holds, all this is in exchange for a brief moment of mastery, that having been attained, vanishes in the air.

I have been climbing more than 30 years. I started as a boulderer and now find myself coming full-circle, still seeking answers in the enigma of difficult movement on steep stone, still finding meaning, however impossible to define, in the shapes of the rocks and my response to them. This quest, I am more certain than ever, will never end.

TOP 10 (FLAGSTAFF):

1. *West Face of Nooks Rock* **V7**
2. *Hagan's Wall* **V5**
3. *Red Wall Standard* **V5**
4. *Just Right* **V7**
5. *Cryptic Magician* **V7**
6. *Hollow's Way* **V8**
7. *North Face Traverse, Nook's Rock* **V8**
8. *Undercling Traverse* **V9**
9. *Mongolian Cosmonaut* **V8**
10. *Window Shopper* **V11/12**

Cameron Cross on the Green Lantern V4. Photo: Andy Man...

FLATIRONS SOUTH

ALADDIN'S LAMP AND UPPER BLUES BOULDERS

Flatirons bouldering doesn't get much better—or more obscure—than this. These stellar secluded boulders sit in an idyllic grassy gully two canyons south of the Terrain Boulders. Though the approach hike is lengthy, it's not especially steep, and the views of the spires and needles around Shadow Canyon are outstanding. The incredible Mamoonious Boulder offers a plethora of highball problems on impeccable Fountain Sandstone, while a recent find, the PB Boulders, offers stacks of varied problems in a Font-like forest.

Directions: Because of erosion, habitat and social trail issues, OSMP is planning on putting a cairned trail from the Terrain Boulders south to the Upper Blues Boulders, thus avoiding the original approach described below. Nevertheless, your first time in to the boulders it might be useful to use the old approach just to get oriented. Please avoid this approach in the fall, when the gully becomes an active bear habitat.

Take Broadway south out of Boulder to the junction with Highway 170 (the Eldorado Market is at this intersection). Turn west to Eldorado Springs. Drive west on Highway 170 for 1.6 miles to the South Mesa Trailhead down and right (an easy turn to miss). Hike north on the Mesa Trail for 20 minutes until you hit the "To Big Bluestem Trail" sign. Follow this cut-off north for about 3-4 minutes to the Big Bluestem Trail (Aladdin's Lamp is about 6-7 minutes up this trail in a small wash just beyond an orderly row of four pine trees to the south), which you then follow west toward the Mesa Trail (another 20-25 minutes).

For the Upper Blues Boulders walk north 60 feet on the Mesa Trail, then cut into the gully diagonaling northwest and up. The boulders are scattered along the length of this gully. The Atom Boulder is about five minutes up the gully, Zoofarsus is about seven minutes, and the enormous Mamoonious sits about 12 minutes up the gully from the trail. The PB Boulders are another three minutes past Mamoonious, heading west on an old trail in the gully.

Alternate approach: From the Bob Boulder at the Terrain Boulders, walk due south along old trail beds for approximately 10 minutes, hugging the base of the steep hillside to the west, to reach Mamoonious. Please reverse this approach when leaving and don't cut east to the Mesa Trail. This approach should be cairned in the near future.

Approach time: one hour.

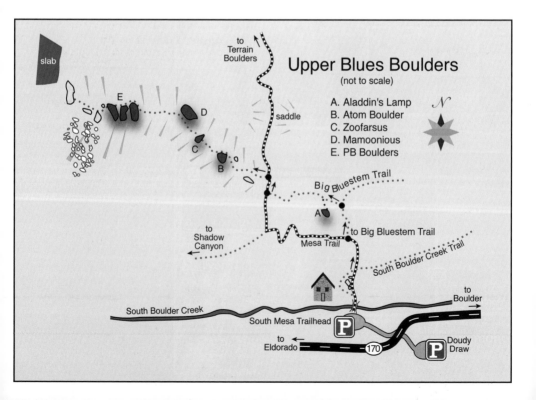

A. ALADDIN'S LAMP

A curious little cave boulder but well worth a visit on your way to the Upper Blues Boulders. Good landings, juggy rails and a fine southerly exposure make this an excellent bumbling and picnic venue. Hollow but seemingly solid jug-flakes abound. Aladdin's Lamp is not pictured.

❒ **1. Genie V3** ★
From the cave's far left side, traverse right across incuts rails. Finish on #2, 13 feet to the right.

❒ **2. Magic Carpet V2** ★
Tug on edges up the maroon wall just right of the grass-filled ledge. Sds on the hanging disk.

❒ **3. Climb Aladdin V3** ★
Crouch-start on the white-stained horizontal then amble up the crimpy face. Many variations possible. V4 if you traverse into it from the left.

UPPER BLUES BOULDERS

B. ATOM BOULDER

This is the first developed boulder in the Upper Blues area and sits in the gully floor 150 feet past a pointy slab/spire on the right. Though the holds are somewhat sharp, the landings are cush and the ripply grips attract the eye. The Atom Boulder is not pictured.

❒ **1. Doodlely Dud V4** ★
Sds on pockets in the gray band, then undercling on crystals out the low roof and turn the lip on grungy slopers.

❒ **2. Curly Merl V4** ★
Start on #1. Traverse the lip of the disk six feet, and finish on crimps right of the little tree.

❒ **3. Mighty Dude V4?** ★★
Start on a low, right-hand sidepull and reef up and left to bad holds over the lip. Burly. Perhaps harder since a hold broke.

❒ **4. Adam's Roof V4** ★★
Start matched in a positive, white-stained hueco at waist height then move up and left to a sharp slot. V2 if you start in the slot.

❒ **5. Teeny Babies V4** ★
Bust up the white pebbles, then huff your way up the blunt prow.

❒ **6. Jumpin' Gymnee V1**
The rounded, mossy northeast arête of the block.

C. ZOOFARSUS

A low, east-facing cave boulder just two minutes up the gully from the Atom Boulder. Though short, the problems offer athletic moves on pocketed purple stone. Zoofarus is not pictured.

❒ **1. Zooloo V3**
Start on the pockets and crank for a slot, then grunge up and over the nappy lip.

❒ **2. Zoofarsus Traverse V6** ★
Start far left on a flat jug and traverse across pockets in the roof, finishing far right on the crumbly face. Twenty feet long.

❒ **3. Zoo TV V6** ★★
Gymnastic and fun. Start on #2 and traverse into #4.

❒ **4. Zoofarsus Roof V4** ★
Sds on the low pocket band and punch straight out the roof to a grainy flake. Thuggy and gymnastic.

D. MAMOONIOUS

This monstrous erratic, blessed with flat piney landings and perfect rock, is way-the-heck up in the woods, making for a great escape. Horns, flakes, ripples and pockets dot the iron-hard maroon and tan stone on three sides of the boulder. Expect high problems.

Mamoonious

SOUTH FACE

❒ **1. Chaugle Pants V5** ★★★ ●
The leftmost line on the south face, starting five feet left of #2 and moving into a scooped dish at the lip of the overhang.

❒ **2. South Face Direct V3** ★★★ ●
Start about eight feet left along the flake and hit a sloper at the lip, then move up the varnished face above to a good pocket. Finish out the upper bulge for full value.

❒ **3. Crystal Reach V3** ★★ ●
From the bottom of the flake fire up and right to the obvious jug crystal then cruise up the face above.

❒ **4. Mamoonious Flake V3** ★ ●●
Climb along the flake/crack on the steep southwest side of the boulder, moving left around the corner to finish. Pumpy.

❒ **5. Easy Skeazin V0** ★★ ●
The downclimb. The path of least resistance on the buckets right of the crystal.

❒ **6. Crimp-Wah V4** ★★ ●
Sds six feet left of the southeast arête on slopers, then pimp your way up tinies to the good, maroon jug rail.

❒ **7. Southeast Arête V7** ★★ ●
Climb the prominent nose, off-routing the jug rails out left and using the textured sloper instead. Top out direct via the committing bulge.

❒ **8. Traverse V6** ★★ ●
Start on #6 and move left (west) across the wall, staying low on crimpers then moving high on the diagonaling slopers to finish on #2 (without stepping down to the flake). Pumpy and technical.

SOUTHEAST FACE

❒ **9. Southeast Wall V5** ★★★ ●
The excellent maroon face. Start standing on the block and fire up and right to an incut, then trend back left along the diagonal seams. Can also be started further left.

❒ **10. East Arête V4** ★★ ●
Start on #9 but go straight up to funky pockets over the lip, finishing up in the rounded groove. Freakous.

EAST FACE

❒ **11. Mamoonia V3** ★
Climb flakes in the bulging, black streak just left of the long white stain. Worthy.

❒ **12. Moonbeam V6** ★
The diagonaling seam six feet right of #10. Hard to achieve lift-off.

❒ **13. Squeezin' and Skeezin' V4** ★
A difficult line just left of the large tree growing against the northeast face. Start with your right hand on a good flake/sidepull.

E. THE PB BOULDERS

Discovered in spring 2001, this recent find makes the approach trudge to the Blues Boulders all the more worthwhile, adding a tightly grouped cluster of six impressive boulders to this gully. Surrounded by trees, these sandstone blocks are mostly shady, providing a good venue on warmer days. Problems vary from highballs to fun slabs and pumpy overhangs, almost all on perfect rock. Walk three steep minutes up the gully from Mamoonious. Many forgotten classics and looming FA's await another 20 minutes uphill.

BOULDER #1

The enormous, glassy boulder at the bottom (east side) of the cluster. It's the first boulder you'll encounter.

☐ 1. **Blajack V9** ★★★
From the middle of the south face bust to a left-hand sidepull, drive-by to the jug, then rock onto the arête. A lower start to *Blajack* is proper and still undone.

☐ 2. **The Altruist V13** ★★★★
Climb the clean southeast arête on the super-aesthetic south face. Big reaches to micro crimps on a flat, overhanging wall.

☐ 3. **Project V?** ★★★
From high miserable holds on the east face climb to sidepulls and the highball finish.

Boulder #1

BIG ORANGE (BOULDER #2)

This is the giant block just uphill and west with its characteristic, highball, orange-colored north face. Two must-do problems on Eldo-hard stone await the intrepid!

☐ 1. **Big Orange V1** ★★★
The tall face. Start on the right in a faint groove and work left on the jugs, topping out on the left side of the face past a white-stained flake. The stellar direct start through a perfect mono is still a project.

☐ 2. **Kurious Oranj V6** ★★★
Sds on the block, your left hand on the good horizontal edge, then work straight up the face on crimps to a lunge move. Top out direct to finish. A super low start left of *KO* with the same finish is V9.

☐ 3. **Orange Groove V0** ★
The easy groove on the right side of the north face.

Boulder #2

THE SAG WAGON (BOULDER #3)

Another super-sized block just west again, easily recognized by its flat, highball, black-colored west face. The dueling highballs on the monolithic west face will loosen your stool and the corner on the north side offers a good challenge for the aspiring hardperson.

☐ 1. **Sag and Bag V5** ★
Low-baggins. Sds on opposing pinch holds on the south side of the boulder left of the tree. Out the cave and up the slab.

☐ 2. **Deuto's Pride V3** ★★
The rightmost problem on the west face, working past an undercling flake to jugs.

☐ 3. **Black Wall V5** ★★★
The central line on the face, starting from a sds and working right from the left-trending ramp up the black wall.

☐ 4. **Green Lantern V4** ★★★
Climb the green lichen stripe on the left side of the west face.

☐ 5. **Corner V8** ★★
The overhanging dihedral on the north side from a sds. Would get another star if the boulder out right weren't so annoyingly close.

Boulder #3

THE SLAB WAGON (BOULDER #4)

The next boulder west with the high, slabby, licheny faces. With some travel these problems should end up being fairly fun.

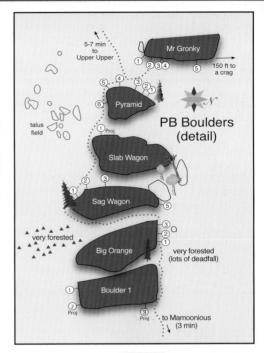

Boulder #4

❏ **1. Project V?** 🌐

Climbs on the right, west steep overhang on less than ideal stone. A fine lip traverse from down and right could be done.

❏ **2. Slip V5** ★★

Surf the southeast arête. A low start will be desparado! Be careful topping out as one person has taken the slip onto the leg breaking boulder below. See page174.

THE PYRAMID (BOULDER #5)

This pleasing, pyramidal block stands alone, just above the lower four blocks, and features good slab and arête problems on which to warm up.

❏ **1. The Downclimb V0**

This is the groove feature just right of the arête on the boulder's west face.

❏ **2. Arête Master V1**

The blunt arête feature just right of #9.

❏ **3. Phillip's Slab V2** ★

The left-of-center line up the west face on small sharpies.

❏ **4. Undone Slab V2** ★★

A harder but similar line up the right side of the wall.

❏ **5. Arête Meister V0** ★

The sharp southwest arête with a slightly mossy top-out. Fun.

❏ **6. South Face V3** ★★

An engaging line on the aesthetic, lichen-streaked south face. Start low on sidepulls and yank for a jug over the small roof, then move up the wall above.

MR. GRONKY (BOULDER #6)

This is the highest boulder in the cluster and just uphill and right (north) 40 feet from The Pyramid. It's also the best boulder in the cluster, with tall—but not highball—problems on splitter purple and maroon stone.

❏ **1. Funkarête V4** ★★

The left arête of the boulder from a low sds. Gymnastic.

❏ **2. Slickhedral V5** ★★

Sds with a small but incut right-hand flake then head up the obtuse, slippery dihedral. Puzzling.

❏ **3. One Trick Pony V5** ★★★

Jump start onto the sloping arête feature and surf it up untill you can rock over the lip. The sds once done from #1 has broken and will be much harder.

❏ **4. The Full Gronky V7** ★★★

An unrelenting pumpfest on smooth, purple slopers. Traverse right along the horizontal lip of the purple plate, finishing on #5. A straight up project is in the middle of the traverse.

❏ **5. Mr. Gronky V5** ★★★

The vertical climb of the purple plate. Sds and bear-hug your way up this crazy feature to a taxing lip encounter. Starting here, rolling right into the face on crimps, and gaining the right arête/lip is a project.

PB Boulders (detail)

Boulder #5

Boulder #6

*** Further south, and best approached from South Mesa Trail Parking, is Shadow Canyon. New developments beckon visitors. Many giant blocks and wicked power problems line the trail and hillsides. Problems up to V11 exist with plenty of room for further development. Please respect the season closures.

*** Further south one gully directly below the Matron, lie some of the most aethestic bouldering in the Flatirons. You'll find a good 30 problems in the gully, many bordering on mega-classic. Please respect the seasonal closures.

*** OK troopers, even further south one gully, tucked quietly in the trees, resides The Shadow Cube Boulder. This maroon beauty will become visible 200 yards to the west as one walks 10 minutes south down the Old Mesa Trail toward Eldorado Springs. It is home to at least four really good problems up to V6.

Scott Neel on Golden Kashmir Sleeper V8 Matron Boulders

Justin Roth makes the first ascent of Slip V5

Photos: Andy Mann

Miah Jones sends What About Bob V4 Photo: Jay Droeger

TERRAIN BOULDERS

Jay Droeger led the rediscovery of this fine cluster of blocks in the late 1990s, thus the area also bears the moniker *Droegerland*. This shady hang offers one of the better concentrations of bouldering in the Flatirons (meaning, once you drop your pad you don't have to hike another mile to get to the next boulder, as is often the case up here). The boulders are well protected from the elements by a dense forest, making them uninviting during Boulder's chilly winters but excellent in the spring and fall.

The rock is a solid, tight-grained Fountain sandstone featured with huecos, nubbins and crimps—smacking more of Eldo than Flagstaff. The superb Tower of Power might just be the best boulder problem of its grade in the Boulder area. Highballs abound, though the landings are often soft and flat. Simply put, the Terrain is a great bouldering area in a beautiful, relaxing setting at the foot of Bear Peak.

Directions: From the intersection of Broadway and Table Mesa in Boulder turn right (west) onto Table Mesa and drive 0.6 miles to Lehigh, where you take a left (south). Drive another 0.8 miles up the big hill and turn right onto Cragmoor Road (the first right past the light at Mesa Elementary School). Drive 0.1 miles west on Cragmoor and park in the dead-end.

From the parking lot walk west and stay right, following the sign for the North Fork Shanahan Trail to its junction with the Mesa Trail. Then head south on the Mesa Trail for five to seven minutes, contouring into, then out of, a drainage. As you climb out and crest a ridge, the trail bends from east to south. Walk roughly 70 yards from this bend to a slight ridge overlooking a grassy bowl. Cruise up this ridge, rock hopping to minimize impact, for one third of a mile to the Bob Boulder. The Animal Chin Boulder and Fairview Boulder are about two minutes northwest of here across a meadow. Expect an approach time of about 45-50 minutes.

Will LeMaire on Flower Power V10   Photo: Jay Droeger

MAIN TERRAIN BOULDERS

WANKA ROCK (AKA THE BOB BOULDER)

This is a choice, 17-foot high blob of Fountain Sandstone plopped down in a pleasant, sunny meadow just 200 yards southeast of Fairview Boulder. Though the holds are somewhat sharp, most of these problems are "must-dos."

☐ **1. Golden Ticket V2** ★

Up dishes and crimps on the bulging left side of the south face. Nearly as rad as Hueco's *Hobbit in a Blender*.

☐ **2. Bob's Crack V1** ★

Crank past good huecos into the black-stained water groove.

☐ **3. Dude's Face V4** ★★

Harder than it looks and still a bit mossy. Work past strange fluted rails just left of the rounded arête.

☐ **4. Trust Arête V4** ★★

Start on #5 then yard left for the arête at the hueco. More fun than *Dude's Face*.

☐ **5. Bob's Wall/What About Bob? V4** ★★★

Continuous, highball, and interesting on appealing red rock. Punch up to the hueco then move slightly right to finish on crimps. One of Boulder's best.

☐ **6. All About Bob V2** ★

Up incuts on the right side of the boulder, starting on a white-stained flake and moving right.

Wanka Rock

FUNK SOUL BOULDER

This is a decent little warm-up block, with kind jugs along its lip to get the big muscle groups working. It features a perfect landing and one of the world's worst lowball traverses. It lies just downhill and south, 50 feet from the Fairview Boulder.

☐ **1. Madam Assey V0** ★

The fun warm-up slab(s) on the southeast side of the rock.

☐ **2. Schnitzel Bock V2** ★

The left to right traverse, using the jugs along the lip of the wall and topping out as for #5. Fun and pumpy.

☐ **3. Schweinhund V9**

A worthless butt-dragging traverse across the bottom three feet of an already diminutive wall. Does bouldering get any stupider than this?

☐ **4. Funk Soul Roof V4** ★

Sds on chalked-up finger slots, below and slightly left of a jug/horn in the middle of the northeast face. V1 starting from the horn.

☐ **5. V2**

Sds on a purple rail near the wall's right margin, then move up past slopers, finishing just left of two small trees growing out of the boulder.

Funk Soul Boulder

FAIRVIEW BOULDER

This house-sized block is the rightmost of the two huge boulders in the main area. The top features commanding views of Fairview High School—great if high schools are your thing. There are good problems in the V1 to V5 range on almost all its faces, ranging from the sit-down crimpfests of the northwest face to the high, juggy problems around the front side.

□ 1. GFP V1 ★
Girl Friend Problem. Past ripples and horizontals on the southwest corner of the rock.

□ 2. GFT V1
Girl Friend Traverse. Sds on huecos underneath the finish to #3 and reel left on jugs, standing up onto a large, purple ledge feature. Low and uninspiring.

□ 3. Kleine Schlampe V3 ★
Ouch! Start low in the horizontal crack as for #4 and #5 but reel left onto the sharp, crimpy lip, moving around the corner and topping out left of the large ponderosa.

□ 4. Eara Fuchin Schmuckin V3 ★★★
The poor-man's *Warm-up Roof.* Start low in the crack, move left 10 feet, then head up past sloping crimps to a juggy, highball top-out.

□ 5. Shoots and Ladders V4 ★
From low in the crack, punch right onto a gritty sloper then head straight over the bulge above to an easy but dirty finish.

□ 6. Snuff V1
Sds on the northeast arête, moving right to a horn at the lip behind the large ponderosa tree.

□ 7. Parasol V4 ★★
The leftmost problem on the low northwest face. Sds on purple undercling blocks, then head out the bulge to a funky lip move.

□ 8. Corner V2
Six feet right of #7 is the obvious crack/corner feature covered in pine needles, rat feces and mud. Don't bother.

□ 9. Kenny G's Meat Whistle V5 ★
A long name for a short problem. Start on a good purple undercling beneath the undercut roof right of #8, then head up the face on sharp slopers.

□ 10. Plush V7 ★★
The best and most obvious line on the wall, starting on a rail below the tallest part of the face and moving past a sharp pocket to a sloper with a crystal embedded in its left side.

Fairview

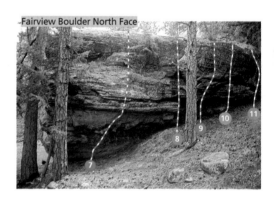
Fairview Boulder North Face

□ 11. Shag V2 ★
The rightmost problem on the wall. Work past pebbles in the seam from a sds on a good rail at knee height.

□ 12. For Her Pleasure V4 ★
Sds at a good four-finger left-hand pocket and a sharp bidoigt for the right on the west face, then move past sharp holds on the ribbed bulge.

ANIMAL CHIN BOULDER

This huecoed sandstone behemoth, 10 feet left (southwest) of the Fairview Boulder hosts the area's showcase problem *Tower of Power*, a sequential, highball journey up a 30-degree overhanging wall on perfect rock, as well as a handful of good highballs.

□ 1. Ejector Seat V5 ★★
This tricky rig climbs the rounded dihedral feature behind a copse of small pine trees on the south edge of the enormous east face. Start on the right and move left through the corner to a dastardly lip move.

□ 2. Highball/Solo V5 ★★★
This 20-foot high vertical face is mandatory fare for the highball enthusiast. Begin on left-leaning ramps around the arête from *Tower of Power* and move right onto the red face. Thin and pebbly up high.

□ 3. MBT V4
Matt's Bad Traverse. Start as for *Tower of Power* but traverse right across the entirety of the north face, finishing right around the corner onto the slab. Forty-five feet of awkward, pointless traversing.

Animal Chin

□ 4. Tower of Power V10 ★★★★
The striking line up the right side of the hanging arête, starting from a sds on underclings and voyaging through continuous, overhanging territory. *Flower Power* goes at hard V10 and stays on the arête.

❏ 5. It Satisfies V5 ★★ 🌀

Boy—does it ever! Begin just right of #3 with a sds at the small crack/corner. Head right to a rail, crank a hard move straight up, then trend right on strange, rampy rock.

❏ 6. Under the Influence V2 ★★★ 🌀🌀

An awesome jug haul taking the line of least resistance up the middle of the north face. Continuously interesting.

❏ 7. Bilinski's New Van V4 🌀🌀

Friable, mankus and mungy.

❏ 8. Trench Mouth V2 ★★★ 🌀

On the west face, move right along a crack/flake feature into a black streak, then head up on crispy flakes.

❏ 9. V3 🌀🌀

Up the bulging wall with a slab at its base just right of #8. Crimpy, flaky and horrible.

Animal Chin

UPPER TERRAIN BOULDERS

THE LOVE BOAT

These highballs are as close as you'll ever get to cocktail hour on The Love Boat. This enormous gray-green block floats 200 yards uphill (west) of the Main Terrain Boulders, and 100 yards above Terror Slab Boulder (a 35-foot high boulder with a highball V1 slab on it's broad northeast face and a decent V4 on its south side). The Love Boat is only about half developed, with room for some very bold highballs both on its bulging east face and on the impeccable, swirly rock of the perennially shady Nordwand.

The Love Boat

❏ 1. Southeast Corner V3 🌀🌀

What, are you kidding me? Up the rounded southeast arête past dirty horizontals over a hideous slab landing.

❏ 2. Hot Buttered Cock Porn V4 ★★ 🌀

Harder than it looks, this scary problem moves left across the bulge then goes up behind the large ponderosa pine abutting the east face.

Problems #3-#6 all top out into the obvious bowl 15 feet up before moving left across the big slab. Descend to the west.

❏ 3. Tall Boy V3 ★★ 🌀

Begin just right of the tree and move past scoops and ledges into the big bowl.

❏ 4. Glass Plate V3 ★ 🌀

For genuine scat connoisseurs only! Start four feet right of #3 and move up past laybacks and underclings into the middle of the bowl.

❏ 5. Famous V4 ★★ 🌀

Move up the smooth red face to a small undercling, then crimp your way into the right side of the bowl.

❏ 6. Northeast Corner V7 ★★ 🌀

Start on an undercling and follow sharp, shallow dishes near the arête, moving left into #5 to finish.

❏ 7. Having a Moment V3 ★★★ 🌀

Perhaps the finest highball at the Terrain Boulders. This problem cruises up a series of scoops in the dark, swirly rock right of the highest, blankest part of the north face. Continuous, slopey, and TALL!

❏ 8. Fag Hag V2 ★★ 🌀

Start on a horizontal rail four feet right of #7 and surmount the slightly mossy bulges above. Good stone.

HAVING A MOVEMENT PART DEUX BOULDER

Two hundred yards southwest and uphill from The Love Boat, this isolated ridgetop area offers a few choice lines on compact red rock. The boulder comprises a small, red spire poking up from the south side of the faint ridgeline.Not pictured

❏ 1. Having a Movement V5 ★★★ 🌀🌀

The leftmost problem, on pocketed rock with a hard red veneer. This problem faces southeast.

❏ 2. Paulious Maximus V4 ★

Sds on the south face, eight feet down and right of #1. Slightly chossy.

❏ 3. Uberhangin V3 ★

Just right again is this west-facing line up an overhang past pockets.

NORTH TERRAIN BOULDERS

THE MILLENNIUM FALCON

This is an overhanging disc-shaped plate of good, steep sandstone two minutes north of the main area via a faint track crossing the forested gully (also filled with blocks). Excellent thuggy climbing on user-friendly stone. The overhang points east.

❑ 1. Hand Solo V3 ★
This problem would get an extra star if it didn't have a back-slapper landing at the crux. Start in finger slots around the southeast side of the rock, crank left off an undercling, then huck to the lip.

❑ 2. Spewbacca V4 ★★★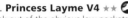
Stellar roof climbing on bizarre but solid holds. Start just right of the pillar/slab abutting the east face with your hands matched on a good flake. V5 if you come in from the low pockets on #3.

❑ 3. Princess Layme V4 ★★
Crank out of the obvious low pockets to the ramp at the lip, then grovel over.

THE EVIL KNIEVEL BOULDER

A less-steep but equally as highball version of The Millennium Falcon about 100 yards due west (uphill) from the Falcon, offering good problems on interesting stone with a few lines right of #2 to establish.

❑ 1. Evil Knievel V3 ★★
Up the left side of the east face, six feet right of a small crack. Long reaches to super-kibby huecos, pods and horns.

❑ 2. Evil Twin V5 ★★
The tallest line on the rock with a big move to a good edge/rail at the top. A little grainy.

DEATH ARÊTE GROTTO

Closer to the Go-Go than the actual Terrain Boulders, this shady little venue merits a visit on a hot day. Head north through deadfall for two minutes from the Millennium Falcon.

❑ 1. East Face Center V3 ★
Straight up crimps in the middle of the east-facing block forming the right wall of the grotto.

❑ 2. The P-Link V6 ★
Begin on #3, move left to a slot in the face, then dyno into #1 to finish. Height-dependent.

❑ 3. Alpine Pansy V5 ★★★
The technical, devious and strenuous prow/arête on the right side of the wall. A unique, Font-like feature with an ugly, back-slapper landing.

Millennium Falcon

Evil Knievel Boulder

Death Arête Grotto

Mike Banuelos on Evil Knievel Boulder   Photo: Andy Mann

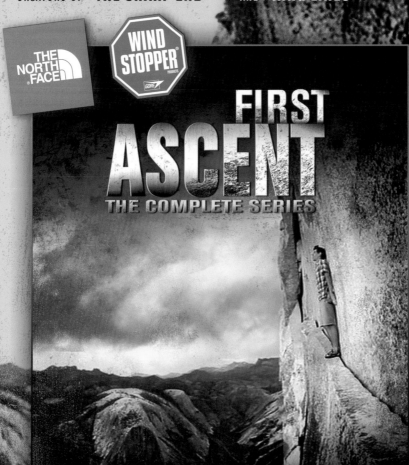

PAUL ROBINSON

To me Colorado bouldering is a special gift. Growing up on the east coast, in New Jersey, I was unable to climb outside most of the time living so far from any decent rock climbing. It was a hard life for a growing climber. But, once I moved to Colorado, I felt truly lucky to know that there are an infinite number of boulders here along the Front Range, most of which are of the utmost quality. So now, having lived here for almost four years, and having seen only a small portion of Colorado's infinite boulders, it seems as if this place will never be climbed out. I've traveled the globe for bouldering and in most places there seems to be a finite amount of rocks to be climbed on, but it is different here on Colorado's Front Range. Everytime I leave my house to go climbing I seem to stumble across something new that catches

my eyes. And, I know that there is more. Right now just sitting in the forest of Colorado are massive boulders that have never been seen by the human eye and may never be. These boulders are bigger and better than anything ever found before, and the crazy thing is, there probably isn't just one set of these, there are tons and tons of them. Some will be discovered one day and others won't. I think that's really what makes Colorado bouldering so special. There is truly no end. Exploring will continue and new amazing FA's will be done and all it will take is a little creativity and a strive for the unknown.

PAUL'S 2007 FRONTRANGE TICKLIST (not bad for a full-time student)

- ☑ *Midnight Express* V14 (Boulder Canyon)
- ☑ *Echale* V14 (Clear Creek Canyon)
- ☑ *Suspension of Disbelief Stand* V12 (Eldorado Canyon)
- ☑ *Free Range* V13 (Boulder Canyon)
- ☑ *Formula 500* V12 *FA* (Clear Creek Canyon)
- ☑ *Dark Waters* V12 (Clear Creek Canyon)
- ☑ *Lost* V11 (Eldorado Canyon)
- ☑ *Elegant Universe* V11 (Eldorado Canyon)
- ☑ *The Hug* V11 (Boulder Canyon)
- ☑ *Left Graham* V11 (Arête Boulder Canyon)
- ☑ *Carrea Gt* V11 (Clear Creek Canyon)
- ☑ *Stanley Kubrick* V11 (Clear Creek Canyon)
- ☑ *Formula 50* V10 (Clear Creek Canyon)
- ☑ *Honeymilker* V11 *FA* (Micky Meadows)
- ☑ *Muddy Waters* V11 (Clear Creek Canyon)
- ☑ *Moon Arête* V10 (Horsetooth Reservoir)
- ☑ *Animal* V10 (Clear Creek Canyon)
- ☑ *Where the Monkey Sleeps* V10 (Boulder Canyon)
- ☑ *Fluid Mechanics* V10 (Clear Creek Canyon)
- ☑ *Open Season Stand* V10 (Clear Creek Canyon)
- ☑ *Purity Control* V10 (Mathews-Winter Park)
- ☑ *The Infinite* V10 *FA* (East Draw)
- ☑ *Qigong* V10 (Eldorado Canyon)
- ☑ *Dave's Problem* V10 (Eldorado Canyon)

Paul Robinson on the FA of Resonated V9   Photo: Andy Mann

ELDORADO SPRINGS CANYON

Boulder's most famous and historic climbing venue has long been host to a myriad of good boulder problems, yet only recently have climbers begun developing the large, promising blocks up and out of the canyon proper. With its enchanting ambience, solid rock, and unexplored bouldering possibilities, good old Eldo promises to keep yielding great new problems in the years to come. The rock, subject to different geologic forces than the rest of the Fountain formation in the nearby Flatirons, is generally bullet hard—sometimes so bullet it's blank!

Directions: Drive south on Highway 93 (Broadway) out of Boulder, to the junction with Highway 170, (1.7 miles south of the last stoplight in town, at Greenbriar). Turn right and drive 3.1 miles west through the town of Eldorado Springs to the park entrance, where you must pay a daily entrance fee (or an annual Colorado State Parks pass, valid also at Castlewood Canyon).

PARKING BETA:

For the East Draw: Park in the lowest lots just inside the Park and walk back east across the bridge to the Springs. There is no public parking in the town.

For the Whale's Tail and the Wisdom Simulator Simulator: Park in one of the lower lots just past the entrance station.

For West World: Drive roughly 0.4 miles up the canyon and park at the road-side Milton Boulder on the right, when the creek is low or frozen, otherwise park in one of the lower lots and approach via the West Ridge Trail.

For the Eldorado Canyon Trail Boulders (Pony Keg, Musical Boulders and Nightmare Block): Drive 0.7 miles up the canyon and park at the Gill Boulder on the right (just over the bridge) or continue west toward the Ranger Station (the low road) and park in one of the lots there.

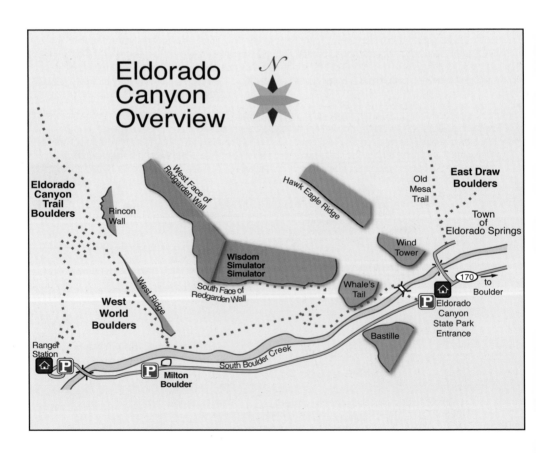

EAST DRAW

Perched on the sunny hogback above the quiet town of Eldorado Springs, these secluded boulders saw only sporadic action until they were rediscovered by Eldo residents Eric Johnson and Chip Ruckgaber in the fall of 2000. Home to The Couch Potato, a 5.12 toprope wall dating back to the 80s, this sheltered ridge is a perfect winter destination, catching sun until early evening and melting out quickly after snowstorms. The rock varies from bullet Dakota to a pebbly sort of hand-eating conglomerate reminiscent of the more rubbly stuff at Pile Tor or Biglandia 40 miles north. Though the boulders are on public land, access is somewhat tricky and your every move can be seen and heard from the town below. Best to limit your group size and maintain a low profile!

Directions: Drive west through the town of Eldorado Springs and park in the lower lot in the Park. Walk back east across the bridge, hang a left across the other bridge to the Springs then follow the road east as it goes behind the pool. Just after the pool the road splits into three; take the middle fork, heading uphill and east through a trailer park. Follow the road back around behind the trailer park (west) until it forks again into two driveways. Walk 100 feet up the righthand driveway, then take the trail that heads off right onto the hillside (this is the Old Mesa Trail). Follow the trail 50 yards to a large pine tree, then branch right on a faint climber's trail and make your way up the hill as best you can.

Chip Phillips on Block One's V5 Photo: Andy Mann

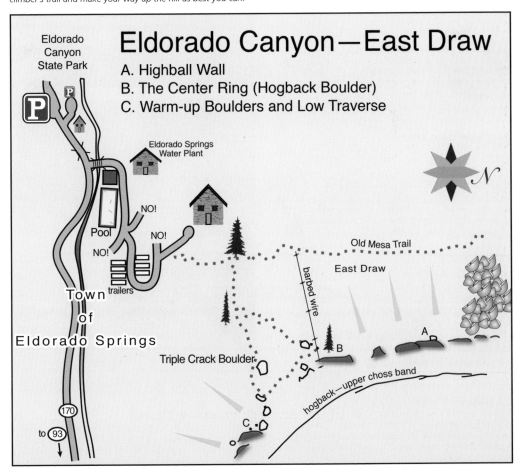

Eldorado Canyon State Park

Eldorado Canyon—East Draw

A. Highball Wall
B. The Center Ring (Hogback Boulder)
C. Warm-up Boulders and Low Traverse

Eldorado Springs Water Plant

NO!
NO!
NO!
Pool

Town of Eldorado Springs

trailers

Old Mesa Trail

East Draw

barbed wire

Triple Crack Boulder

hogback—upper choss band

A
B
C

170
to 93

A. Highball Wall

Tall problems with committing moves and butt-clenching top-outs, well above a grassy landing. This diamond-shaped wall is approximately 60 yards northwest of the Center Ring, just past an equally appealing toprope up a tall black face. The left sector of the wall over the terrible block landing has yet to see a ropeless ascent.

☐ 1. Pervertical Sanctuary V2 ★
Climb the left side of the diamond-shaped wall via an incipient crack, moving right onto #3 to finish.

☐ 2. D1 V4 ★★
The direct line up the middle of the diamond. From the horizontal rail, two feet above the small roof, move left onto crimps and laybacks in the burnished patch of tan rock.

☐ 3. King of Swords V2 ★★★
The right side of the wall. Continuous climbing on good holds past a sinker pocket to a bizarre, disconcerting top-out. Twenty-plus feet tall.

*** Even further north, five minutes along this hillside, are old 5.12 topropes that have since been bouldered. It is the obvious, orange, overhanging boulder you'll see from Eldorado Springs. Beware loose flakes and bring a thousand crashpads.*

B. The Center Ring
(aka The Hogback Boulder)

This varied wall of rugged conglomerate is the main hang in the East Draw, offering a 60-foot, schralper traverse and a handful of good up-problems. To get there wind your way northeast up the hill, eventually crossing an old barbed-wire fence up high. The fence abuts the right end of the wall.

☐ 1. Hooey's Back Porch V3 ★
Start on the sloping horizontal at arm's length on the wall's left end and reel straight up over the lip to a hidden finger pocket. It's a great V8 from a low-as-you-can-go sit start.

☐ 2. V3 ★
Same start as #1 but reel right along the lip, topping out past a loose-looking block feature.

☐ 3. The Infinite V10 ★★
The line left of *Pig-Dog*. Start as for #4, roll left into the face, grab some horrendous crimps and chuck for the seam.

☐ 4. Pig-Dog V6 ★★★
One of the steeper problems on the Front Range, taking a tempting line of holds out a flat, 30-degree overhanging wall. Sit start, ass in the dirt, left hand in a four-finger pocket, right hand on a sidepull, then go straight out the overhang.

☐ 5. Crack V2
Start on #4 but crank right along the painful, pebbly crack under the roof.

☐ 6. Pig's Nose V3 ★★
A superb jug haul! Start just right of #4, sitting down with your right hand in a deep, incut letterbox. Crank past horizontals and the pig's nose to good holds at the lip.

☐ 7. Slopers V3 ★
Climb the face on the right side of the wall, 10 feet left of the big tree, via glassy slopers. Challenging.

☐ 8. Undercling Mantle V2
The face just right of #6, starting on funky holds in the brown rock and hitting mossy jugs at the lip.

☐ 9. Barb-Wire Traverse V7 ★
Sixty feet long and very rugged. Begin as far right as possible, just left of the ponderosa. Stay low (five feet and under) through the beginning and middle on funky horns, slopers and pockets to finish out on #6. Knee-bar rests are on. The traverse into #4 is *Pig-Dog Girl* V9 ★★.

Highball Wall

The Center Ring

Paul Robinson on the first ascent of The Infinite V10
Photo: Andy Mann

C. Warm-up Blocks

This trio of Carter Lake-style cubes of brown and green sandstone is situated along the hillside down (60-70 yards) and southeast of The Center Ring. As the name implies, this is a great place to warm up.

Block One

This block has a challenging, crimpy problem on its southeast face and a handful of mossy slabs (V0-V2) on its northwest side.

❏ 1. **Crimpy Face V5** ★★
A steeper-than-it-looks type problem on the aesthetic southeast face. Start just right of the arête on pebbly crimpers, make a big move up and right to another set of crimps, then finish out past the loose flake (no grab!) in the black rock.

❏ 2. **V2** ★
The stand-up finish to #1, moving to the jug at mid-height from a crisp, right-hand undercling.

Block Two

This block faces almost due south, making it a good place to catch morning sun on your warm-up circuit. Melts out quickly.

❏ 1. **Left Side V2** ★
Climb the tan rock right of the arête, eventually moving left around the arête into a finger crack.

❏ 2. **Black Dike V1** ★
The most pleasant line on the wall. Follow the pebbly, black striation just left of the center.

❏ 3. **Scoop-Face V3** ★
Climb the scoop feature in the center of the wall, starting with your left hand on an undercling and your right hand on a good sidepull, then up the grainy face above.

❏ 4. **Right Arête V2** ★
Start with a chest-high right-hand crimp around the corner then slap up to the big plate on the left and mantle over.

❏ 5. **Overhanging Crack V1**
The steep crack/flake feature around the corner from the arête.

Block Three

This 20-foot high block leans against the top of the Low Traverse, forming a small alcove.

❏ 1. **Crack V0**
Climb the loose, spooky, right-leaning crack up the left side of the southwest face.

❏ 2. **Face V2** ★★
Trend diagonally right across the big face, passing a couple of ledges en route to the mortifyingly technical top-out.

❏ 3. **Scoop V2** ★★
This career-ending line takes the scoop and arête on the right side of the block over the terrible landing. Committing, though not especially difficult.

Low Traverse

This excellent power-endurance problem on the steep, recessed wall abutting the lowest of the Warm-up Blocks is a good place to finish off, as the holds are much smoother than those at the other walls.

❏ 1. **Crack V2** ★★
The excellent finger-to-hand crack on the left side of the wall. Start sitting down on the horn for full value.

❏ 2. **Face V5** ★★
The dark-brown face just right of the crack. Shoulder roll from the horn to a left-hand mini-horn, then punch straight out the bulge on good holds. Worthy.

❏ 3. **Traverse V7** ★★★
Begin far right on a good block then cruise left past flat holds to reach a sloping ledge, which you follow to #1. Top out via the crack. Finishing left past the crack on glassy slopers adds 12 feet of climbing and a V-grade. Aesthetically pleasing. A few variants exist.

Block One

Block Two

Block Three

Low Traverse

TRAILSIDE BOULDER

This squatty, isolated boulder is actually in the bottom of the East Draw, another four minutes north up the Old Mesa Trail. Though not as sunny as its counterparts on the ridge, this rock offers a hard, hueco-esque line up the south overhang just off the trail. The Trailside Boulder is not pictured.

❑ 1. Trailside Overhang V10? ★★

A recently broken low flake makes this line substantiallly harder. Start sitting and work your way past slopers and crimps to the lip. A thuggy and unique anomaly. A fierce project climbs the maroon streak on right side of the west face. See the final text in the Flatirons South chapter for good bouldering just a bit further north.

THE BASTILLE

The Bastille is the obvious and popular cliff on the south side of the canyon. It remains shady in the winter months but is swarming with climbers during the warmer seasons. Numerous traverses and crack problems exist on the lower face above the dirt road. The Bastille is not pictured.

❑ 1. Micro Traverse V8

Ultra thin crimps and sloping feet define this problem on the far left of the Bastille. This problem ends at *Shield Traverse*.

❑ 2. Shield Traverse V3 ★★

A superb Eldo slab with one difficult move. A V4 climbs up just left of the start.

❑ 3. Zorro Crack V3 ★★ 🌑🌑

Starts left of *March of Dimes Direct*. A couple of hard moves climb through the intersecting seam/cracks.

❑ 4. March of Dimes V2 ★★ 🌑🌑

A fun move off the ground leads to easier ground. This highball problem is most often toproped.

❑ 5. Slope Face V2 ★

Starts just right of two bolt holes and traverse right to the Northcutt Start dihedral.

❑ 6. Lower Bastille Traverse V2

On the right of the face just above the road is a long traverse skirting around the right side of the face.

THE WIND TOWER

This is the cliff first encountered on the right after crossing the footbridge that is located just after the main parking area. The bouldering is located on the south face (the wall facing the creek) and stretches from the southwest corner of Wind Tower across the entire south face.

❑ 1. Swoopy V0

Underclings below the initial roof on *Kings X* and left of #2. A simple circular boulder problem with a multitude of contrivances. Part of the *Wind Tower Traverse* V6 (a haphazard collection of slabs, corners, no-hands rests and slopers).

❑ 2. Access Corner V0

The slabby corner leading up to *Rainbow Wall* (an obvious bolted route on a lichen-streaked wall). This corner and the adjacent wall to the right are the down climbs for all the problems to the right stopping at #8.

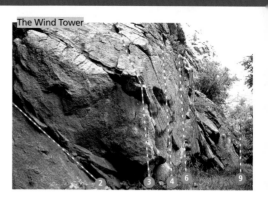
The Wind Tower

SOUTH WALL PROBLEMS:

❑ 3. V1 ★

Start on the white chockstone and reach the diagonal sloping edge. Pull up to better holds and the top. A V0 reaches around left from the white chockstone to a good crack then a massive jug. A V3 sit down starts on the sharp arête below the chockstone and climbs the sloping ramp on the south face.

❑ 4. Crystal Lift V2 ★

The problem nine feet right of the white chockstone. Start in a shallow, stepped dihedral and pull up to a gray crystal. A difficult reach with polished footholds up the arête to a sloping hold on *South Wall*.

❑ 5. South Wall Left V0

Just right of *Crystal Lift* is an open dihedral.

❑ 6. South Wall Center V2 ★★ 🌑

The smooth, tall face a couple of feet right of *South Wall Left*. This is a polished nightmare and one of the best problems on Wind Tower. A spotter is comforting for the top-out moves.

❑ 7. South Wall Right V0

Start on good holds and climbs above the massive jug at mid-height.

❑ 8. Traverse V3 ★★

A superb butt-scraping traverse (right to left) on sloping edges finishes at the *South Wall*. The problems listed below have different downclimbs. Either use the awkward dihedral right of # 9 or the slab right of *Round Up*.

❑ 9. V5 ★

Fourteen feet right of #8. A small, flat face with a broken band of stone running across the bottom. Start underclinging below the seam splitting the face and pinching the right arête. A vicious highstep and slap reach the top and fun groveling.

❑ 10. Round Up V6 ★★★

An 11-foot traverse ending just right of the awkward dihedral. Climb right to left on the terrible slopers on the edge of the vertical wall to a mantel. Bad feet and sloping handholds epitomize this problem. A V2 starts on the first holds on *Round Up* and climbs the slab to a small right-facing dihedral eight feet up.

❑ 11. Gold Rush V4 ★ 🌑🌑

A thin, vertical face right of the slab above *Round Up*. Start on the white boulder sitting on the ground and climb the left side of the miniature rainbow-colored face. Huge jugs are hidden in the far-left dihedral, which makes the problem a V0 cruise.

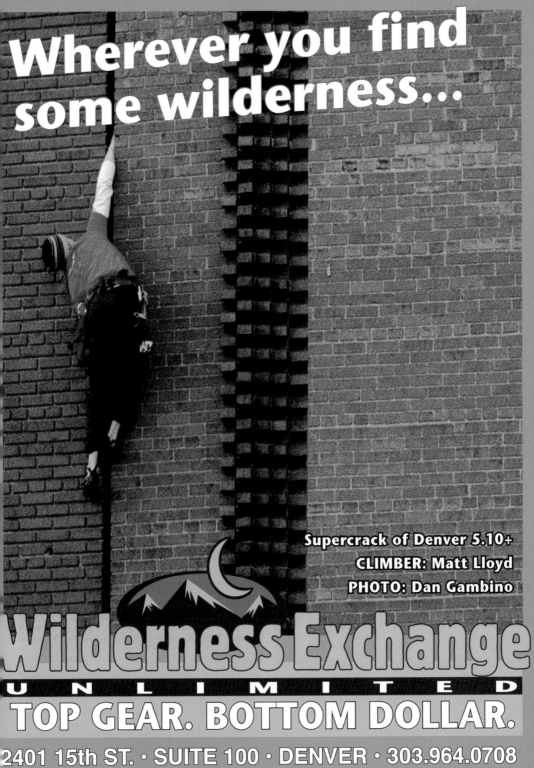

WHALE'S TAIL

This is the rock found directly left after crossing the footbridge. The most-traveled bouldering area, which will become all too obvious from the horrendously polished holds. Descents for the problems before the Monument Cave (the big cave on the Whale's Tail) are either achieved by climbing up and over the Tail or by hasty retreats (i.e, downjumps, downclimbs or frightening traverses on slick rock). Caution is warranted on these problems due to polished footholds.

The Whale's Tail

☐ 1. **Pocket Bulge V1** 🌐
The problem left of *Just Left* that climbs through a big pocket up on the wall.

☐ 2. **Just Left V0** 🌐
A good hold fest. This problem is mindless due to the chalk trail.

☐ 3. **Dihedral 2 V0** 🌐
Just left of *Scary Cling* is a simple, although polished, dihedral that surmounts a small overhang.

☐ 4. **Scary Cling V4** 🌐
Left of *Throw Back* arête is a tall face with the crux coming well off the deck.

☐ 5. **Throw Back V3** 🌐
An arête left of #7. Caution is necessary to avoid falls on the boulder protruding from the ground like a bungee stick.

☐ 6. **Slick Traverse V6**
For the butter lover in all of us. A short traverse from *Dihedral 1* across *Slipper Face* to the easy exit moves.

☐ 7. **Dihedral 1 V2** 🌐
The dihedral left of *Slipper Face*. Not overly exciting.

☐ 8. **Slipper Face V2** 🌐
A polished nightmare for the feet. Good technique is the key, not good boots.

MONUMENT CAVE AREA

The big blocky cave covered in sporadic chalked holds on the left of the Whale's Tail south face.

☐ 1. **The Arête V2** ★★
On the block next to *Lunge Break* is a good arête. A sit down start makes this problem rather horrific on the tips.

☐ 2. **Micro Pull V9** ★★
The direct start to #3. Grab the small crimps down and left and make the long pulls on slopey holds into #3.

☐ 3. **Lunge Break V2** ★★
A superb problem left of the crack. Crimp the right-facing layback and reach up and left to good slopers.

☐ 4. **Clementine Direct V0** ★★ 🌐🌐
The crack left of *Off the Couch*. A great crack because you never have to jam.

☐ 5. **Off the Couch V0**
Starts around the corner from the left wall forming the mouth of the cave.

☐ 6. **Cave Traverse V4**
Dark, dirty, and dingy. Best started right of the beginning moves on *The Monument* sport climb. The further one starts near the mouth of the cave the less wet and sooty your body will get. Starting from the rear of the cave doesn't make for a recommended problem, unless you love struggling in the dark.

☐ 7. **Around the World V4**
Starts on the right side of the cave's opening and circles through the jugs and slopers, which are so polished you can check unmanageable hairs. Fun for up and down problems. *Vertical Polish* V3 crimps up the smallest edge on the left of *Around the World*.

CLOSE TO THE EDGE SLABS V0-V3 🌐
Two boulders located above the cement platform and *The Arête*.

Monument Cave Area

CREEK SLAB
The long slab on the left just over the stone wall after crossing the footbridge. Traverse the multitude of holds for problems in the V0 to V2 range.

CREEK BOULDER
Another boulder in the creek bed just past Creek Slab boulder and before Monument Cave.

☐ 1. **East Bulge V5** ★★★
A classic for the boulderer with a sloper fetish. The problem starts in the creekbed (not accessible during spring run off). Pull on two thin crimps and slap up to the rounded top, traverse slightly left, and pull up and over. Just left of East Bulge is the classic *Three Feet High and Rising V7*.

Creek Boulder

Chuck Fryberger enjoying Crank Rock's Crankakee V3   Photo: Andy Mann

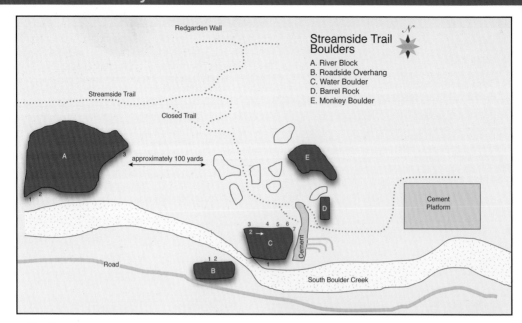

Streamside Trail Boulders

A. River Block
B. Roadside Overhang
C. Water Boulder
D. Barrel Rock
E. Monkey Boulder

Redgarden Wall

Streamside Trail

Closed Trail

approximately 100 yards

Cement Platform

Cement

Road

South Boulder Creek

STREAMSIDE TRAIL BOULDERS

This set of Eldorado boulders is rife with excellent slabs and finger-wrenching problems. The classic *Over the Water Traverse* provides the full Eldo experience, with casual climbing over the roaring creek. Located just west from the Whale's Tail and stretching to the far reaches of the Redgarden Wall.

A. RIVER BLOCK

Walk west approximately 10 yards down the Streamside Trail to the junction where the trail heads up to the west face of the Redgarden Wall. Look down the trail for a massive boulder lying in the creekbed. It is partially blocked by a large pine and shrubs. The boulder reaches right next to the trail on the left. To reach the problems in the creekbed walk beside the boulder on the left side (facing down hill).

☐ 1. **Fall Line V0** ★
The crack left of *Eastern Priest*. Starts over the water.

☐ 2. **Eastern Priest V4** ★★★
A highball problem on the wall facing the creek. After a thorough cleaning job the line is now an amazing highball. One of the best for the grade anywhere. A direct finish from the starting hold awaits.

☐ 3. **Projects V?**
A righteous project (or two) under the roof between #2 and #4.

☐ 4. **The Kiss of Life V7** ★
Climbs the south face corner. Undercling start from the ramp.

☐ 5. **Gunk Roof V0** ★
A veritable jug haul right across the lip of a small cave near the boulder's southeast corner. A sds adds spice. Top-out is grovely.

CRANK ROCK

The boulder lies about 100 yards upstream from the River Block on the north side of the river and has a perfect little patch for landing. Look for the tan and maroon bands.

☐ 1. **Crankakee V3** ★★★
A classic problem that climbs the center of the south face to a disconcerting topout.

☐ 2. **Methamphetamine V3** ★★
This new route climbs the arête immediately to the right.

River Block

Crank Rock

B. Roadside Overhang

On the road side of the creek and directly across from the Water Boulder is a chossy roof.

❐ 1. **Standard Route V2**

The easiest problem on the overhang that finishes on the left.

❐ 2. **Psychit V4**

The straight-out variation using all the scary choss.

Roadside Overhang

C. Water Boulder

Water Boulder

The prominent boulder located after hopping over the cement barrier found just upstream from the cement platform. This boulder sits in a pool of water through the spring months so get there late in the year as the winter also leaves its mark with a glacier at the base. The northwest-facing wall has some awesome slab problems.

❐ 1. **Over Water Traverse V1** ★★★

A super-classic traverse starting on the downclimb slab and skirting the boulder on the creek side. A blast!

❐ 2. **Water Boulder Traverse V4** ★

A traverse across the northwest face. As if the straight-up crimpers did not do enough damage.

❐ 3. **Undercling Face V1** ★★

The problem that climbs the right side of the northwest face.

❐ 4. **Center Route V3** ★

The most difficult and most entertaining problem up the slab.

❐ 5. **To the Side V1** ★★

Left of *Center Route*. A fine outing on little crimps.

❐ 6. **Left V1** ★★

On the far-left side of the west face is a fun problem.

❐ 7. **Arête V1** ★★

A blunt, slabby arête that faces the cement barrier. A hard move off the ground gets you situated on the slab.

D. Barrel Rock

The first boulder encountered after walking southwest past the cement platform. Another polished boulder with short V3 problems (the center problem being the most demanding) on its south face. A vicious traverse can be done from left to right staying below the lips' jugs. Not pictured.

E. Monkey Boulder

Directly uphill from Barrel Rock. One problem climbs up the overhanging side. Not recommended, as the stone is dirty and fragile. The Monkey Boulder is not pictured.

TJ Birchfield sends the Eastern Priest V4   Photo: Andy Mann

WEST WORLD BOULDERS

Home to the mega-classic *Germ Free Adolescence*, this steep, slippery hillside of polished blocks has seen a few quality problems go in recently. Although there aren't many good moderate problems to warm up on and landings tend toward the sloping, this area is still worth a visit, mostly for the tall pine and quiet maroon block ambience. Though south-facing, this hillside is also quite wooded; landings can be sloppy and wet a day or two after big snowstorms, but the rock is quick to dry.

Directions: *Drive west through the town of Eldorado Springs into the Park and park at the Milton Boulder (during low water, or when the creek is frozen over). For West World, cross the creek via a series of slippery rocks just downstream from Milton and head straight up the hill and left (west) to the boulders. Alternately, when the creek is high, park at the lower lot in the Park and approach as for the West Ridge, heading left across the hill to the boulders once you've made the greasy traverse on the slabs just above the creek. Approach time: five to ten minutes.*

A. WEST END ROCK

Farther west from the Spotless Boulder is a lone boulder with a fine V0 problem on its southeast face. Not pictured.

B. SPOTLESS BOULDER

Walk west from Roofus Rock roughly 40 yards to a ridge covered with miscellaneous boulders. One of the first boulders encountered has a small, thrutchy overhang on its south face, which is V4. The Spotless Boulder is just around and over the top from the V4 overhang and has three main problems in a small gap with another boulder. The problems are all covered in a healthy layer of lichen. Not pictured.

❑ 1. V0
Climb the obvious lichen-infested slot using your butt as an appendage for an easy outing.

❑ 2. Punky Reggae Party V1
The leftmost problem outside the gap. Follows a right-leaning ramp.

❑ 3. Don't Touch I-Man Locks V3 ★
The center of the three. Five feet left of *Venus*.

❑ 4. Venus and the Razor Blades V2 ★
The rightmost problem within the gap. Starts at the small, right-facing dihedral.

❑ 5. Slabilicious V0 ★
The low angle slab found above the gap where *Venus* and *I-Man* are located.

C. ROOFUS ROCK

Directly to the left from Germ Free Boulder this maroon overhanging face has two distinct problems that are V4 with vicious mantle finishes (numbers 3 & 4 on topo).

❑ 1. Sheep Thrills V4 ★★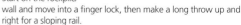
A terrible name for a beautiful problem. Lime-colored lichen the shape of an open hand outlines a slightly overhanging face littered with good edges. The top-out is a little spooky.

Roofus Rock

❑ 2. When the Chips are Down V9 ★★★
This stellar line, put up by Colin Lantz in the fall of 2000, takes the high, lichen-streaked face right of *Sheep Thrills* on the boulder's west face. Start on the rockpile/wall and move into a finger lock, then make a long throw up and right for a sloping rail.

❑ 3. John's Scoop V0 ★
In the west scoop around the corner from the maroon-colored overhang. Start on thin holds and reach out and right to huge edges.

❑ 4. Colin's Highball V2 ★
This ultra-sandbag rating was provided by the first ascensionist. Start on the old V0 in the scoop on the right side of the west face then work back left along the lip of the ramping arête.

❑ 5. High Slab V0 ★
Step onto the southwest arête of the boulder from the big block, then realm up the monolithic southern slab above. Harder if you stay left on the small edges.

D. MIND BOGGLE ROCK

This is the rock just left of The High Spire with an overhanging southwest face with a discontinuous shelf at mid-height. Highball, dirty and wet is the name of the game. Not recommended. Problems on the west face, from left to right, are cleaner, thin and range from V0 to V5.

❑ 1. Bringer of Light V10 ★★
Climb from a sds under the roof and pull the desperate moves in the face to a spooky top-out. A nice one!

Mind Boggle

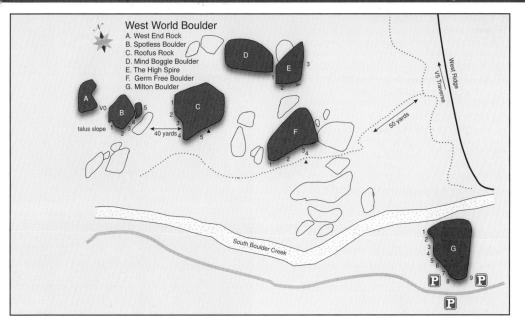

West World Boulder

A. West End Rock
B. Spotless Boulder
C. Roofus Rock
D. Mind Boggle Boulder
E. The High Spire
F. Germ Free Boulder
G. Milton Boulder

E. THE HIGH SPIRE AKA STRATOSFEAR

A tall boulder rests uphill from Germ Free Boulder. Attached to its west face is Mind Boggle Rock. A descent is found in the notch between High Spire and Mind Boggle.

❑ 1. **Squealer V4** ★★
A thin face on the west side of the spire. One difficult move from the starting holds gains a good edge then a dynamic move to reach a flat, ten-finger edge. A V5 is just right.

❑ 2. **Three Beers V4** ★★ 🌐🌀
Start on the southwest corner and angle up and left. Spooky.

❑ 3. **Stratosfear V2** ★★ 🌐🌀
A deep crack system on the south face that climbs up and right. Or, finish straight up on small edges for *Two Beers* V3.

❑ 4. **Klingon V0** ★ 🌐🌀
An easy face route on the east face. Climb up the face on positive edges then up and over.

Daniel Woods sends When the Chips are Down V9

Photo: Andy Mann

High Spire

F. GERM FREE BOULDER

The severely overhanging boulder with pounds of chalk on the holds. The problems on this boulder beg for attentive spotters and a go-for-it attitude. If tall problems are appealing this will satisfy any craving.

Germ Free Boulder

❑ 1. Genetic Engineering V5 ★ 🪨🪨
On the far left of the boulder, five feet left of *Day-Glo*. Start on two decent holds up to slopers. The moves pulling on to the slab are true thrutching.

❑ 2. The Day the World Turned Day-Glo V6 🪨🪨
A hard to ascertain problem 11 feet left of *Germ Free*. The starting holds are at arms reach if you are seven feet tall. A hard move from a good edge gains a thin vertical seam and the difficult top-out.

❑ 3. Twisted Adolescence V8 ★ 🪨🪨
This powerful variation climbs out the cave just left of *Germ Free Adolescence*. Start on *Germ Free* but take the flake/hueco with your right hand and bust high and left to a three-finger pocket, then the lip.

❑ 4. Germ Free Adolescence V5 ★★★ 🪨🪨
It doesn't get any better. A committing problem that starts matched on an obvious jug system. Reach up to the hueco and out on the face to a bomber edge. Reach the lip and grovel up and over on good, although not good enough crimps. Two other starts can be found to this problem. The right direct is *Here Comes Sickness* V8 and the left direct sds is V7.

Park Tech Boulder

TRUTH BLOCK

This recently unearthed little gem reveals its charms only upon close inspection. The crimpy, positive nature of the rock and the boulder's sunny position above the creek make for a good outing. This boulder is roughly 100 feet below the Germ Free Boulder and about 60 feet above the creek. Stiff for the grades. The Truth Block is not pictured.

❑ 1. Truth or Dare V4 ★ 🪨
A crimpy problem in the slot on the left (west) side of the boulder, starting from two good square-cut edges at head-height.

❑ 2. Dare V2 ★ 🪨
Start on the incut flake and move left over the drop off. Mega scary!

❑ 3. Nice Move V3 🪨
Start on the same incut flake and punch up and right to a sloper.

❑ 4. Truth V4 ★★ 🪨
The center line up the southeast face, topping out just right of the big dead tree. Sds for extra value. A V5 traverse starts on *Truth* and crimps rightward 13 feet to finish on a rounded purple horn.

❑ 5. Lies V1 🪨
Start from the rampy rock and climb the short wall via sidepulls.

LOW TIDE BLOCK

Below Truth Block and right next to the river, Low Tide Block offers a few short nice problems hidden in the trees. See photo on next page.

Justin Williams bares down on Tone's Warm-up V4　Photo: Andy Mann

Park Tech Boulder

This is a tiny block with fun problems and good landings, nestled in a flat pine grove just 50 feet from the creek, about 150 feet upstream (west) of Milton Boulder on the opposite side of the creek.

❏ **1. Left Side V4** ★

Sds on the horizontal and move right then back left into the funky seam.

❏ **2. Tone's Warm-up V4** ★★

From the same sds go right and up the crack.

❏ **3. Park Tech V5** ★★

From the crimps on the right side of the wall make a big toss to the sinker hueco at the lip. A V6 variation moves right a few feet from the start on sharp crimpers.

West Ridge Traverse

Though somewhat friable, this fun traverse provides a good lactic burn on interesting blocky stone. It's also a decent place to mess around and warm-up, as the holds tend to be bigger than the unforgiving crimps of West World. The traverse is at the lower (southern) end of the West Ridge about 100 feet above the creek.

❏ **1. West Ridge Traverse V5** ★★

Traverse the diagonaling break from right to left, either finishing direct up the steep face via chossy holds on the traverse's left end or simply stepping off. The *Terminator Version* V6 starts all the way down and right and crosses the lower wall on sharp crystals to join the traverse.

G. Milton Boulder

The large, lone boulder on the right side of the road and past the Bastille (0.4 mile from the bridge entrance). One of the most vicious slabs in the state. Be prepared for footwork intensive climbing to sloping exits. The descent is down the slab next to *Leaning Arête*.

❏ **1. Ridge Face V0** ★

The problem that climbs the far-left side of the west face.

❏ **2. Layaway V0** ★

A sidepull fest. Climb the good sidepulls up and right to the top.

❏ **3. Micro Slab V6**

One of the brutal slabs on the west face. Starts on a lichen-covered bulge just left of a burgundy/white patch of rock.

❏ **4. Standard V1** ★★

Right of *Micro Slab* is an easy problem that climbs into the positive laybacks and higher underclings.

❏ **5. Undercling Route V3**

Start on two opposing sidepulls and climb up using a difficult to hold undercling.

❏ **6. Donna V4** ★

In the scoop to the right of *Undercling* use a small two-finger sidepull and high right-hand edge outside the shallow scoop to gain the sloping top-out.

❏ **7. Milton V3** ★★

A fun slab problem with fairly good crystals to yank on that starts like *Donna* but goes straight up. The move to the top is the crux.

❏ **8. Never Say Never V9** ★

A friction masterpiece. On the far-right face before the blunt arête. Uses the small right-facing sidepull of Milton. A V9 Skip Guerin problem climbs the blunt right arête making up the *Never Say Never* scoop.

❏ **9. Leaning Arête V0** ★★

The obvious arête around the right corner from all the difficult slabs. Climb the slabby arête on the left side of the giant low-angle slab.

Pete's Prow Boulder

This is the north-facing prow-shaped boulder directly across the road from Milton Boulder.

❏ **1. Pete's Prow V5** ★

Slap moves to glassy slopers take you up this tricky double-arête rig. A henious sds project climbs in from the roof.

Low Tide Block

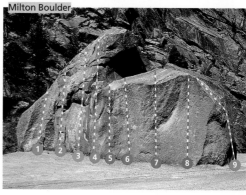

West Ridge

Milton Boulder

Pete's Prow

QUIGONG

Hidden in the talus across the road from Milton Boulder is a superb steep affair. A west-facing overhang 40 yards southeast from the road Start through the talus at *Pete's Prow* scrabbling to the southeast (left).

Quigong

❑ 1. **Quigong V10** ★★
Starts low on a big pinch and move into the upper arête with a bad landing every move of the way.

THE GILL BOULDER AREA

At the western bridge where the road splits and heads to the Ranger Station many boulders surround the right parking area and sit in the creek.

A. GILL BOULDER

On the left of the parking lot after the final bridge in the canyon sits a huge square boulder. Every problem borders on classic status, even though the footholds have been worn smooth as glass. Don't be discouraged and beg for a higher grade if the low-angle slabs thwart technically imperfect efforts.

❑ 1. **South Face V2** ★
An Ament problem from the 60s. Start on two small crimps and pull up to a right-hand crimp. A good jug is over the lip. The downclimb for all problems is just left where a worn tree hugs the face.

❑ 2. **V4** ★
With your right hand pinch the blunt arête that makes up the left side of *Southeast Slab*. Numerous small slopes and crimps for the left hand and a dynamic move up the face.

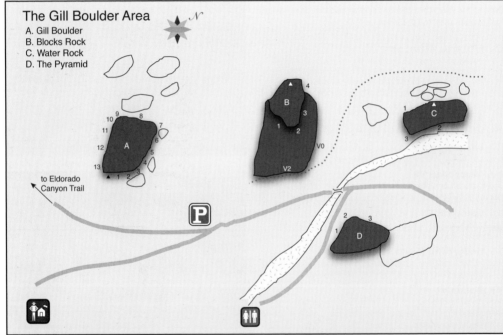

The Gill Boulder Area
A. Gill Boulder
B. Blocks Rock
C. Water Rock
D. The Pyramid

to Eldorado Canyon Trail

Gill Boulder South face

Gill Boulder East & North faces

❏ 3. **Southeast Slab V0** ★
A small slab four feet wide is on the southeast corner above a small boulder.

The slabs on the east face from left to right:

❏ 4. **Left V2** ★
The easiest of the three slabs problems. As with *Center*, be prepared for a long reach and belly flopping to top out. The king of all sandbags!

❏ 5. **Center V3** ★
Climb the delicate face in the middle of the slab.

❏ 6. **Right V3** ★
Thin, thin, thin slab climbing. Two by fours with sticky rubber are the choice footwear.

❏ 7. **Northeast Corner V0** ★★
A veritable cruise through good laybacks. Many contrived starts exist for this problem.

❏ 8. **North Dihedral V0** ★★★
Super classic! Climb the open dihedral on the north face. Good holds are reached from the small layback in the dihedral.

❏ 9. **North Reach V1** ★★
Climb the well-featured face on the right of the north face. Fairly highball but reasonable.

❏10. **The Blunt Corner V3** ★★
Just around the corner from #9 is a set of positive edges that lead to a stance at an open scoop/dihedral. A substantial throw or reach gets one to the top of the dihedral from a small intermediate.

❏ 11. **Standard Face V5/V10** ★★★
Follow the crimp ladder and move right to gain the high shallow, right-facing dihedral. A new V10 direct sds called *606* begins on the lowest matched edge/sidepull way down and right and somehow uses the worst micro-edges on the face to gain the high dihedral/corner. V8 as a direct stand start.

❏ 12. **The Grinch V8**
Right of *606* and 10 feet left of *Gill Face* are thin crimps and tiny pockets that climb to the top. The problem, long forgotten but recently made popular again, is said to be V8 and newly named *The Grinch*. It's considered quite the sandbag.

❏ 13. **Gill Face V2** ★★
The right arête on the west face. Start laying back the arête and using the flat edge on the face. A sit down makes the problem V3.

Gill Boulder West face

The slabs on the east face from left to right:

Swiss Legend, Fred Nicole, focusing hard on The Gill Boulder's Center Slab V3   Photo: Andy Mann

B. BLOCKS ROCKS

A few feet right from the picnic table at the Gill Boulder parking lot is a boulder that rests on top of a large flat slab. The slab has a sit down start (V2) on the southeast corner that pinches a sharp arête up to good solution pockets. A V0 slab on the east face has also been done.

☐ I. Left Face V0 ★
Climb a selection of the huge edges to the top.

☐ 2. West Arête V1 ★
Start the problem standing and climb up the arête. A sit down start to this problem boosts the grade to V3.

☐ 3. V0 ★
On the flat east face climb the thin edges to the top.

☐ 4. V1 ★
On the far right side, standing on the ground next to the slab, pull on with your feet under the roof. A throw up the face reaches an excellent edge and the top.

C. WATER ROCK

Park at the Gill Boulder parking area and walk due east down the trial past Blocks Rocks. A few yards down the trail and in the creek sits a tall boulder with several good problems.

☐ 1. V0 ★ 🌀
Climb the far right face on the uphill side that leads to a good flake system.

☐ 2. East Scoop V0 ★★ 🌀
On the southeast face above the creek. Traverse around the boulder and climb up and past a large crystal. Despite a very bad landing, this is an idyllic line above the creek.

☐ 3. Resonated V9 ★★★ 🌀
The west face to the overhanging arête above the creek. Best climbed in winter when the pool is frozen. Start on left jug.

☐ 4. Echo V5 ★
Start on the jug in the face as for #3 and move left around the arête and finish on #1. Looks lame but moves well.

D. THE PYRAMID

The small slab at the west end of the canyon and below Supremacy Rock. It is directly above the road. The descent is down a small gully on the backside of the slab.

☐ 1. West Face V1 ★ 🌀
A fun challenge that climbs up the solid crimps. The problem starts in the road.

Blocks Rocks

Water Rock

☐ 2. Northeast Arête V0 ★ 🌀
Climb the blunt arête directly left of the near-vertical face starting in the road.

☐ 3. Simple Simon Slab V0 ★ 🌀
Climb the obvious big crack on the north face.

THE WISDOM SIMULATOR SIMULATOR

This esoteric, somewhat intimidating slot problem follows a continuous line of small but positive holds along the lip of the slot cave between *Dangerous Acquaintances* and *The Wisdom* on the upper (west) end of the Roof Wall. A good place to climb if you're already up there. Not pictured.

☐ 1. Wisdom Simulator Simulator V8 ★★ 🌀
Approach as for the Roof Wall routes. This problem is in the upper slot just above the approach slab used to reach *Rosy Crucifixion*. Start on a good, flat jug up and left of *Dangerous Acquaintances* and traverse 60 feet up and left along the lip of the slot, stepping off where the wall turns slabby at the base. of the first pitch of *The Wisdom*. Needs traffic.

The Pyramid

Wisdom Simulator Simulator

Steve Mammen knows to Never Say Never V9   Photo: John Sherman

JOHN SHERMAN

"West World's big draw is *Germ Free Adolescence*—seldom attempted, less seldom topped. *Germ Free* is a sweeping, 16-foot, 60-degree overhang, featuring a landing which slopes away dramatically toward the creek a hundred yards below. In the middle is a suitcase-sized flake, followed by a series of evenly spaced, but decreasingly smaller holds leading to a four finger wide, doorjamb-width edge perfectly situated at the lip. Above that the holds continue to shrink. Topping out is the crux—basically, a nightmare for both climber and spotter. A favorite ploy to rattle would-be ascentionists is to wait until they've grasped the initial jug, then tell them the tale of Rufus Miller. "You heard about Rufus Miller on this one?" "Who?" "Big Roof. Former gymnast. Built like The Hulk. Clamped the lip, cut his feet loose, then pulled half a one-arm giant before dismounting. Sheez, he looked like Superman flying in reverse. I thought he was gonna clear the river for sure." Sometimes this ploy works. The climber gazes down the steep hillside, glances up at the lip, then lies to his partner. "You know, this doesn't really look like the best line on the Front Range. Let's check out the Whales Tail." Both then hurriedly vacate West World and head downstream."

John Sherman - *Sherman Exposed, Slightly Censored Climbing Stories*

TOP 5:

1. *Pinch Overhang* V5 (Horsetooth Reservior)
2. *King Conquer* V3 (Flagstaff)
3. *Germ Free Adolescence* V5 (Eldorado Canyon)
4. *Breashear's Crack* V3 (Morrison)
5. *Kahuna Roof* V6 (Carter Lake)

Sarah Marvez on the Walrus V5   Photo: Brian Solano

ELDORADO CANYON TRAIL BOULDERS

THE RON AND PONY KEGS, AND THE MUSICAL BOULDERS

Though technically two separate areas, these two clusters of rock are similar enough and close enough together to combine into a single circuit. Blessed with perfect landings in grassy meadows, clean maroon stone, and a kind southerly exposure, both areas are quick to melt out after snowstorms and offer pleasant, quiet getaways from urban encroachment. Given their very sunny exposure and the crimpy nature of the problems, these boulders are best visited from October through April.

Directions: For both the Pony Keg and the Musical Boulders take the Eldorado Canyon Trail, which heads up and north out of the western end of the park. For Ron's Keg and the Pony Keg follow the trail up past two switchbacks then north along a split-rail fence. The fence soon ends. Just before a set of new wooden steps, head left into the grassy, open gully below the burn area on the ridge to the west.

Approach time: five minutes.

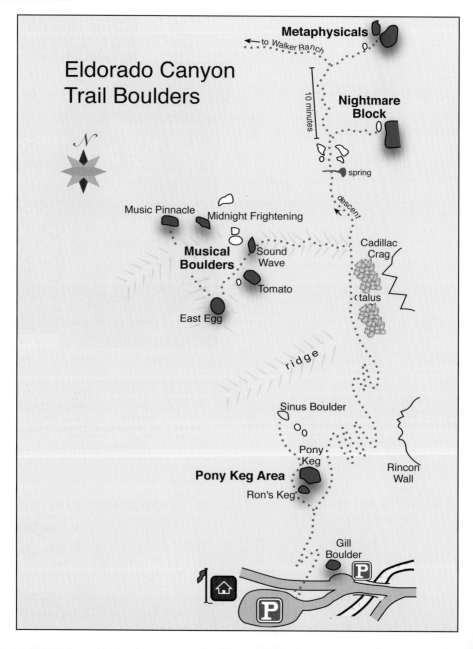

Ron's Keg

Though short and somewhat sharp, this sunny blob of maroon rock plopped down in a soft meadow is not without merit. Combine the short approach with perfect landings and a crack at the harder problems on the adjacent Pony Keg to sweeten the deal.

❑ 1. Chip's Arête V2 ✶
Climb the slabby, rounded northwest arête via thin sharpies.

❑ 2. Ron's Keg Traverse V5 ✶✶
Start on #1 and traverse right across the entire rock, cruising past the hueco on the south face to finish out on #8. Tricky.

❑ 3. Easy Crack V0
Amble up the fun crack four feet right.

❑ 4. Horn's Mudda V2 ✶
Start on the good horn and move up and left to a pinch. Moving right and up to the small pine is V1 and slightly crumbly.

❑ 5. Southwest Arête V2 ✶
Climb the arête/prow starting around its south side and working your way past crimps to a good horn.

❑ 6. South Face V3
Start with your right hand on the undercling seam and fire up and left to a sloping pocket, then top out via sharp crimpers. Painful and unnecessary.

❑ 7. Direct South Face V5 ✶✶
Start in the lone hueco and move up and right to a small slit pocket, then surmount the glassy bulge as best you can. Unruly.

❑ 8. V0
Climb the short but appealing water groove on the right side of the south face via pockets and layaways.

Pony Keg

This glassy chunk of maroon stone took on an even redder hue in the summer of 2000, when slurry bombers inundated the area in effort to contain a nearby wildfire. The already slippery holds took on an even glossier sheen. Nevertheless, the improbable lines on this rock provide a unique challenge.

❑ 1. Left Side V2
Start on the head-high jug rail where the angle changes on the north face and traverse five feet left on crimps, then head up the slab. Weird.

❑ 2. Center Route V4 ✶✶
This is the easiest way up the foothold-free north face. Start with your left hand on a good incut at head-height and your right hand in the horizontal three feet to the right, then slap over the bulge for a dish.

❑ 3. Fingertip Traverse V6 ✶✶
Start on the northwest corner and move left along the obvious seam, topping out 20 feet left when the wall turns slabby on #1.

❑ 4. The High Traverse V5 ✶ 🌀
Traverse the slopey lip of the wall.

❑ 5. Northwest Corner V5 ✶
Start on the large crystal right of the crack/seam and crank rightwards over the bulge on sharp edges, off-routing the crack to the left. The crack itself is V1.

❑ 6. Woody's Pebble V3
The sharpest boulder problem on earth! Surmount the bulge just left of the southwest arête, off-routing the good holds in the crack and tugging on a shark-tooth crystal. Horrible, awful, execrable.

❑ 7. The Rail V2 ✶✶
Sds on the southwest arête at the crack, then reel right along the crack for 20 feet until the rock turns slabby. Easier up-problems can also be done along the length of the south face.

❑ 8. Pony Keg Traverse V8 ✶✶
Reverse #7 and cross the west face of the boulder using the horizontal seam and a set of crimps just above it to finish out on #4. Continuous and technical—meaning your feet are gonna slop off. Sicker V-grade glory awaits those who off-route the holds above the seam.

Ron's Keg

Pony Keg

The Musical Boulders

Though not particularly extensive, these isolated boulders, when combined with a trip to either the Nightmare Block or the Pony Keg, are part of one of Boulder's better adventure-bouldering circuits. Their sunny aspect high on a ridge below Cadillac Crag guarantees quick meltage after winter snowstorms. Many other fine problems can be found here which are not covered in this guide.

Directions: From Ron's Keg follow the well-traveled trail north and west up the steep hillside to a view of the East Egg due west. Total distance on this trail from Ron's Keg to the East Egg is approximately 800 yards.

EAST EGG

This lone erratic perched high on a scenic ridge (and visible from the ridge above Pony Keg) is a mandatory stop for highball and thin-face aficionados. *The Walrus*, a perfect line on exemplary Eldorado stone, is a must-do for the grade, and the tall slabs around the southwest side of the boulder provide stimulating highball entertainment.

☐ 1. **Downclimb V0**
The easiest way up and down the rock. Climb the high, slabby northwest face.

☐ 2. **Slab I V1** ★
Start four feet left of the vibrant, green lichen on good hue-cos, climbing the rounded bulge to a slightly reachy top-out.

☐ 3. **Slab II V2** ★★
The center line on the wall, heading up the tallest shield of rock to finish out directly below a small pine tree. You can bail either right or left if you get gripped up high.

☐ 4. **Slab III V1** ★
Locate the huecos in the black streak seven feet left of the arête. Head straight up on slightly friable flakes and nubbins.

☐ 5. **Southern Prow V0** ★★
Climb the high, rampy prow where the east face meets the southwest slabs. A mini-solo.

☐ 6. **The Walrus V5** ★★★
One of Boulder's finest, to be sure. Climb the faint black streak up the blankest part of the east face, starting with your right hand on an undercling flake. Continuously thin and committing up high.

☐ 7. **Eggman V3** ★★
This classic line climbs the vibrant, green lichen streak up the middle of the east face, starting from a small, round boulder at the base. Finish up the faint water groove on the left for *Tone's Variation* V3.

☐ 8. **Steak Knife V4** ★
Climb the slightly mossy face five feet left of the northeast arête. Quite thin.

THE WORLD'S SMALLEST BOULDER

This diminutive blob is 100 feet uphill and northeast of the East Egg. No spotter required.

☐ 1. **Shortest Hardest V3** ★
The line up the bulging left side of the west face to a mantle crux at the lip.

☐ 2. **Shortest Easiest V1**
Sds on pockets and climb the southwest face via nice red stone.

☐ 3. **Shortest Medium V2** ★
Actually sort of fun for a lowly lowball. Sds on the bottom, southern end of the diagonaling seam on the east face and follow it rightwards to a roofy conclusion.

THE TOMATO

This rounded red orb just uphill of The World's Smallest Boulder offers similar problems on frustratingly bald stone.

Tomato

East Egg

World's Smallest

THE MUSIC PINNACLE

Head due north from the East Egg 100 yards into the trees to find this appealing boulder, the lowest of the northern-most cluster of boulders. Expect high problems with thin, sharp holds.

Music Pinnacle

☐ 1. **West Crack V5** ★★
Sds low and left on small pockets then work up and right into the twin crack/groove systems, eventually jamming the rightmost one to finish.

☐ 2. **Pinnacle Crack V0** ★
This is the obvious crack/corner line on the south face. It's also the best way off the boulder.

☐ 3. **Sherman's Seam V1** ★★
The leftmost line on the east face and also the most obvious. Follow the seam/faint dihedral up slick rock to the top of the boulder.

☐ 4. **Funk V3** ★

Just right of the seam climb the faint arête feature with pockets, entering it from the scoop on the right. Thin and technical.

☐ 5. **East Face Center V3** ★

Follow the scoop all the way to the top, tugging on thin crimps and suspect crystals en route. Beware the ankle-breaker landing on embedded rocks.

☐ 6. **East Face Arête V2** ★

Move right out of the scoop onto the round arête then slap right for a good edge up high.

LIGHTNING SPIRE AKA HERTZ ROCK

This block sits 30 feet east and uphill from the Music Pinnacle.

☐ 1. **Midnight Frightening V10** ★★★★

This fine line was finally opened by Dave Graham directly up the scoop from two horrendous crimps (V11) and done starting on the wide crack to the left (V10). The arête to the right is *The Frederick Arête* V7.

☐ 2. **Process of Belief V9** ★

The chalked bulge to the left (south) from *MF* starting from a right-hand hueco to big slaps and bad, although rough, slopers in the bulge.

☐ 3. **V6-V9**

Lowballish lines on the southwest face.

Kevin Jorgeson on Midnight Frightening V10   Photo: Andy Mann

SOUND WAVE BOULDER

Though low and squatty, this block is blessed with perfect Eldo sandstone and fun huecos, pinch ribs, and crimps along its overhanging east face. Walk east and uphill from the Lightning Spire about 50 yards, passing a huge perched boulder en route.

❏ 1. **Sound Wave Traverse V5** ★★

Traverse the east face from right to left, either finishing out on its south end where it turns slabby or staying low around the corner and topping out via a cobbled alcove on the west side. A problem of the same grade sits down and left on the east face and climbs direct into a henious mantle at the apex of the lip.

C. NIGHTMARE BLOCK

This hunk of 20-foot-high and 15-degree-overhanging maroon sandstone offers steep, powerful climbing in a secreted-away, forested setting. Most of the block's monolithic west face is composed of dark maroon rock laced with sidepulls, incuts and spikes, similar to the rock on Eldo's classic sport route *Your Mother* (12d). The ten-odd up-problems, numerous variations and two traverses will have you pumped hellishly fast—the rock is very smooth, and you'll find yourself over-gripping, especially on the higher problems. The arduous approach (30-40 minutes uphill) is a great idiot-barrier, making this a wonderful place to come when you want to be left the fuck alone.

Approach: Walk 100 yards on the upper road leading west from the Gill Boulder until you hit the Eldorado Canyon Trail. After two quick switchbacks the trail levels out and heads north. After passing a split rail fence on the left, you'll see a faint trail leading down and left to the Pony Keg boulder. Stay on the main trail past another nine switchbacks (passing the cut-off to Rincon Wall at the fifth switchback). A couple of minutes up from the last switchback you'll cross the grassy ridge leading down to the Musical Boulders and East Egg.

The trail levels out then drops down through a talus field shaded by large ponderosa pines. Pass a marker in the trail, then a small spring five yards further along with a culvert running under the trail. Hike another 35 yards, passing through a cluster of boulders, then turn right (east) and hike uphill 50 yards along a faint ridge, coming to the Nightmare Block, a west-facing, 10- to 20-foot-high maroon wall.

Approach time: 30-40 thigh-burning minutes.

Sound Wave

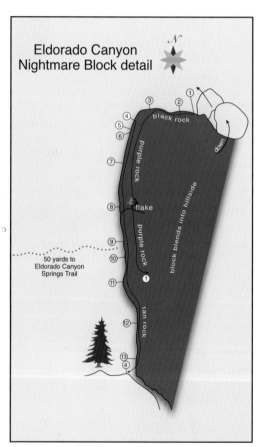

Eldorado Canyon
Nightmare Block detail

Nightmare Block

NORTH FACE

❏ 1. **Cameron's Way V5** ★

A lip traverse of the entire block. Begin atop the easternmost boulder stacked against the north face of the block (you use this boulder to descend from the problems) and step onto the wall, sagging low onto a slopey rail that leads you down to the top of #2. Hand traverse around the corner, staying on the lip of the wall until you reach #8, then mantle.

❏ 2. **One Move Makes You Wonder V4** ★★

Start in the whitish corner above a rocky landing and fire up and right to a jug at the lip. V7 from a low start, down and right.

❏ 3. **All Dogs Must Die V3** ★★

Just big, wet, stupid ones. Begin above the perfect landing just left of the arête on underclings and fire for an edge. V6 from a low start.

West Face

❏ 4. Nightmare Traverse V10 ★★★
One of the best power-endurance problems in the Front Range. This 45-foot traverse isn't so bad move-for-move, but the pump factor is hideous. Stay roughly below eight-foot height, beginning on the left arête (#5) and finishing out by stepping off the slab on the wall's south end. Unrelenting, shouldery, and tough.

❏ 5. Derek and the Sentinel V2 ★
The line up the arête, moving right on slopers to an awkward top-out.

❏ 6. Gumby Hell V2 ★
Start on the arête but punch right to large sidepulls, topping out as for #5. Fun in a weird-ass, barn-door sort of way.

❏ 7. One Cigarette Makes it Murder V5 ★★
Six feet right of *Gumby Hell*, this fine, powerful problem makes its way past sloping gastons, sidepulls and an obvious pinch rib into a set of twin cracks that meet in a V-notch at the lip. V7 from a sds on a large, left-facing undercling.

❏ 8. Standard Nightmare V5 ★★★
The directissima of the wall and perhaps its purest line. Start just right of the obvious pinch rail on #6 and punch up past slopers into jugs. Pant-loader exit.

❏ 9. Salvator V3 ★★★
Almost as good as *Standard Nightmare*, the direct line cruises up incuts and sidepulls in the faint, diagonaling seams on the right side of the maroon plaque. V4 from the sds.

❏ 10. My Liver Talks to Me V6 ★★
Sds directly under the faint arête where the purple plaque of rock meets the brown sandstone on the right. Grunt your way past crimpers and sidepulls without using the right arête, heading for the jug 15 feet up on #9.

❏ 11. The Optimator V3 ★★★
Begin just right of #9 at the border between the maroon and the tan rock, then crank past sidepulls, spikes, and a crimper on the right to a juggy but tricky top-out. V4 with a sds.

❏ 12. You Can Do It V1 ★
Well, maybe. Start on the juggy spikes seven feet left of the right margin of the block. Climb past a faint corner, then move left on the slab to top out. The area warm-up.

❏ 13. Ants V2 ★
Start as for #11 but head straight up the slab right of the corner. Crimpy in the slabbiest of ways.

Nightmare Block

The Metaphysical Boulders

Extra-super bonus blocks for those who just can't get enough steep hiking! Five minutues further up the trial brings you within spitting distance to an obvious zone on the right. Here you'll find a selection of problems including *Trailside Overhang* V7, *Paradigm Shift* V7, and *Diaphanous Sea Project* V?

Continue another five minutes further along the Eldorado Canyon Trail to the point at which the trail makes its final bend westward toward Walker Ranch. The trail passes over a small wooden bridge in the bottom of a steep ravine leading northeast. Either follow the ravine or better, hike along the right lip of the ravine for roughly 6-9 minutes until you encounter a cluster of house-sized blocks. An obvious classic, *Seven Inch Gumby* V5, climbs the right side of the tall, purple wall on the lower block. The middle block offers fun slab and traverse problems in the V1-V6 range, and the upper block offers an ultra-highball V4 called *Pocahontas* up the pocketed wall just left of the obvious, blank overhang. There are more boulders up the hill; the potential for futuristic highballs at this area is just beginning to be tapped.

Please be aware that this area is under study by the City of Boulder Open Space and Mountain Parks and that access issues could arise.

ELDORADO BOULDERS

Directions to Eldorado Boulder: Note: All trails go from well-trodden to faint at best. From the Music Pinnacle head north down the distinct, steep, rocky trail approximately 160 yards to a small drainage.

To reach the Eldorado Boulder go left (west) on the flat trail 40 yards (DO NOT CONTINUE DOWN THIS TRAIL AS IT HEADS INTO PRIVATE PROPERTY) then right on a faint trail (cairns may be present) contouring slightly uphill west then northwest for approximately 110 yards to a more distinct trail contouring north. Go approximately 120 yards to the bad-assest monster block with bolted lines on the steep southeast face. Go around the left side of the boulder to the west face.

Lost Boulder is reached from the north side of the Eldorado Boulder headed north approximately 50 yards.

Suspension of Disbelief is located by leaving the west side of Lost Boulder headed west up the trail that contours west then north. Approximately 125 yards along this trail head downhill (WNW) then up slightly to 150 total yards. A couple of large boulders are down in the drainage called Gully Block (a few lines have been done). Continue another 50 yards down a steep part of the trail to a small meadow/clearing then up (north) staying on the right side of a drainage for approximately 80 yards to two seemingly insignificant blocks on the left (Suspension of Disbelief is on the west face of the second boulder).

Blue Whale Area is found by heading north from SOD's east side on a faint trail staying above the drainage and always going up the hillside and moving slightly northeast approximately 250 yards to a conglomeration of boulders.

Carpe Diem

CARPE DIEM BOULDER

☐ **1. Carpe Diem V2** ★ 😊😊
25 yards to the north from the drainage at the base of the trail to Music Pinnacle is a tall south facing vertical face with a disconcerting reach at the top. A large overgrown boulder, 50 yards up gully, has seen some action as well.

HIDDEN WALL

A secluded vertical wall found approximately 30 yards back up the trail to Music Pinnacle then northeast 125 yards to a south-facing wall hidden behind a stand of pines. A little puddle usually keeps the middle of the wall's base sopping wet. Extremely thin lines ranging from left V4 to right V3 give or take a number grade. Walk uphill from here to the Eldorado Trail and find a treasure chest of obscure classic boulders.

LOST BOULDER

A shorter and safer block littered with difficult lines. Wow.

☐ **1. Elegant Universe V10** ★★★ 😊
Climbs the north face moving left to a HUGE throw. V11 from a sds.

☐ **2. Elegant Infinite V9** ★★★ 😊
Same start as #1. Sds but straight up to crimp in middle of face then reach almost to the top.

☐ **3. Lost V11** ★★★ 😊
Climbs the obvious west face seam.

☐ **4. Elegant Traverse V5** ★ 😊
Same start as *Lost* but bust right on crimps to a finish above the big pine. Start as for #2 for V7.

Lost Boulder

Nick Sherman on Lost V11   Photo: Andy Mann

Cameron Cross on The Streaked Corner V5   Photo: An

ELDORADO BOULDER

The magnificent and massive boulder with a gorgeous lichen-striped southwest face. A perfect highball wall with obsolete bolts up the right-facing corner and two sport climbs on the gully side. A few unlisted problems may have been done on the far left side of the north face.

❑ 1. Dave's Problem V9 ★★★★ 🪨🏃
Starts on an obvious matched hueco on the northwest bulge then up high to the left-facing corner and committing final move.

❑ 2. The Streaked Corner V5 ★★★★ 🪨🏃
An ultra-classic highball that climbs the lichen-stripes right of the bolts to the same finish as *DP.* A great V0 is 20 feet right.

❑ 3. Will's Problem V6 🪨🏃
On the far left side of the north face above the steep hillside climb the initial slopers moving up and slightly left if necessary.

SUSPENSION BOULDER

❑ 1. Suspension of Disbelief V14 ★★★ 🪨🏃
An absolutely killer line on the west face above a small creek/drainage covered with logs, first opened by Dave Graham in 2005. Starts low on a jug and moves into the left-facing corner, then a crystal, slapping the blunt left arête, and ending with a substantial throw to a glorious flat jug. The stand start from opposing slopey gastons is V12.

❑ 2. Project V? ★ 🪨🏃
Right of #1 on the west face pulling over the low roof/bulge and finishing up the face or on the arête. Possibly doesn't go.

*** Down gully south 200 yards is a little zone of three boulders, highlighted by the 30-footer resting on the edge of a drop-off. A fine project lies on the cleaned black northwest prow. A short V5, *Gonzo Roof,* climbs out the boulder behind it from a sit start.

BLUE WHALE AREA

A nicely shaded area littered with boulders of all sizes. Up in the gully five minutes to the southwest of this zone is the amazing highball arête *Eye in the Sky* V3, and *Captain Underpants* V5, which climbs the desperate slab on the north face.

LEMAIRE BLOCK

❑ 1. Tie Tree V8 ★★ 🏃
The first boulder encountered from *SOD.* Climb the black west face from a good right-hand pocket to bad slopers and super obvious jugs that looks like eyeballs.

❑ 2. Pocket Problems V0-V2 ★★ 🏃
To the the right of #1 are a variety of great short probems on fun holds.

❑ 3. The Fontainbleau Slab V2 ★★ 🏃
On a seperate boulder to the right (south) of #1 is a super low angle slab with perfect slopers.

Eldorado Boulder

Suspension Boulder

LeMaire Block

Paul Robinson on Suspension of Disbelief V14   Photo: Andy Mann

BLUE WHALE BOULDER

Go approximately 35 yards to the north from the V8 to the largest boulder in the wooded area. A nice little V5 roof problem can be found directly across from this block.

❐ 1. Blue Whale V8 ★★★ 🪨🤚

Super deluxe classic line on the south face climbs from a head-high matched edge to the right-sloping mini-arête with a crux getting the left foot up and over the low roof to stand up.

❐ 2. V1 ★★ 🪨🤚

To the right of *Blue Whale* is an excellent slab on the east face between two pines.

❐ 3. South Paw V4 ★ 🤚

The northeast arête has a decent little problem.

❐ 4. Projects V? ★★★ 🪨🤚

On the southwest bulge and west face scoop/corner are two lovely lines waiting for ascents.

Blue Whale Boulder

Blue Whale Boulder

Bennett Scott on Blue Whale V8   Photo: Andy Mann

Greg Johnson on the first ascent of Mavericks V5   Photo: Matt Samet

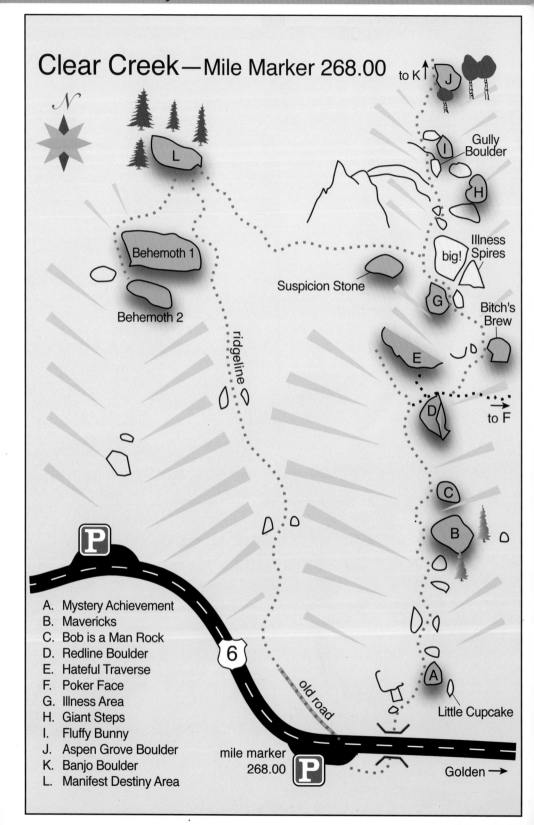

Clear Creek—Mile Marker 268.00

to K

N

Gully Boulder

Illness Spires

big!

Bitch's Brew

Suspicion Stone

Behemoth 1

Behemoth 2

ridgeline

to F

old road

mile marker 268.00

Golden →

Little Cupcake

A. Mystery Achievement
B. Mavericks
C. Bob is a Man Rock
D. Redline Boulder
E. Hateful Traverse
F. Poker Face
G. Illness Area
H. Giant Steps
I. Fluffy Bunny
J. Aspen Grove Boulder
K. Banjo Boulder
L. Manifest Destiny Area

CLEAR CREEK CANYON GULLY 268

There's bouldering in Clear Creek? You've got to be kidding me! Though this highly-traveled canyon has become a semi-tolerable sport climbing area over the last decade, it wasn't until hyper-motivated college professor and diaper-changer Greg Johnson took a look in one of the canyon's rugged lower gullies that any bouldering was found.

The rock, a metamorphic gneiss, ranges from sublimely solid to appallingly loose along the length of the canyon. Fortunately, the milling action of the small stream in Gully 268 has endowed these boulders with a smooth, solid veneer, much like the rock on nearby Anarchy Wall.

Once up bouldering in Gully 268 you'll quickly forget the traffic, smut and noise of Route 6 below, where countless busloads of folks are shuttled up to cookie-cutter casinos in Black Hawk and Central City. Expect lots of highballs ... and don't bother showing up during the warmer months—unless your idea of a good time is total sun exposure on a hot, overgrown hillside and sliding off of greasy slopers. This is a perfect winter area, even during the coldest months, melting out as quickly as Morrison and holding sun for most of the day.

Directions: Drive 3.6 miles up Clear Creek Canyon (US 6 west out of Golden) to a large pull-out on the left (south) side of the road before a road cut. This pull-out is at mile marker 268.00. Walk east out of the parking lot to the tunnel under the road. The tunnel drops you off at the base of the gully where the bouldering is found. A path can also be taken directly across the highway from the parking. An overview road map can be found in the Morrison Chapter, page 230.

A. Mystery Achievement	**E. Hateful Traverse**	**I. Fluffy Bunny Bouldering**
B. Mavericks	**F. The Poker Face**	**J. Aspen Grove Boulder**
C. Bob is a Man	**G. Illness Area**	**K. The Banjo Boulder**
D. Redline Boulder	**H. Giant Steps**	

A. Mystery Achievement Area

Though the road noise is a bit oppressive, the stone is nice and you can warm up well for the thuggier problems at Mavericks. Climb a sliding dirt chute on the right, 100 feet past the tunnel, onto the bench below these boulders. Follow the gully back down to the entrance of the tunnel and you'll find the lowball power problem *Carrera GT* V11.

Mystery Achievement Boulder

The big boulder on your right once atop the chute. The landing presents an exemplary model of erosion control. Let us praise those ancient stone-workers who built their home beneath the boulder.

❏ **1. The Spooky Spanker V5** ★
Yikes! Start with your right hand on an undercling then slap your way up into the thin crack and rounded prominence above.

❏ **2. Mystery Achievement V3** ★★★
Climb the proud face over the center of the platform, aiming for the rounded crack up high. If you blow the exit you'll pitch past the platform.

The Little Cupcake

This diminutive, though fun, block sits just behind and east of Mystery Achievement. It's a good place to warm-up, especially if you milk the traverse for a lap or two.

❏ **1. Leftinski V0**
Climb the small bulge on the left side of the boulder.

❏ **2. Slopeski V3** ★
Climb past slopers in the center of the boulder onto the rounded ramp above.

❏ **3. Rightinski V1**
Fumble your way past slots up the right end of the wall.

❏ **4. Traverski V2** ★
Monkey swing left across good holds on the lower part of the wall, doing your best to keep your feet out of the dirt.

The Nuisance Boulder

This is the low, flat-topped boulder on the left 50 feet up the trail from Mystery Achievement. The problems climb the bulging, surprisingly slopey west face.

❏ **1. Left V3**
Climb thin holds on the left side of the face to the baby's-bottom top-out.

❏ **2. Right V3**
The line just right of the groove.

❏ **3. Full V5** ★
From jugs on the south face traverse the lip and finish on #2.

Echale Boulder

❏ **1. Echale V14**
Cross the road and hike uphill 170 yards, staying right of the chute, to a very low distinct roof right of the drainage. An extremely steep line dug out for the purpose of making a problem only a couple of superstars can ascend.

B. Mavericks

The premier boulder in the gully, boasting a handful of superb lines on perfect rock, as well as a few stimulating moderates. Continue three minutes up the gully from Mystery Achievement to get here. A fun warm-up cave is just east.

❏ **1. North Shore V9** ★★★
Begin on sloping pods down and left of the *Mavericks* corner and bust a huge move up to a sloping horizontal, then finish on *Mavericks*.

❏ **2. The Plunge V4**
Mountaineer up onto the block left of #3. Pinch a rounded hole with the left hand and reach out into the crack. Spooky!

❏ **3. Mavericks V5** ★★★★
Simply brilliant. Start low under the hanging arête with your right hand in a good mailbox slot. Slap moves take you to a lip "moment." *The Two Jack Start* (V6 ★★★) begins at the good right-hand hand jam below #4 and traverses the diagonaling crack leftwards into *Mavericks*.

❏ **4. Dry Dock V2** ★
Scary as shit. Start atop the block and move right to the lip, then bust a scummy mantle over the worst landing.

❏ **5. Tsunami V9** ★★
Move from the crack to the big, sloping bump. Yank on it (left hand) and fire to the lip.

Little Cupcake

Echale

Mavericks

❑ 6. Tube Direct V7

Sds four feet right with your hands in sloper jams. Crimp up the face to the crack feature above you. Jingus yet pointless.

❑ 7. The Tube V3 ★

Sds on the southwest arête, ramp left along the lip until you hit the diagonaling crack, undercling it and bust over the lip. Harder if you take the crack hold as a finger lock.

❑ 8. Shore Break V3 ★

Sds low and left on the southwest prow over the blocks, your left hand on an incut flake. Bust right along sloping ramps until you hit the top of #7.

❑ 9. 41st Street V7 ★★★

The plumb line on the triangular south face. Start in the underclings at chest height, then do what must be done to gain the top. Powerful and classic.

C. Bob is a Man Rock

This aesthetic little block is 50 feet up the gully from Mavericks, just above the whitewash. Swirly, man.

❑ 1. Bob is a Man V5 ★★

Step up onto a block below the middle of the northwest face then grapple past crimps to gain the lip. A fun lip traverse can be done in from the left as well.

❑ 2. V2

Sds under the southwest arête, then surf along its length to the top.

D. The Redline Boulder

This pointy, isolated block offers some of the better moderates in the area on grippy, brown and red stone (though the sloping landing leaves something to be desired). Traverse down and right across the gully just 3-5 minutes uphill from Mavericks (this is the start of the trail out to The Poker Face). The boulder is 50 feet east of the gully on a bench.

❑ 1. Bulge I V1

Climb the leftmost line on the southwest face, then amble up the big slab above. Start with your right hand on a cracked flake.

❑ 2. Bulge II V2

Begin four feet right of #1 and climb the rough, crystalline groove feature to the slab.

❑ 3. The Red Line V3 ★★

This semi-classic follows the obvious clean dihedral to the crack traverse. Easier up high.

❑ 4. Thin Red Line V5 ★★

Sds on crimpers on the southeast arête (just right of the dihedral) and climb into the finger traverse crack above, which you follow 10 feet right to finish on #5.

❑ 5. Red V2 ★★

Step off the boulder against the east face and yard on the good crack holds to a distant jug/ledge and then the lip.

❑ 6. North Slabs ★

Fun problems and variations in the V0-V1 range can be done on the licheny north face.

E. Hateful Traverse Wall

Named such because no one seems to like it, except the climber who put up all the problems. This red-and-beige wall sits just right of the black-streaked waterfall and forms the base of a large cliff approximately 100 feet uphill from the Redline Boulder. Hateful Traverse Wall is not pictured.

❑ 1. Hateful Traverse V5 ★

Begin left (just right of the perennially wet black streak) and move right across the horizontal crack onto the face. Head up into the obvious break via #3, just left of a glassy bulge.

Bob is a Man

Redline Boulder

❑ 2. Hateful Downclimb V1 ★

The easiest way on, and off the wall. Climb slots up the arête-feature on the left end of the wall.

❑ 3. Hateful Upclimb V3 ★

Sds below the end of the traverse and climb up either past the flake or into the groove, eventually topping out over a second bulge. Many variations are possible.

F. THE POKER FACE

This boulder sits well out of the gully on the hillside, more or less level with the Illness Boulders and 150 yards east (down canyon). The offerings here range from dynamic bulges on impeccable stone to a long, powerful traverse of the diagonal crack line on the south face. Approach time: 10 minutes. Not pictured.

❏ **1. Trundle of Love V6** ★★
The fun problem six feet right of the wall's left margin. Ass low, crimp your way off the rail and up the bulge. V2 from the stand.

❏ **2. Texas Hold'Em V9** ★★ 🌑
Start sitting down on #1 and follow the diagonal crack system up and right across the boulder, topping out where the crack ends on the east face. Feature climbing at its finest. This problem is much easier if you start further right.

❏ **3. Chucky Cheese V7** ★★
Start four feet right of #1 with your right hand in a good pocket. Heel hook left and reef up to a good inset, then huck high and right to finish. Much easier (V3) if you move left from the inset.

❏ **4. Bulge V2** ★ 🌑
Start on good jugs over the large block and move out and left into the bulge on nice, grippy stone.

❏ **5. Low Seam V6** ★★ 🌑
This problem can be done either as a sds to the crack or taken a little further right for full difficulty. Sds three feet right of the block on a good jug and work right along the seam to its end, eventually hitting a crimp out right and throwing back into the crack to finish.

❏ **6. Wretch Like Me V3** ★
Climb out the cave onto the dark rock of the east face, starting with your left hand on a sloper in the obvious V-notch below the lip and your right on a low crimper.

❏ **7. Calipula V4** ★
Start on #6 but traverse right just below the lip, off-routing the jugs up and over. Hit the arête on the right and climb the thin face above, off-routing the arête for the left hand.

G. THE ILLNESS AREA

This sunny zone is 10 steep minutes up the gully from Mavericks and has yielded the highest density of problems in the gully. These blocks are scattered on the hillside just east of the gully below the large crag, which is easily distinguished by a smiling blue face spray-painted on the rock. Head straight up the hill above the Redline Boulder on a trail that takes you past the RSV Cave and the Bitch's Brew Boulder before traversing back left to the Illness proper. Approach time: 10 minutes.

RSV CAVE

What it lacks in stature this wall more than makes up for in terms of steeps. This west-facing cave is perched on the hillside about 100 feet up and east from The Hateful Traverse Wall.

❏ **1. V V4** ★
Sds start hyper-low on the left side of the cave, your hands on a sloping rail. Move right up the prow on bizarro holds.

❏ **2. S V2** ★
The center line. Sds on a good, incut flake then press out the lip.

❏ **3. R V4** ★★
Low-start in the very back of the rightmost part of the cave, then twist your way lipwards into the dihedral. Thuggy. *RSV* (V5) climbs *R* to the lip before traversing left across *S* to finish on *V*.

Giant Steps Left
Giant Steps Right
Illness Spires
Left Illness
Right Illness

BITCH'S BREW BOULDER

Just up and right from RSV, this giant boulder has a proud problem waiting to be done on the deadly southeast overhang. Though a handful of crummy lines have been done over the eroding dirt hillside on the boulder's northwest face, the real gems climb the southwest face. Not pictured.

❏ **1. Arête V2** ★
Climb the funky, hanging prow on the southwest corner of the boulder.

❏ **2. Scoop V3** ★
This line takes the pegmatite scoop right of the prow.

❏ **3. Bitch's Brew V7** ★★
Powerful and fussy. Sds with your left on a crimp in the peg band and your right higher on a flat hold, then slap your way up the bulging face above the slab-slapper landing.

Alden Short on Squid V8   Photo: Andy Mann

Illness Boulders

Left Illness

Right Illness

ILLNESS BOULDERS

Traverse left from the top of Bitch's Brew to get here (one minute). Two radically undercut blocks with perfect, flat landings and lots of sun make this one of the choicest zones on the hillside.

LEFT ILLNESS

This is the higher, pointy block to the west. The recently-completed cave problem facing the gully offers the promise of double-digit sickness and elite four-star athleticism.

☐ 1. Squid V8 ★★

Start on the south face, just left of the hanging prow, with your left hand on a pinch and your right hand on a crimp. Reel right past slopers around the corner, then traverse right along the low seam, off-routing the upper jug rail. V4 if you use the jug rail.

☐ 2. Battling Seizure Robots V5 ★★

Do the easy variation on #1 then dice your way past sloping crimpers on the gold face/prow just left of #3. Have your spotter stand below the pads so you don't go off the 100-foot cliff.

☐ 3. Dead Lizard V1 ★★★

Up the steep southeast face of the giant boulder on creaky jugs/horns. The low start off the bad crimps is *Rhino* V10. Traversing the crack rightwards goes at V2 and has an eerie finish.

☐ 4. Stanley Kubrik V11 ★★

On the backside of the Left Illness Boulder (the opposite side of *Rhino*), is *Stanley Kubrik*. It starts just before you go out the first lip, on a right hand crimper and a left-hand flat side-pull. And you also have *Stanley Kubrik SDS* V12. You start way under the roof on a bad undercling, then fire out to the start of *Stanley Kubrik*, and finish.

☐ 5. Paths of Glory V11 ★★

Start as *Stanly Kubrick SDS* and trend left staying under the roof the whole way.

RIGHT ILLNESS

This is the roof/boulder perched on the east side of the grotto.

☐ 6. Squeeze Job V3

A useless little campus move up the wall left of the choss heap at the base of the block.

Left Illness

☐ 7. Heaping Helping V2 ★

Ascend the heap, make a long stretch for a jug over the lip of the boulder and press it out.

Note: Problems #8, #9 and #10 share a common sds on the right with your hands matched in a good, low horizontal.

☐ 8. Bacterial V5 ★★

Thuggy and acrobatic. Head up and left along the lip on inset seams, off-routing the jugs to the right. Turn the lip on good holds right of the heap.

☐ 9. Viral V3 ★

Lock off and stretch right for jugs from the sds.

☐ 10. Ebola V7 ★★

The integral lip traverse, crossing #8 and #9 to finish with an exit crux on the far left (north) end of the boulder over the jingus landing. Potent.

ILLNESS SPIRES

These two massive, pointy blocks abut each other on the bench just uphill and east of the Illness Boulders.

LEFT SPIRE

☐ 1. Sport Park is Neither V2 ★★
Climb the left line, directly below the prominent arête. Either bail right into the bowl or finish on the 40-foot arête (5.9+).

☐ 2. Puss in Boots V3 ★
This line starts on low underclings then fires past fragile crimpers on the brown face four feet right of #1. Elegant.

☐ 3. The Skirted Snail V4 ★
Slap your way up the rounded prow on the southwest corner of the boulder. Slabby.

☐ 4. The Downclimb V0
This is the best way off for #1-3. It follows the seams in the black streak on the south face of the boulder, just right of #3.

RIGHT SPIRE

☐ 5. High Slab V0 ★★
A beautiful line on positive edges up the middle of the high slab just right of the chimney. Good, heady bouldering.

H. GIANT STEPS

This is the jumble of enormous boulders 50 yards uphill and north from the Illness Area. Many proud, high (20+ feet) lines have been done on these austere brown rocks, yet the hardest lines have yet to cede. Bring at least three crash pads or you're unlikely to leave the ground. This zone is more-or-less directly below the big crag with the blue smiley face and holds sun most of the day in the winter. Approach time: 15 minutes.

SUSPICION STONE

This easy-to-spot, south-facing overhang is left (west of the gully) on the small bench across from and slightly uphill of the Illness Area. Not pictured.

☐ 1. Nietzche V3
The leftmost line, on funky flakes and holds into the groove.

☐ 2. Marx V3 ★
The tall center line, which more or less follows the rib/prow. *Eastwood* V6 tackles the face right of the prow, off-routing the prow for the left hand.

☐ 3. Freud V1
The rightmost problem up the featured but dirty groove.

GULLY BOULDER

The sds to the one problem here will be horrendously hard. The rock is perfect—polished to an alarmingly slick sheen by the milling action of water and covered in grey and white swirls. This boulder is in the wash, level with Giant Steps Left and just below the big slab in the gully. Not pictured.

☐ 1. The Italian Stallion V5 ★★★★
Start low and left on a sloping jug and work right across the horizontal until you can punch straight out the slippery prow. Simply brilliant!

GIANT STEPS LEFT

This is the left of the two huge blocks that faces almost due west. The problems are high and the footholds still slightly friable, but the landings are for the most part flat. This wall holds sun most of the day in the winter.

NORTH FACE

☐ 1. Slaves of Truth V1 ★
This fine pocket climb takes the inside face around the corner and uphill from the arête.

☐ 2. Masters of Irony V3 ★
Begin on #1 but work your way up the rounded prow just right via underclings and slopers.

WEST FACE

☐ 3. Speed Zoo V4 ★★
Begin just right of the arête on high underclings. Punch straight up the wall above, past another undercling and rig hand sidepull to a crimpy finish.

☐ 4. The Moose V4 ★★
Begin on #3 and continue right on good underclings (or climb directly into these on plate-crimpers), bust for a left-hand sloper, and fire high and right to a made-to-order handlebar jug. Tall and classic.

☐ 5. Undone I V? ★★
The line up the center of the wall over the rectangular block. Groovy.

☐ 6. Undone II V? ★★★★
The very distinct rightmost line on the wall, following a vein of quartz up a black streak.

GIANT STEPS RIGHT

This is the rightmost of the two blocks, easily distinguished by an aesthetic prow on its right end, just north of a huge, dead tree. The landings are a bit worse here, despite efforts to shore up the eroding hillside.

☐ 1. Headbanger's Ball V6 ★
Ouch! This short but fierce problem tackles the bulging wall left of the black-stained dihedral on the wall's uphill end. Start with your ass in the dirt!

☐ 2. Star Drive V0 ★
Climb the corner, taking care with mossy footholds. Check out the mank bolt on top!

☐ 3. Rolly-Polly V5 ★★
Though the first move is the hardest, this line ain't over 'til it's over. Begin on a good right-hand crimp six feet right of the dihedral and fire up to the sloping horizontal, then trend right and up to finish.

☐ 4. La Fissura V1 ★
Climb out the obvious right-leaning dihedral in the middle of the wall over the shite-ous block landing.

☐ 5. Il Precario V6 ★★
Precarious in Italian. Climb the face right of the crack, aiming for a juggy seam up high and right. Crimpy and committing on psychedelic, swirly rock.

Giant Steps Left & Right

...ple V4 ★★★
...g on good holds at head-height and
... for a sloper before wrapping back left
... Aren't people great?

...n with People V6 ★★
...-up combines a low (read: groundhog) traverse of the
...west cave behind the dead tree with #6. Needless to say,
...e prow is much scarier when you're pumped.

I. FLUFFY BUNNY BOULDERING

Sixty feet straight up the gully from Giant Steps (at the top of the whitewash) sit these deceptively steep and polished chunks of bullet rock. Though seemingly downright lame, the left wall of the alcove is completely devoid of texture, especially on the top-outs, making for some hilarious beached-whale maneuvering.

FLUFFY BOULDER

The squatty, slopey, and south-facing left wall of the alcove above the nice, grassy landings. Not pictured.

❐ **1. Smooth Operator V2** ★★
Climb the rippled face past horizontals to finish on glass.

❐ **2. Scrumpy V0** ★
The dihedral/seam up the middle of the wall.

❐ **3. Frumpy V2** ★★
The rightmost line up the glassy bulge. Harder if you off-route the rounded three-finger pocket and anything right of that.

BUNNY BOULDER

The overhanging, right wall of the alcove. Featured with jugs, crimps and horns, this little gem climbs quite steeply and powerfully on surprisingly bomber stone. Bring a spotter for the rightmost problems, which hang out over a nasty mini-couloir.

❐ **4. Fuzzy Bunny V2** ★★
Sds on good incuts, then fire up the polished face above. One variation powers into the jug undercling up and right.

❐ **5. Blood Bunny V4** ★★
Sds on a good right-hand layaway and left-hand pinch, then power on and slap your way up the prow/rib feature to the top of the wall.

❐ **6. Funny Bunny V3** ★
Sds with your hands in a good crack down and right of the rib, then work your way up the juggy groove above on good flakes.

❐ **7. Bunny's Traverse V6** ★★
Powerful and harder than it looks. Traverse the wall from right to left, dropping in from the jug/horns on #5 to a pair of flakes that lead into #4. Add a V-grade if you off-route these horns.

J. THE ASPEN GROVE BOULDER

Climb the whitewash immediately above the Giant Steps and follow the gully northeast. Find this large, pleasant boulder 30 yards up from the top of the whitewash. There is plenty of potential for new problems in and around the grove. Approach time: 20 minutes.

❐ **1. V4** ★
The leftmost line, on wavy rock directly above the large pit. Undercling low and left then punch past slopers to the lip. Tricky.

❐ **2. Center V3** ★
Climb this pretty little line by kneel-starting with your left hand on a gray edge and your right hand on a crimp, six feet right of #1.

❐ **3. Right V2**
Take the aforementioned crimp with your left hand and move right to a layback, then up.

K. THE BANJO BOULDER

Despite the arduous approach, this mobile-home sized slab of good, gray stone 30 minutes uphill from the car is worth a visit. The wall offers everything from thuggy cave problems to testy vertical face climbs, with plenty of highball top-outs to keep things spicy. Its idyllic setting in a grassy meadow bisected by a small stream makes for a fun hang in the warmer months. To get here, hike out of the gully onto its right (east) side above the Aspen Grove Boulder then contour back left into the gully across from an attractive, multi-tiered crag to the west. Beware the sketch hobo encampment. Approach time: 30 minutes.

❐ **1. Undone** ★★★
The highball arête-to-face line starting on the north arête of the wall and turning a terrifying roof at 13 feet.

❐ **2. Eric's Highball V3** ★
Cruise up the crack to the roof, move left, then up and over on knobular holds via a committing rock-over.

Bunny

Aspen Grove

Banjo Boulder

❏ 3. Dihedral V0 ★★

The obvious crack/dihedral splitting the wall.

Note: #4-7 all begin on the right side of the cave, sitting down with your hands on a large horn and moving left into underclings.

❏ 4. Traverse V7 ★

From the sds cross the entirety of the cave until you can move out on the layaways of #5 and backhand left into the crack at seven feet. Either climb the crack to finish or drop off.

❏ 5. Sandcastle (aka The Coveted Double Bird Toe) V8 ★★

Every thug's wet dream. Stay low across the cave until you hit the sloper/corner system on the left side. Head out the slopes to a painful vertical slot over the lip, slap right to a beach-ball, then fire up to a diagonaling finger slot. The good holds out right over the lip on #6 are off. Finish out on the crack.

❏ 6. Banjos V6 ★★★

Work left through the cave to the last good undercling, then climb straight out onto the lip and head for the diagonaling finger slot. Finish via the crack.

❏ 7. Rufus's Wonder Move V4 ★★

Go left five feet from the horn, grab crimps over the lip, and stand up right into a flake/groove system. Technical and strange.

❏ 8. Courtesy V2 ★

The high problem up the center of the vertical wall, aiming for a finger slot at 12 feet.

❏ 9. Sympathy V3 ★★

The slanting finger crack on the right side of the wall, eight feet left of a trough with a bush. Finish by staying left on flakes or punching right to a horn at the top of the crack.

L. MANIFEST DESTINY AREA

"Go West, young man!" Perched high on the hillside in the faint gully 200 yards west of the main area, this collection of bigger-than-they-look-from-below boulders offers the superlative Manifest Destiny boulder and two barely-touched behemoths just downhill. Be careful not to dislodge any rocks from here, as they may very well tumble all the way down to the road!

Directions: Either hike directly up the ridge west of the gully from the parking area via a faint climber's trail or approach from the gully itself via a trail cutting west from Giant Steps across the base of the large crag. Manifest Destiny is another 100 yards up the hill once you hit the ridge and can be distinguished by the large dead pine tree just below its southwest face. The Behemoth Boulders are just two minutes downhill from here.

Manifest Destiny

MANIFEST DESTINY

The main draw, offering over a dozen steep, deceptively problems on interesting, black- and gray-streaked stone a well as good views of the canyon and the jerky-selling weir in the large pull-out directly below. Much walking.

❏ 1. Traverse of Bliss to Arête of Piss V4 ★★

A long name for a long problem. Leftward traverse the obvious horizontal on the northwest face, finishing out on the tricky arête all the way uphill.

❏ 2. Slab Oneski V1

The leftmost slab problem on the face via small edges, just uphill from the rock-pile landing.

❏ 3. Slab Twoski V1

From good holds near the start of the traverse, rock up past crimps to good holds on the slab.

❏ 4. Josh's Roof V8 ★

Awkward and difficult. Climb the roof six feet right of the start of the traverse. Full V8 rating assumes you start with your hands under the lip on the crimp and the undercling, bro.

❏ 5. THC Engineering V6 ★★

The engaging prow just over the Nepalese rice-paddy terrace. Start low on the flake, slap up and right to a jug then reel back left on crimpers to gain the crack above.

❏ 6. Mangina Crack V?

The obvious, not-too-hard-looking crack on the south/south-west face of the boulder, just above the huge dead tree. To fall is to be impaled.

❏ 7. Jade's Variation V3 ★

Climb the crack to mid-height, then bust right onto the head-wall through good holds.

❏ 8. Flaps V6 ★★★

The classic face line up the bulging black wall six feet right of the crack. Catch the finger lock at mid-height with your right hand and finish via a committing lunge to a horn.

❏ 9. Kilgore V6 ★★★

A dynamic excursion on underclings and sidepulls just four feet right of #8. Snag the finger lock with your left hand and finish just left of the large groove.

❏ 10. Cephalic Index V7 ★★★

The prominent nose on the boulder's south face, starting left below the spiny bush. Roll through from the honking-huge sidepull jug to a phat pinch, then slap your way up the rounded prow.

❏ 11. Manifest Destiny V2 ★

The splitter hand crack in the alcove above the big bush. Harder from a sds.

❏ 12. Divine Right V5 ★

Start on the double underclings at head-height, then paw your way through the overlaps, eventually moving left into the crack.

❏ 13. Prowling V8 ★★

The long prow on the southeast side of boulder, right of a small tree. Start low, just right of the tree, and move up and right on poor crimps, eventually finishing out on #15.

❏ 14. Rape V3 ★

Climb the groove from an undercling halfway up the prow. *Rape and Pillage* (V4) starts on this problem and links into #15.

❏ 15. Pillage V1

Start at a good hold on the steep face and pull for the lip jug.

15 feet east of Manifest Destiny, offers
roblems.

...ng with Jocasta V1
steep left prow of the rock.

..de's Line V5 ★★
. on the low jug on the left and slap your way up the
overhang without using the prow.

☐ 3. Philoctetes V3 ★
The funky, powerful seam up the middle of the face.

The Fin

BEHEMOTH I
Why does this boulder only look five feet tall from the highway?
A few problems have been done on the low, wavy southeast
face, but the proud line out the left side of the south face needs
to be done in a big way. This boulder is directly downhill from
Behemoth II.

Behemoth 1

BEHEMOTH II
Big as a house and (mostly) blank as shit, this hard-to-miss
chunk of gray stone sits in the faint gully about 70 yards
below Manifest Destiny.

☐ 1. Creaky Flake V0 ★
The thuggy, juggy romp on the obvious flake splitting the west
face. Use caution on the blocky top-out.

☐ 2. Mr. Bitchy V6 ★★
Sds on the pink quartz horn then battle up the scenic arête at
the junction of the massive south face and the more manage-
able west face. Super-steep and super-highball. Climb near
the crystalline crack on the left to finish. The prow proper, out
right, is *Mrs. Bitchy* V7, and scary as hell.

Behemoth II

TUNNEL 2 BOULDER
*Directions: Head West on Hwy 6, into Clear Creek Canyon,
until just before Tunnel 2. Park at pullouts (near Sonic Youth,
same as parking for New River Wall & Wall of Justice) and
walk over the bridge that's before Tunnel 2. Head down a sandy slope, back toward Sonic Youth, following the creek. The
Tunnel 2 boulder is on the north side, a few hundred yards
down the creek. (Will be visible from road as you approach).*

☐ 1. Flash Flood V6 ★★
Climbs the right arête. Start very low with right hand low on
a flat crimp and left hand on left side of arête on a sloping
edge. Move up the arête using crimps, heel hooks and pinches
and exit either direct or moving left into a good rail system.

☐ 2. Aqua Huck V5 ★★★
Start left hand on obvious jug in the middle of the face, and
right hand on an incut crimp. Make a big move right to a sloping pinch, and move left through crimps to the good top-out.
Grade is probably height dependent. A classic!

☐ 3. High Waters V7 ★
Start on same jug as *Aqua Huck*, but move left through a
sharp, right gaston, and a left sloping edge. Body tension and
contact strength required for this one.

Tunnel 2 Boulder

New River Boulder

New River Boulder

Walking back down-canyon roughly 100 yards from Tunnel 2 Boulder you'll find a small, streamside cave just west of *Sonic Youth* that provides thuggy variations on positive rock, with the possibility for highball top-outs. More hard varations than you can count. A 2011 excavation effort created countless butt-dragging variations which are not shown here.

☐ 1. Fluid Mechanics V10 ★★★
Sds down on a good rounded jug in the middle of the roof and work out onto the finish of *Dark Waters*.

☐ 2. Dark Waters V12 ★★★★
Sds way back on the obvious undercling in the center of the cave. Work directly out to the sloping lip, traverse left and finsh out the cave as for *Fluid Mechanics*. Be careful topping out on the brittle choss for it has claimed at least one ankle. One of the best thuggy testpieces on the Front Range.

☐ 3. Than's Problem V8 ★★
Pull onto sloping laybacks several moves in to *Dark Waters*, pull the crux move to the sloping lip and traverse out right, staying low the whole way around the corner and finishing on the highest jug. The first hard line in the cave to go down. Sds as for *Fluid Mechanics* and joining this line is *The Swamp Traverse* V9.

☐ 4. Formula 500 V12 ★★★
Sds as for *Dark Waters* but formulate yourself to head right under the roof into a different crux sequence utilizing a sidepull rail under the roof to get out into the lip of the cave and head back left into the finish of *DW*. Finishing right as for *Than's* is *Formula 50* V10.

☐ 5. Wet Carrot V4 ★★
Start halfway through the finish on *Than's* on a jug and finish around the corner right to an obvious highest jug. Many varations exist on this side of the cave that mere mortals can enjoy!

Clear Creek Also-Rans

Not surprisingly, this craggy canyon offers other bouldering possibilities. These other areas suffer two major drawbacks, however. They are either so close to the road as to be completely noisome and annoying, or they sit in the creek and are inaccessible during high water—or both. Nevertheless, for the bored boulderer looking for something different or for those who just can't get enough of the tranquil, pristine ambience of the canyon, we've listed a few choicer areas below. Don't forget to bring hip waders and earplugs!

Mile Marker 270.00

Look for this mile marker 1.6 miles up the canyon and park where you can (there's a small pull-out on the left just before the mile marker). These boulders are on an elevated bench on the right (north) side of the canyon and can be reached via a steep scramble along the road-cut. Not much else is known.

Mile Marker 269.50

Look for this mile marker 2.7 miles up the canyon and park in an ample pull-out on the left where a large, white cross reading *Brandy* commemorates a tragic car accident. On the other (south) side of the creek find a smooth, left-leaning, overhanging arête (V4 ★★★), accessible only when the creek is frozen.

Little Eiger Bouldering

Drive 3.1 miles up canyon, cross a bridge and park on the right. Animal V9 faces downcanyon on a large boulder just over the guardrail. Start on a right hand sidepull and a low left hand underling for full credit. Starting matched in the undercling is V7. Other small boulders are around.

Anarchy Wall Bouldering

Drive 6.8 miles up the canyon, parking on the left just after you pass through Tunnel 3. A small cluster of solid, featured blocks has tumbled down the hill from the Anarchy Wall above. The twin slabs at the bottom are a great place to teach beginning climbers.

The Wave Wall

This varnished piece of bullet granite is only accessible during the colder months, unless your idea of a landing is three feet of icy, swiftly-moving water! Drive 11.5 miles up the canyon, taking a left onto US 6 at the stoplight which marks the junction with Highway 119. The Primo Wall will be on your right after Tunnel 6, 1.2 miles from the stoplight; the Wave Wall is at 1.4 miles, just upstream. The Wave Wall is the polished, concave golden wall forming a sort of mini-alcove right above the river. Park where you can and ford across. Though not exceptionally hard, the problems here are quiet aesthetic. Home to the infamous V8 dyno *Zion*. Down stream is the Nomad Cave, home to Off the Books V11, which climbs a compression feature from opposing sidepulls into a jug finish. Drop off from here, or continue up the 5.13d for Ali Nomad 5.14b.

The Dike Wall

This sunny traverse wall is 1.6 miles above the stoplight at the junction of US 6 and Hwy 119. It is just above Hwy 6 to the right (north), directly across from an old, reddish, abandoned building on the south side of the creek. The traverse starts on the left at an undercling and moves right along the sloping ripples. There is also potential for a few up-problems.

Annette Bunge on Helicopter V6   Photo: Fred Knapp

MORRISON

Morrison Wall is pure undistilled urban bouldering. The business is on a south-facing ridge above the small tourist trap of Morrison. These sandstone walls have the incredible advantage of being especially kind to the fingers (although tough on the calluses); hence an excellent area for extended sessions. Hordes of boulderers, topropers and training fanatics brave the crowds for the readily available self-torture. Morrison's greatest asset is the endless bouldering contrivances. The severely overhanging walls of The Lobby Area and The Black Hole offer the most concentrated sections of desperate bouldering in Colorado and possibly in the States. The Nautilus Area and Spike Rock tend toward moderate bouldering. Another Morrison asset is its wintertime usability. The south-facing wall works like a solar collector on even the coldest days, yet summer mornings are pleasantly cool. Vicious boulder problems, easy access, and a focused environment creates an area with everything but seclusion. Across the highway and creek from Morrison Wall is an extension of the sandstone ridge. The north-facing hillside is littered with less-visited boulders of superb quality. Many distinct cracks, arêtes and faces make up the selection of quality problems on the South Side. Always tread lightly when visiting the South Side.

Directions: From the north off Interstate 70 drive south down State Route 26 past Red Rocks Amphitheater and into the town of Morrison. At the stop light take a left and parallel park at the end of town (on the right) and next to the creek, which is adjacent to the road. Alternately, take the Morrison Road exit off C-470 and drive 0.3 mile to the parking on the left before entering the town of Morrison. The wall can be seen directly above the road opposite the parking. Since Jefferson County Open Space recently created a new trail, the south side parking is now south of Morrison Road on the east side of the hogback.

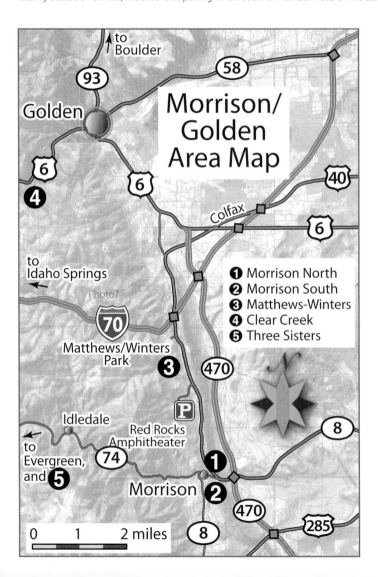

to Boulder

93   58

Golden

Morrison/ Golden Area Map

6

6   40

4

Colfax   6

to Idaho Springs

Photo?

70

❶ Morrison North
❷ Morrison South
❸ Matthews-Winters
❹ Clear Creek
❺ Three Sisters

Matthews/Winters Park   ❸   470

Idledale   8

Red Rocks Amphitheater

to Evergreen, and ❺   74

Morrison   ❶

❷

470

0   1   2 miles   8   285

THE BLACK HOLE

Near the right end of the cliff after walking up the southern-most trail (which starts at the chain link fence next to the road) is a Mecca, a cornucopia of contrived problems. The smoke-stained rock —the remnants of many fires— stands in sharp contrast to the hundreds of chalked handholds. The variations within the hole probably near a hundred. Many classics are listed and detailed along with brief descriptions and grades for other commonly tried problems. The near-impossible chore of outlining each problem has been left to the active boulderers. To learn the exact sequence of a problem ask a local (even then a handhold or two may have been changed or been forgotten since the first ascent). Problems are listed from left to right.

❑ **1. Helicopter V6** ★★
An ultra-classic for Morrison but the original rightward-traversing-start is falling off. The direct start begins from underclings to reach slopers a series of slopers. A knee-bar is helpful halfway through the traverse to make the transfer to the upper sloping edges. A big move leads to the lip.

❑ **2. Air Loopis V8** ★★★
A popular circular problem that traverses left from the jugs at the base of the Hole, then out *Helicopter Direct* (a low V7 start to *Helicopter* off a bad right-hand undercling and terrible left-hand gaston edge/hole to join the middle of *Helicopter*), then finishes *Helicopter*, and continues across the top of the Hole before reversing *Breashear's Crack* (the only line of jugs leading out the Hole) to the starting jugs.

❑ **3. Center Route V10** ★★
The same start as *Cytogrinder*. Reach up left hand to a small and sharp crimp, then right hand to a very small incut. Left hand to an intermediate, the left again to a large sloper. Finish by matching "the deck of cards" edge, just over the lip. Considered a standard for the grade, it has been done in tennis shoes.

❑ **4. Cytogrinder V8** ★★
From the lowest jugs at the base of the cave climb up to the optional sickeningly sharp crimper with the right hand, then undercling a chipped two-finger pocket with the left and punch up on sloping edges. The large foot out right is off. The final throw to the lip is difficult after the lower crux.

❑ **5. McTwist V5** ★
From the starting sds jugs at the base of *Breashear's Crack* move up to a sloping hold, which is still in the crack with the right hand then up to a painful two-finger pocket for the left then to the top via sloping edges and underclings just left of #6.

❑ **6. Breashear's Crack V1** ★★★
The most obvious and best problem coming out the cave. This isn't really a crack climb, rather a line of obvious weakness.

❑ **7. Tendonitis Traverse V5** ★★★
Midway up the *Breashear's Crack* is a long line of holds (jugs to big edges to crimps) leading out right. Start from the small set of crimpers at the far right of this obvious horizontal line of edges (at head-height) and traverse left to *Breashear's Crack*.

Black Hole

Black Hole Right

❑ **8. CJMD V8** ★★★
One of the few independent lines. On the far right of the Black Hole is a small open landing area before walking south (away from the Hole and toward the spot everyone defecates). Start on a low sloping handhold with miserable feet and go straight up and right from the far right holds of *Tendonitis Traverse* using a limiting crimper with the right hand. Follow this with a couple of throws up the sloping arête, and a right-hand throw for a hidden jug up and right. *Smurf* V10 is the evil sds from a left crimp pinch and heinous right sidepull.

❑ **9. Extra Otis V11** ★★
Possibly the longest traverse (approximately 75 feet) at Morrison. Starts on the highest rightmost handholds (right of *CJMD*) and traverse left through the Hole and the *Wisdom Simulator* to the ending holds at the top of the ramp. *Otis* V10 starts on *Tendonitis Traverse* and finishes the same as *Extra*.

Additional Black Hole problems, left to right:

❑ **Point of Impact V10** ★★
A left to right traverse across the base of the Hole ending with minute edges just right of *Breashear's*.

❑ **Miss Clairol V8** ★★
A contrived problem on bad holds up and through the *Helicopter* area.

❑ **Lady Revlon V7** ★★★
The better more popular version of *Miss Clairol*.

❑ **Death by Drowning V7** ★★
Sds problem below then through the *Helicopter* area.

❑ **Pop Goes the Weasel V9** ★
Another contrived sds problem that begins at *Helicopter Direct* (the original Direct off a bad right hand undercling) then up and through the *Helicopter* area.

❑ **Power's Boring V8** ★
Climbs up the slot just right of the underclings on *Helicopter*.

❑ **Going to the Airport V7** ★★
Just right of *Breashear's Crack* are separate low underclings. Throw up to *Tendonitis'* rail then all the way to the top slopers without matching on *Tendonitis*. Finish by pulling up to the jug at the top of the arête.

❑ **5. Air Jordan V6** ★
Starts as for *Going to the Airport* but allows moving on *Tendonitis* before throwing all the way to the top slopers (one hand on each side of the arête) and then finishing on the jug at the top of the arête.

❑ **Illegally Insane V10** ★★
This problem deserves three but, alas, it is contrived. Traverse *Tendonitis* down *Breashear's Crack*, then do *Air Loopis*.

❑ **Taxi Driver V10** ★★
The same problem as *Illegally Insane* but do *Death By Drowning* instead of *Helicopter Direct*, to gain the upper holds and finish of *Air Loopis*.

Wisdom Simulator

The upper section of The Black Hole (above the block on the left of The Black Hole proper). Many problems pull straight out from the *Wisdom Simulator's* beginning jug section in the V3 to V5 range, as well as other fun problems in the middle and upper sections of the traverse.

☐ 1. Wisdom Simulator V7 ★★

Starts in the nook below the adjacent block to the Black Hole's left side and traverse left on good jugs to a crux section on thin edges before more bomber edges and jugs. Finishes at the far left end of the upper area on easy rock.

☐ 2. Upper Wisdom Simulator V3 ★★★

Sds on the obvious large jug underneath the rock and above the crimper crux of *Wisdom*.

The Lobby aka The Warm-up Wall

From the southernmost trail beginning at the chain link fence walk straight uphill. This is the first part of the wall encountered from the trail. Numerous small boulders have been retro-placed at the base of the wall to add to the comfort level of already spoiled boulderers. As with The Black Hole, problems are too contrived to fully describe each one. Ask some buff dude for the sequence to the more obscure problems. Problems are listed from left to right.

☐ 1. Holloway's Route V7 ★★★

An independent problem just down and right from an obvious roof crack that leads out left. Look for opposing crimpers on an extremely overhanging wall with a small edge just over the lip. Get hold of the opposing crimpers and smear a terrible right foot heel hook for the throw to the lip. Many ugly top-out sequences can be done to reach the upside down crack at the top of the slab.

☐ 2. Willow's Wart V5 / My Sharonna V6 ★★

From the lower right-facing layback jug at the right end of the wall, traverse left to the V-slot holds keeping the feet always above the low chalk line just below the small edges. At the base of the V-slot go left with the left hand onto a small sloping edge (below the midway jug) then catch the big sloper in the right-facing dihedral (left side of V-slot) with the right hand and pop with the left to an obvious mini-jug. Cross with the right to a tiny crimper above and left from the mini jug and then match on a positive, thin horizontal slot just before the wall becomes devoid of holds. Finish with a relatively easy but long move from the horizontal crack to the jug that is up and left. *My Sharonna* goes straight up to a sharp incut from the horizontal crack and then over the lip.

☐ 3. Some Biceps Are Bigger Than Others V6 ★★

From the lower right-facing layback jug at the right end of the wall, without further matching traverse left with left hand on the crimper above and right of the base of the V-slot— keeping the feet always above the low chalk line. Cross right hand under to the hold just to the right of the V-slot. Move left to an atrocious left-hand gaston on the sloping right-facing dihedral then crosses with the right hand to a good incut edge right of the wall's middle-height jug. With the left hand grab the small pocket on the left side of the massive jug in the middle of the wall and cross with the right hand to a high incut edge on a left angling line of edges. Then finish by moving further left on small edges and slots under the pointed arête and over the lip.

The Lobby

Rob Raker on Wisdom Simulator V7   Photo: Fred Knapp

Additional Lobby problems, left to right:

☐ **Life's about Nothing V6** ★
& Life's about Fucking V6 ★★

These two extremely contrived problems begin on the far low left of the Lobby before *Holloway's Route*.

☐ **Chasing Pennies V7** ★★

Starts on the left and fiddles through contrived sequences to end in the same vicinity as *Life's About Nothing*.

☐ **Electric Nork V6** ★★★

One of the original difficult problems in The Lobby. Start as for *Some Biceps*. Without matching, go from the right hand hold just right of the base of the V-slot directly up to a small crimp in the middle of the face just left of the huge jug and then up right hand to the triangular-shaped hold just below the lip With no further rules, finish by moving to the top rail.

☐ **Lascivious V9** ★

Same as *Some Biceps* until reaching the midway jug. Do not go to the left-hand pocket but pull straight up to the small crimps above with the left and over.

☐ **Vulgar Display of Power V9** ★

Too contrived to even begin a description. If small, shoulder-torturing holds are your forte then hop aboard.

☐ **The Occasionalist V8** ★★ 🌣

From the lower right-facing layback jug at the right end of the wall, without further matching, traverse left with the right hand to the crimper used by the left hand in *Some Biceps* and *Nork*. Left hand goes to the sloping edge above and just right of the base of the V-slot (feet above the low chalk line of course). Continue as for *Willows Wart* for two moves and then cross right hand to the mini-jug. Go left straight up to the pocket on the left side of the midway jug and then right to the small incut edge just below the lip. Finish by moving further left on small edges and slots under the pointed arête and over the lip.

☐ **White Men Can't Jump V10** 🌣

Dyno from the holds at the base of the V-corner system to the huge mid-height jug two-handed then double-dyno again to the flat jug up and left from the top arête.

HAIRY SCARY WALL

Uphill to the north from The Lobby, approximately 25 yards, is a short traverse wall with a couple of straight-up problems on the right side.

☐ 1. **V0** ★★ 🌣

Climb up the dihedral on the far right of the traverse.

☐ 2. **V1** ★★ 🌣

Start in the dihedral and move left on the face on edges and sloping pinches.

☐ 3. **Traverse V2** ★★ 🌣

Traverse the wall from right to left.

Hairy Scary

SAILOR'S DELIGHT BLOCK

North from Hairy Scary about 10 yards is a block that over-hangs the trail.

☐ **Sailor's Delight V2** 🌣

Climb from under the roof to flakes out the roof and over to big, flat jugs.

Sailor's Delight Rock

THE COCKPIT

Just up and around to the northeast from *Sailor's Delight* is a small cave. A few variations can be done out the cave starting at V1. The Cockpit is not pictured.

5.8 BOULDER

The lowest boulder on the hillside (down and left from Sailor's Delight) with a V0 on the south face and V1's on the east and west faces.

5.8 Boulder

TREE SLAB

Just north of The Cockpit about 15 feet is a slabby wall that is right of a tree.

☐ 1. **Corner Overhang V0** ★

Climb the excellent holds just right of the arête.

☐ 2. **Low Traverse V0** ★

Traverse the upper set of left-angling holds from the right. The lower traverse into *Corner Overhang* is thin and harder.

☐ 3. **High Traverse V2** ★

Traverse from the right side with feet on holds used in the *Low Traverse* using thin vertical seam and crimper edges for hands. The top of the boulder is off. Top out at the left side of the front face.

Tree Slab

MAGNUM BLOCK

This is approximately 10 yards left of the Tree Slab and defined by a miniature overhang at the base with a vicious slab to finish the problems. A tree is directly right of the wall.

☐ 1. Magnum Force V5 ★ 🔾

Surely considered a classic slab problem but the pain of crimping through the slab may bring different thoughts to mind. Starts low on the triangular point under the roof and moves left and then up the ultra-thin slab.

☐ 2. Make My Day V4 ★★ 🔾

Can be climbed via a low left start or a more difficult right start. Finish up the crack and arête.

Magnum Wall

SPIKE ROCK

The short block just below Magnum Wall with an overhang on the north face.

☐ 1. V2 ★★

Climbs the north face to a reasonable mantel.

☐ 2. V1 ★

Climb the slabby arête on the west face.

Shawn Raboutou on Spike Rock V2

BOWLING BALL WALL

Again to the north from *Magnum Force* is a wall with a few fun, easy problems reminiscent of the Nautilus Wall. Both traverses and straight-up problems can be done in the V0 to V1 range.

Bowling Ball Wall

NAUTILUS WALL

The upper, northernmost wall at Morrison. It is best defined by being just left of a large cave (look for the prominent chalked arête). A superb area for getting a pump on good edges and jugs.

☐ 1. Nemo V0 ★★

The furthest left problem on the face that climbs straight up.

☐ 2. League V0 ★★

Up the middle of the wall on good edges. Escape left.

☐ 3. V0 ★

Just left of the arête is another fun face problem. Escape off to the left.

☐ 4. Nautilus Traverse V3 ★★★

An excellent traverse that can be lapped for a pump. Of course, low eliminates can make it harder.

Nautilus

Austin Lankford on Nautilus Traverse V3   Photo: Fred Knapp

Scott Blunk

October 1972. My first Front Range climbing experience, bouldering around the base of a scruffy crag in Poudre Canyon. I had no idea at the time it was my introduction to a lifetime of adventure on world class stone...

Memories from the past 36 years flash by: absolute terror while manteling the top of *Pinch Overhang* without a spot on a blazing summer day. Golden aspen and perfect tacky rock in Poudre Canyon. Spending the entire summer in Pueblo bouldering with John Gill when I was 21 years old. Breezy, dreamy summer evenings at Flagstaff. And finally, exclaiming "Oh my God! Look at that!" over and over the first time I walked in to Mt. Evans.

To me the best bouldering areas absolutely must meet two criteria: great rock and great conditions. The Front Range has a unique combination of different rock types for each part of the year. In winter, the Dakota and Fountain sandstone hogbacks reign supreme. Dakota sandstone is the quintessential bouldering stone. It is solid, grippy, sports a wide variety of holds and above all forms into lines simply begging to be climbed. I've been to Fontainebleau five times and have rarely seen a line there as compelling as *Kahuna Roof* or *Ripper Traverse*. For spring and fall, Boulder and Poudre Canyons have some of the best granite I have ever touched. Smooth, crimpy, sloping, hard, and perfect. And there simply is no finer summer bouldering than the alpine areas of Rocky Mountain National Park and Mt. Evans. Here, huge talus fields yield over a thousand world class problems on fantastically weathered gneiss. No matter how hot, windy or cold the day might be you can find a perfect place to climb somewhere in the 200 miles of exposed rock between Red Feather and Pueblo.

Steve Mammen said "climbing at Horsetooth in the 70s was more fun than you should be allowed to have." I know each successive generation of boulderers has felt the same way. The beauty, freedom and adventure of Colorado bouldering are an unbelievable privilege. Please, let's work together to keep it that way.

Top 10:

1. **Middle Eliminator with Gill jump start** (Horsetooth Reservoir)
2. **Ripper Traverse** *(private property)*
3. **Days of Whining Posers** V7 (Carter Lake)
4. **Mental Block Standard** V4 (Horsetooth Reservoir)
5. **The Big Pickle** V6 (Carter Lake)
6. **Against Humanity** V7 (Poudre Canyon)
7. **Sloper Chief** V5 (Carter Lake)
8. **Hank's Lunge** V5 (Poudre Canyon)
9. **Hagan's Wall** V5 (Flagstaff)
10. **Left Eliminator** V5 (Horsetooth Reservoir)

Phillip Benningfield sends Rupture V6   Photo: Phillip Benningfield Collection

MORRISON SOUTH SIDE

Across Bear Creek from the madhouse of Morrison's main bouldering area is a quiet zone of superb problems. As the standards have been pushed on the north side, things have remained relatively the same on the south side since the 1980's when a couple of genius boulderers began to develop these fine blocks. On these separate blocks a number of high quality and seldom-ascended problems can be done. If the masses get to be too much on the popular north side, venture over to the south side for a welcome relief. Many landings are sloping and rocky.

Directions: *From the north off Interstate 70 drive south down State Route 26 past Red Rocks Amphitheater and into the town of Morrison. At the stop light take a right. Alternately, take the Morrison Road exit off C-470. Continue out of town to the south for 0.2 mile and turn right on Soda Lakes Road. Park on the right in a dirt pullout and walk 35 yards to the staircased trail left of the parking area. Go right on a flat trail until reaching a faint trail on the left that heads uphill to the boulders. Do not pass the Jefferson County Open Space Boundary! Please stay on the used trails as an inordinate amount of resource damage has occurred.*

OVERVIEW OF MORRISON SOUTH SIDE

A. The Bottom Boulder	**F. The Tunnel**	**K. The Square Block**
B. Overhang Boulder	**G. The Alcove**	**L. The Bulging Face**
C. The Slab	**H. The Double Arête Boulder**	**M. The Next Level**
D. The Bulge Rock	**I. The Dihedrals**	
E. The Crack Rock	**J. The Massif**	

A. THE BOTTOM BOULDER

The first block up the faint trail 50 yards with problems on the north and west sides. A V-shaped roof caps a beautiful slab on the north face.

The Bottom Boulder

❑ 1. Left Arête V5 ★★ 🪨🌀

Start low and left at the base of the V-roof and climb up to the apex and over. An easier version climbs straight up the slab from below the apex and finishes the same.

❑ 2. West Bulge V1

Climb the west face.

B. OVERHANG BOULDER

Immediately above The Bottom Boulder is a block with a distinct overhang on the north side. Problems climb the very licheny northeast face starting on good rails. Not pictured.

C. THE SLAB

Continue up the hill for approximately 40 yards to the southwest to a slab facing north. Many highball problems V1-V2 have been done on the slab that has a nice sheen of lichen.

D. THE BULGE ROCK

Just east of and almost touching The Slab is a slightly overhanging tan and black striped face.

❑ 1. Center V2 ★ 🌀

Climb the left-angling seam/crack on the north face to high flat shelves.

❑ 2. Right V1

A problem to the right of #1 on the west face.

F. THE TUNNEL

The small tunnel formed between The Crack Rock and the southern block. The Tunnel is pictured on page 238.

❑ 1. Left Boulder-South End V2 ★

Start low on the south face and climb up and over the lip.

❑ 2. Right Boulder-Free Hang V1 ★

Climb up and right on the northeast high holds to a good rail just over the lip. Belly flop onto the top. A low start to this problem called *Cling Free* begins below the chalked crack on an underclinged crack and finishes the same.

❑ 3. Dasani V6 ★★

Climbs the uphill, east facing arête. Start low and right in a mail-slot and trend up and left to the apex. Classic surfing.

G. THE ALCOVE

Continue uphill from The Tunnel for approximately 20 yards to the ridgeline to where two blocks form an overhanging alcove.

❑ 1. Left Arête V2 ★ 🌀

Climb up the far left side of the left block without using the low gray slab for the feet.

❑ 2. Left Finger Traverse V2 ★

On the left block, traverse right on the discontinuous crack, then over before reaching the right block.

❑ 3. Fist Crack V2

Climb the wide crack between the two blocks. A little dirty and loose. Exit to the left.

❑ 4. Left Lunge V4 ★★ 🌀

From the center of the right block get hold of the left part of the crack and dyno to the lip then over.

❑ 5. Squirming Coil V6 ★★ 🌀

From the right arête of the right block climb straight up to the high crack. Sds with hands low on the blocky shelf.

❑ 6. The Right Arête V5 ★ 🌀

Climb the outside right arête of the right block up and left, then exit on the right slab. Sds right hand on arête, left on sidepull.

The Slab

The Bulge Rock

The Alcove

E. THE CRACK ROCK

Continue uphill from The Slab (around the right side) to the next block with discontinuous right-leaning cracks. This block makes up the north part of The Tunnel. The north face has a few straight-up problems in the V0 to V2 range. *A South Face* V5 starts low on the arête and undercling.

Crack Rock

H. THE DOUBLE ARÊTE BOULDER

From The Alcove go west for approximately 10 yards to an obvious east-facing double arête. A slab is just around the corner and is too licheny to climb without serious cleaning. A short steep V1 problem is just to the right on a separate block.

Double Arête Boulder

☐ 1. **Double Arête V6** ★★★ 🌀

Climb the double arêtes from a low start. Gain the left arête and toe and heel hook the right arête to a reasonable top-out.

I. THE DIHEDRALS

The east end of the ridge above and right of The Alcove approximately 40 yards offers low-angle corner systems. Fifteen feet east of the Square Block. The Dihedrals are not pictured.

☐ 1. **V0**
The left most crack that climbs up and left. Not recommended.

☐ 2. **Easy Corner V0** ★
A low-angle corner just right of #1 with a black streak on the right face.

☐ 3. **V4** ★★★
Climb the right sloping arête of the right face that makes up the corner of #2. Exit either left or right.

J. THE MASSIF

Directly right of The Dihedrals is a tall wall undercut at the base.

The Massif

☐ 1. **The Left Crack V0** ★
Climb the crack on the left side of The Massif. Loose holds up top.

☐ 2. **Low Traverse V1** ★ 🌀
Traverse the wall from left to right on good holds. Exit before the lichen slab or continue across to a step-off ending. A higher traverse also climbs left to right.

K. THE SQUARE BLOCK

This beautiful block is next to The Massif and is actually rectangular. It has a distinct crack splitting its north face.

☐ 1. **V2** ★
Climb the short crack on the southeast side (facing The Massif).

☐ 2. **Done Deal Dyno V3** ★★ 🌀
From the starting edges of #1 dyno to the lip.

☐ 3. **Front Left Corner V1** ★ 🌀🌀
Climb up the blunt north arête on lichen-covered flat edges. Watch out for one loose edge.

☐ 4. **Breashear's Crack V3** ★★★ 🌀🌀
Climb the distinct crack right of #3. A classic line that requires a little gumption.

☐ 5. **Northwest Corner V3** ★★★ 🌀🌀
Climb the arête and face right of *Breashear's* on right-hand laybacks and left laybacks and crimps. A superb boulder problem.

☐ 6. **West Face V1** ★★
Climb the west face's white rock on pockets and edges.

Square Bolck

L. THE BULGING FACE

Directly right of The Massif, 20 feet, is a slight bulge on gray rock. The top-outs on this block are extremely lichen-covered. The Bulging Face is not pictured.

☐ 1. **Far Left V1**
Start on the good arête holds and climb up and left on the sloping arête. A sds is V4.

☐ 2. **Left Side V0**
Same start as #1 but move up and right to a flat jug. Exit right or left.

☐ 3. **Far Right V2** ★
Start on a good right-hand edge on the wall's right side and exit off right past the arête.

☐ 4. **Slots V5** ★★
Just right of this wall is a nice short arête bulge with slots in it. Start as low as you can go.

M. The Next Level / The Handcrack Area / Triple Crack / The Prow

The ridge continues up and right from The Bulging Face. Many more cracks, overhangs, faces, unfinished projects and full-fledged bushwhacking is in store. Some of the landings in these areas are atrocious.

☐ 1. Rupture V6 ★★★ 🌑

Top ten V6 problems in the state! Located in The Next Level. Starts low above a ledge and slaps the living hell out of the best, as well as worst, slick as snot sloper sidepulls. A treat on some of the finest rock in the freakin' world!

☐ 2. Arrowhead Arête V10 ★★★ 🌑

An outstanding testpeice for the area. Climb the arrowheaded arête from a low start on underclings or sitting on the sloping shelf down and right, slap your way to a fierce sloping topout. V9 from a stand start.

Slots

Rupture Boulder

Arrowhead Arête

Kristen Kirkland on the Done Deal Dyno V3   Photo: Matt Miller

Jamie Emerson

One of the things I love about bouldering in Colorado is the change of seasons, and this dictates where I climb. In winter, the jet stream blasts its cold torrent off the Continental Divide. The sun sets early and the days are cut short. How appropriate then that low lying areas like Eldorado Canyon, Horsetooth Reservoir, Carter Lake and the Flatirons are all so close, offering perfect friction on their otherwise slippery sandstone. The mild winters and abundant sunshine offer wonderful and surprisingly pleasant afternoons. As the days grow longer, I am afforded more time to drive and hike, and I find myself heading into the hills. Places like Boulder Canyon, Camp Dick and Big Elk Meadows come to mind. Cold air holds in the high peaks providing cool evenings and nice spring conditions. As the air warms, the light lingers and the shadows stretch with the lengthening days. Finally, summer comes into full swing and the heat drives me into the mountains. Few things in this world are more perfect than long summer days underneath monstrous boulders, underneath even more monstrous walls of stone, surrounded by an endless garden of alpine wildflowers. It is these days that I live for. But the season is short, and soon the flurries fly and dust the peaks, giving perspective to the depth of the mountains. For a few weeks, conditions are as brilliant as the golden aspen and all the grandeur of Colorado is on display. Deep in the mountains with a few close friends and the chance to try as hard as I possibly can, we dabble in perfection. As winter closes in, I find myself revisting the local areas and the cycle continues. Constant throughout is the crisp, dry air, and nearly every day is sunny. If all this weren't enough, an endless supply of strong and motivated climbers are ready to offer you a spot, and when they are finished with that, they most likely will show you how its done.

The incredible thing is that this has been going on for a long time, since the legendary John Gill left his mark almost 50 years ago. Few places in the country have the amount of climbing that Colorado has, and fewer still have the history. And the cycle continues. Each year climbers find new boulders, new problems, interpret things in their own way and try to leave their mark, the same way Gill did so long ago. Underneath the same blue sky, tucked away in the same rolling hills. Amazingly, these contributions are not locked away, but they are here to give us passionate, inspriration, frustration, joy, and meaning.

Top 10:

1. *Suspension of Disbelief* V12/V14 sds (Eldorado Canyon)
2. *Cage Free* V11 (Boulder Canyon)
3. *Pinch Overhang* V5 (Horsetooth Reservior)
4. *Black Ice* V10 (Flatirons)
5. *Dark Waters* V12 (Clear Creek Canyon)
6. *Germ Free Adolescence* V5 (Eldorado Canyon)
7. *Doughboy Arête* V7 (Carter Lake)
8. *Super Chief* V9 (Carter Lake)
9. *Moon Arête* V9 (Horsetooth)
10. *Midnight Express* V14 (Boulder Canyon)

Matthews-Winters Park

Joe Kinder sends Ghost Dance V6   Photo: Brian Solano

MATTHEWS-WINTERS PARK (THE MILLENNIUM BOULDER)

With the bouldering mecca of Morrison close by, who would a thunk? Peaceful and pristine despite its situation at the edge of the Denver city limits, this area offers the choice Millennium Boulder, a species of sandstone erratic, as well as a concentration of good bouldering on the hillside and plateau just west. The three-star problems on the Millennium are must-dos for their grades, but don't just stop there. The Ridgetop Area offers great traverses as well as the difficult highball The Holdout, taller and scarier than many of the problems done so far on the north side of The Millennium. This place is a great alternative to the slime and spray of Morrison.

Directions: From the junction of Highway 93 and Highway 6 (to Clear Creek Canyon) continue south on Highway 6 for 2.3 miles and take a right on Heritage Road. Go 0.9 miles past three stoplights to a junction with Highway 40, where you take a right onto 40 west. Continue south on 40 another 2.7 miles, passing under I-70 at 1.2 miles and the entrance to Matthews-Winters Park at 1.6 miles. Turn right into Red Rocks Park and Amphitheater and drive west 0.7 miles to a gate. This is the northern entrance to Red Rocks. Turn left just before the gate into a small dirt parking lot.

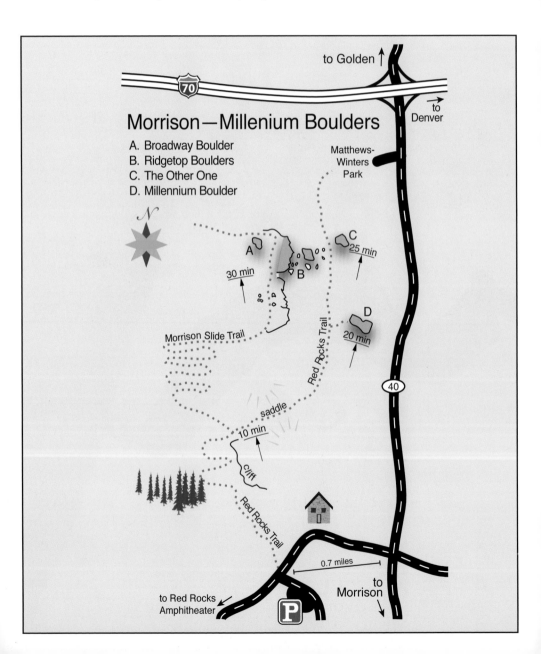

THE RIDGETOP BOULDERS

Directions: *From the parking area head north on the Red Rocks Trail for roughly 10-12 minutes, passing a large pink wall on the right and working your way up switchbacks before arriving at a T-junction. Head left (west) on the Morrison Slide Trail past seven steep switchbacks until you hit a high, scenic plateau with great views of Denver (approximately 25 minutes). Walk north along the plateau, passing a clump of low, red boulders. Approximately 175 yards past these boulders notice a faint draw on the right (east) leading through the cliff band. The Ridgetop Boulders are just north of this draw; the Hillside Boulders are strung out along the slope leading down to the Other One. For the Broadway Boulder, continue on another minute until the trail bends west. Go west 50 yards. The boulder is in the trees, 75 feet off the trail to the south.*
Approach Time: 25-30 minutes.

A. BROADWAY BOULDER

This isolated block, nestled in a pretty forest of scrubby pines, offers fun crimper problems on quality stone and a handful of good moderates. Wedge-shaped and slightly gritty, this block is reminiscent of the good stuff up at Flagstaff Mountain.

☐ **1. V3** ★
Start in funky pockets six feet right of the tree and diagonal right and up.

☐ **2. V3** ★
Start in the good horizontal and cruise up the face past flakes and edges.

☐ **3. Marcelo's Madness V7** ★★
A continuous, crimpy traverse on perfect dark stone. Sds at the northeast corner of the boulder on a rail at knee-height, heading left through a tricky crux to finish on #1. Named for Marcelo's proud winger off the Broadway Brewing Building in Denver.

☐ **4. V0** ★★ 😎
The fun green/black slab on the north side of the boulder.
Start low on a good horn and amble up the dinner plates.
The arête to the left is also V0.

☐ **5. V0** ★ 😎
A slightly harder version of #4 beginning just to the right. Fun!

☐ **6. V4**
A crimpy traverse beginning on the horn and working right on the steeper, low part of the wall, finishing out along the west face at big holes in the horizontal. Sharp.

Broadway Boulder

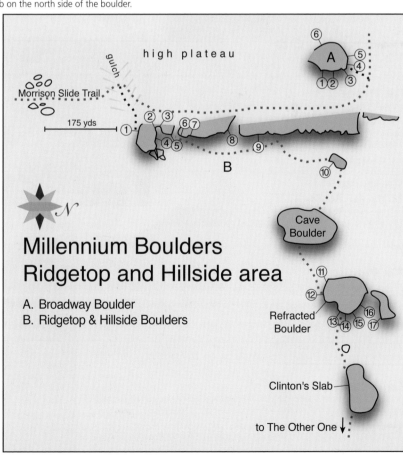

Millennium Boulders
Ridgetop and Hillside area

A. Broadway Boulder
B. Ridgetop & Hillside Boulders

B. Ridgetop Boulders

With the highest concentration of problems along the ridgetop, this intriguing and varied area is worth the hike. The rock is a strange, red sandstone littered with sinker pockets and tiny crimps. The views of the hogback across the road and on into Denver are stunning. Some of the landings tend to slope, so bring a crash pad or two.

The Holdout Boulder

This is the big boulder with the intimidating dark north face, jutting out from the ridgeline.

❏ **1. V2**
Move up the south face on slightly friable crimps and dishes above the rocky landing. Will clean up well.

❏ **2. V5** ★
Start on the uphill side of the boulder and hand traverse left along the horizontal seam. Strenuous.

❏ **3. The Holdout V8** ★★
The stunning line on the north face, straight up the black streak, on solid red stone. Either start on waist-high crimps and crank high to a shallow three-finger pocket, or sds in the little cave for *The Full Holdout* V9.

Fuck Plato Boulder

The small wall just north of The Holdout with a prominent arête on the right side.

❏ **4. V2**
Step right onto a small ledge then crimp your way up the dark green stone.

❏ **5. Fuck Plato V4** ★
Sds on the arête then work past pebbles and crimpers to a sketch-mo top-out. Harder and steeper than it looks.

The Perch

The wall just north again, right of the dirty crack system.

❏ **6. Choss One V0**
Grainy and kinda loose. Start with your left hand in a good basketball-sized hueco on the arête, then up.

❏ **7. Choss Two V2**
Sds. Work over the bulge on loose flakes, passing a good mouth-shaped pocket.

❏ **8. The Perch V5** ★★
The poor-man's *Dogmatics*. Sds this elegant rig low and left (east) under a small cave, then angle up and right across the red, green and black-streaked face to finish at a large white crystal on a ramp. Continuous.

The Porch

Just across the little gully from The Perch find this long wall with striking black and white-streaked rock.

❏ **9. Donkey Traverse V6** ★★
This 48-foot pumpfest has it all, from slopers to tiny pockets to incut rails. Begin far right (north) on the wall at an obvious incut jug and work left, staying low around the corner and finishing up past thin moves in a large hole on the south face. Not to be confused with its cousin, *The Monkey Traverse*, at Flagstaff.

The Ticket

This curious little cave/scoop feature is 100 yards north of the main area just below a prominent prow on the cliff line. Also known as the *World's Shortest Highball*.

❏ **10. The Ticket V6** ★
Sds on double underclings and pimp out the seam to the lip of the cave. Powerful and frustrating.

Holdout Boulder

The Perch

The Porch

The Ticket

movement crew

working hard to set a new standard

movement

2845 valmont road boulder   303-443-1505   movementboulder.com

HILLSIDE BOULDERS

These boulders can either be approached by dropping down from the Ridgetop Boulders or by walking uphill from The Other One. They offer a smattering of pleasant middle-grade problems as well as some easier slabs for beginners.

THE REFRACTED BOULDER

A good, sunny block with technical problems from V1 to V5 on friendly red stone. It's about 200 feet downhill from The Ticket, directly below and north of an enormous boulder with an east-facing choss cave.

☐ 11. Suburban Skyline V1 ★
Layback the ramp on the left (west) side of the south face. Dirty but fun.

☐ 12. Thin Face V5 ★
Start on crimps in the funky white scoops, then move left onto the red face. Technical.

☐ 13. Pain V6
The horrible meat-grinder crack on the east prow of the boulder. Sds in the gnarly bushes. Utterly worthless.

☐ 14. V2 ★
Up the finger crack/seam on the prow just right of #13.

☐ 15. Monomaniac V5 ★
Climb the aesthetic red face via a tips mono and strange gastons. The crack on the right is off. Tendon injury potential.

☐ 16. Refracted V4 ★★
The excellent finger crack up the face right of #15. Slopey, devious, technical.

☐ 17. Fearful Symmetry V3 ★
Locate this fun little problem up a faint corner on the boulder just north. Sds, top out left on nubbins.

THE CLINTON BOULDER

Downhill another 60 yards is this big slabby blob with V0 problems up its flanks. Not pictured.

The Refracted Boulder

The Refracted Boulder

Fearful Symetry

Tyler Hepting on Deseret V2, Millenium Boulder Photo: Kyler Deutmeyer

THE MILLENNIUM BOULDER AND THE OTHER ONE

Directions: *At the T-junction take a right (east), continuing along the Red Rocks Trail over a small saddle. Continue north along the trail into an open, grassy area. 3-4 minutes along the trail you'll see the enormous Millennium Boulder in the meadow down and right. The Other One is another 300 yards along the trail, 80 feet downhill and to the east.*

C. THE OTHER ONE

If it's not the Millennium Boulder then it must be that other one! Though not as compact or aesthetic as the Millennium, The Other One is a great place to warm up or cool down after your session. Though most of the problems are moderate, one vicious V9 and a couple of testy highballs should keep even the hardest of the hard awake.

SOUTHWEST SIDE

☐ 1. **V0**
Start on the far left (west) end of the boulder and traverse eight feet right on flakes.

☐ 2. **Vee-Wonderful V1**
Grab a good hueco with your left hand and pull over the bulge.

☐ 3. **Other One Dyno V2** ★
Huck to a good jug/flake from the finger slots on the left end of the horizontal.

☐ 4. **Angel V3** ★★
Honor student by day, hooker by night. With your right hand, undercling a bomber cobble in a hole then head left to the slopey horizontal and up.

☐ 5. **Little Wing V3** ★★ 🌀🌀
A higher, more continuous version of #4. Start above the rocky landing in sloping holes, then realm up past a nipple hold to good crimps.

☐ 6. **Voodoo Child V5** ★★ 🌀
Sds on a horn just left of the nose of the boulder and punch up to a good hole. Surmount the double bulges straight up for full value or bail right below the crux finish if your underwear needs changing.

☐ 7. **V6**
Sds right under the nose, snag the hole over the lip with your left, and fire high and right to a crumbling edge. Real bad.

THE OTHER ONE NORTH SIDE

☐ 8. **Black Fly V9** ★★
A real tendon test for pocket aficionados. Start on sloping crimps under the tallest part of the north face, then yank past two small, sharp pockets to the lip. Ouch!

☐ 9. **Mike's Muscle Car V4** ★
Vroom, vroom! Sds in a crumbly horizontal behind the trees, crank left and up then reel left along the crispy horizontal, topping out on #8. Gymnastic and pumpy. The straight-up is V4 as well.

☐ 10. **Buttercups V2**
Start in the horizontal and move right past an obvious pebble. Top out via good, but dirty, holes 10 feet right.

The Other One

D. THE MILLENNIUM BOULDER

Strangely overlooked for years by the Morrison crew, who proclaimed it to be either *too blank* or *too chossy*, this geologic anomaly didn't begin to see serious development until Greg Johnson and Bob Williams visited in 1998 for another look. A chunk of bullet, Eldorado Canyon sandstone swallowed by the Earth and spat back up 30 miles to the south, this 16-foot high block embedded in a grassy meadow is nothing short of stellar, especially for highball and thin pocket aficionados.

SOUTH AND EAST FACES

☐ 1. **Warm-up Ledges V0-V3**
The short, upper end of the south face has a myriad of warm-up possibilities.

☐ 2. **B.C. V2** ★
Start on the southeast face where it turns vertical. Pull on via big slopers then head up the glassy rock.

☐ 3. **Cargo Cult V3** ★★
Start on a horizontal pinch, move right to a sidepull, pass a pocket and rocket to the lip.

☐ 4. **Epiphany V5** ★★
The technical southeast prow of the rock. Match the sloper, then heel hook past a dish to finish on deep pockets. Start here and finish by traversing into #2 is *Chef's Mangoes* V6.

☐ 5. **Deseret V2** ★
Six feet right of #4 locate this mini-buttress with a white-stained flake. V7 with the sds. Funky.

☐ 6. **Cannibal Dance V7** ★
Follow the thin, right-leaning seam to a shallow pocket left of the seam in black rock. *Thunderhead* V9 is the sds that trends right and up through the finish of *Purity Control*.

☐ 7. **Purity Control V10** ★★★★
A lot of good climbers threw themselves at this painfully obvious line until it was finally climbed. Straight up the very overhanging northeast face via the widely spaced pockets, starting with your right hand in a sinker three-finger hole.

☐ 8. **Black Heart V9** ★★
Just right of *Purity Control*. This goes from the platform to big huecos, via a huge toss off insultingly small holds.

Millennium Boulder

Millennium Boulder

Millennium Boulder

NORTH FACE

☐ 9. Terminate w/ Extreme Prejudice V8 ★★
Bust up and right from the hole on #10 to finish via the prominent black streak. Sds is V9.

☐ 10. Ghost Dance V6 ★★★★
This is the striking line on small pockets up the east side of the north face. V9 and painful as all hell from the sds. This problem can either be finished left or direct.

☐ 11. Moon Child V10 ★★★
This new line goes directly up from the mailbox-slot of #12. Make a move to a sloper pocket, then trend up and left. Despo.

☐ 12. Old Bones V6 ★★★
Start low in the two-handed mailbox-slot right of the blank middle of the north face. Work right to a pocket, then cruise up past good holds to a right-hand bidoigt and left-hand pinch. Set up and huck for the distant lip. *Nadir* V6, begins here and traverses all the way to the northwest prow and a finishing stance. *Sequel* V2, starts here and busts right, traversing big holds to the hueco/ledge.

☐ 13. Second Coming V4 ★★
Start low in the pockets just right of #10 and fire for the big holes. Throw the exciting Hail Mary toss to the lip.

☐ 14. Lono V3 ★★
Start in the head-height, pancake-shaped hueco and go for a crimp. Same Hail Mary finish.

☐ 15. Revolution V2 ★★
Take the hueco/ledge in the middle, then top out straight up past less-than-obvious holds.

☐ 16. Revelation V1 ★
Move right from the hueco/ledge to a mono, then up and over the northwest prow.

THE CAVE BOULDER
The giant obvious boulder halfway down the hillside.

☐ 1. Bambi V11 ★★
This recently opened line is unique to the Front Range due to its steepness. A once choss covered roof now has become a great problem. The crux comes with a long stab for a two-finger pocket at the lip. Top out the 25 foot slab.

☐ 2. Fantasia V13 ★★
This awesome roof was first climbed in 2011 by Daniel Woods. Start sitting on a good right-facing sidepull down and right, and climb out the massive roof on unique movements and finish on *Bambi*.

Cave Boulder

Three Ball Climbing.com
how does threeball
define quality?
visit us

THREE SISTERS PARK

Three Sisters Park is a mountainside of sporadic granite towers, miniature cliff bands and separate boulders that are easily reached from the myriad trail systems. This Jefferson County Open Space Park is a mixmaster of trails shared by hikers, bikers, runners, elk and deer. The boulders vary from very rough rock—rather taxing on the tips—to pain-free crimping; the top-outs on most blocks require dealing with lichen and grit. Losing interest? In the park's favor are some nice easy problems and a quiet setting with incredible views of Mt. Evans and Mt. Bierstadt and the possibility for finding new lines away from the Front Range crowds.

Directions: Take Highway 74 from Morrison to Evergreen. From Evergreen take Highway 73 headed south (you can only go one way). Go 0.6 mile to the second stoplight and go right on Buffalo Park Road. Continue on this road past the high school for 1.5 miles to the parking area on the right.

*** Make sure to pick up a trail map at the parking areas; there are about a million different trails around here.

Brothers Area: *Walk up The Sisters Trail to a left on Ponderosa Trail. Pass The Brother's Lookout on the right and take a right on The Sisters Trail. Fifty yards down the trail, look up to the right into the woods, where Brothers Boulder can be seen.*

South Face of The Brothers: *The south face has a number of problems skirting the base. These problems are easy to locate as they are seen from Ponderosa Trail. A few uncharted blocks sit on the south hillside between The Brother and Ponderosa Trail.*

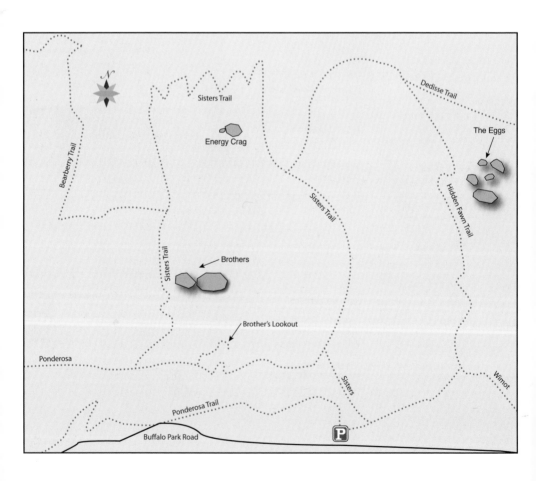

THE EGGS

These blocks—the best and most traveled—are easy to find as they are nestled directly off the Hidden Fawn Trail to the east less than a 10-minute walk from the parking area. A good landmark is a pair of signs indicating Area Closed Revegetation in Progress on the right 50 yards before passing the first Egg. A handful of additional small boulders with undocumented problems litter the hillside.

The Eggs

TRAILSIDE EGG

A chalk-infested block sitting 20 yards off the trail with problems on the south face. It is located just up Hidden Fawn Trail from tight turns in the trail and after the Area Closed signs. Many contrived problems can be done to lengthen a session on this block.

☐ 1. **V0**
The leftmost problem from a sds.

☐ 2. **Dihedral V1** ★★
The dihedral problem, with stemming, to gain a jug above.

☐ 3. **V4** ★★
Just right of #2, on gold rock, is a tough little number. Start off a left-hand undercling and right-hand sidepull to gain a bad hold in the roof, then jugs.

☐ 4. **V3** ★★
Climb the black rock on edges to high jugs. A sds is much harder.

☐ 5. **V0** ★
Follow a white streak right of the black patina face.

Trailside Egg

WEST CRACK EGG

This boulder is located approximately 30 yards up the hill to the east from Trailside Egg. It has a distinctive crack splitting its west side and a glued edge on the south face. No grades are given for the glued problems.

☐ 1. **V2**
The crack on the west face. The lower one starts, the harder it is.

West Crack Egg

IN BETWEEN EGG

This is a few yards southeast from the West Crack Egg.

☐ 1. **V3** ★★
A right-trending layback/crack starting on the west face. Moving left from the low starting holds is harder.

☐ 2. **V1** ★
A sds on the south face, off of decent sloping edges, to very good holds.

WHITE EGG

South 20 feet from In Between Egg. This Egg is not pictured.

☐ 1. **V1** ★
On the north face, start off the jug and use an undercling to reach the top holds.

☐ 2. **V2** ★
Start on the white face, traverse left to jugs, then the undercling to finish the problem.

In Between Egg

UPPER EGG

The best looking block on the hillside. It has a dihedral/scoop on the south side.

❐ **1. V0**

The slab on the southwest face just left of the pine that hugs the boulder.

❐ **2. V6** ★★

Climb the dihedral/scoop. This is the best looking problem at the Eggs but it has the most vicious top-out so two stars will suffice.

❐ **3. V4** ★

The arête right of the dihedral, starting off the good jug. The roll onto the slab is not trivial. A direct start can be done off the horrible slopers just left of the starting hold.

❐ **4. V0** ★

Climb the slab on the east face trying to find the hidden edges.

Bobbi Bensman on West Crack Egg V2   Photo: Fred Knapp

BROTHERS BOULDERS

This is a pair of boulders sitting side-by-side approximately 75 yards east from The Sisters Trail. The left boulder is short and the right block stands a little over 10 feet high.

LEFT BLOCK

☐ 1. **V1**
A one-move problem on the left side.

☐ 2. **V0**
Straight up the face off the jug.

☐ 3. **V5**
A sds on the right side of the boulder starting off a full-pad edge then a terrible edge to the finish.

RIGHT BLOCK

☐ 4. **V2** ★
A traverse across the face through a sloping section.

☐ 5. **V2** ★
The left problem on decent edges to a dirty top-out.

☐ 6. **V0** 😊
On the right side of the face above a small block is a decent warm-up.

THE SISTERS AREA

The easiest way to reach these boulders is to walk Hidden Fawn Trail for 10 minutes to The Eggs. For Elephant Butt take the Hidden Fawn to the intersection with The Sisters Trail (15 minutes). Continue past the intersection for 45 yards and head uphill to the west to reach both Energy Crag (100 yards) and The Blockheads (175 yards).

THE BLOCKHEADS

This selection of boulders is located at the terminus of South Sister. The Sisters' ridgeline peters out before the north side of the Brothers. The main Blockhead is on the south end of South Sister. Numerous alluring west-facing slabs can be done along the ridge headed back north toward Middle Sister. Another way to find the Blockheads is to skirt the hillside headed east from Brothers Boulder past an old road/trail to the ridge between the Sisters and Brothers, then head north about 40 yards toward the Sisters.

BLOCKHEAD

Blockhead is not pictured.

☐ 1. **V2** 😊
The west face, up a discontinuous seam and edges.

☐ 2. **V2** 😊😊
Up the white streak on the left above the block lying on the ground.

☐ 3. **V3** 😊😊
Climb the right-facing corner off a white starting hold through the biggest part of the low roof.

☐ 4. **V0** 😊
The east-face gully with a beautiful offset crack.

Brother's Boulders

ENERGY CRAG (HIDDEN WALL)

A condensed set of south-facing cracks and face problems on a short cliff band below The Blockheads (75 yards east). From The Sisters Trail/Hidden Fawn Trail intersection head south (45 yards) and the cliff band is above (100 yards west) from the Sisters Trail; it is located on the south side of a large northeast-facing slab. The problems listed are the main attractions with many more contrived problems offered. The Energy Crag shows *Thievery*.

☐ 1. **Thievery V6** ★★★
On the left side of the crag is a burnt-orange face. Start low on the incut jug and move up the overhanging face to a full-pad edge, then a left-hand sidepull to jugs. A great problem worth the trip on its own.

☐ 2. **V3** ★
Just right of *Thievery* is an arête. Climb up the laybacks and gastons using the feet on the adjacent wall.

☐ 3. **V4** ★ 😊
To the right of the dead tree is a low start off of an undercling to a right-hand slot, then a tough mantle over the lip.

☐ 4. **V4**
Just right is a dynamic problem off an arête to a sloping top.

☐ 5. **V0**
The rightmost problem on the crag, with a small tree to climb through.

Rufus Miller on Thievery V6   photo: Miller collection

ELEPHANT BUTT

A squat little affair found at the junction of The Sisters Trail and Hidden Fawn Trail. The block is located 25 yards up The Sisters Trail on the right. There are some problems on this boulder, but they are extremely sharp and grating. Elephant Butt is not pictured.

ANDY MANN

Being a professional photographer living on Colorado's Front Range is my dream come true. Each day, and everywhere I go, I am blessed with beautiful scenery, classic boulder problems, and amazing subjects. For me, it has just always been about being at the right place at the right time, not forcing the shot, but being aware of it. Most of the photos you see in this guide are raw moments in time. I just happen to have been there, rooting for my friends on their projects. I believe that each and every boulder problem has its own "proverbial moment of truth," and that single moment is, for both the photographer and the climber, something we are driven to better understand. I hope that the photos in this guide inspire you, as a climber, or as an apiring photographer, to try and find these little special moments. Cheers.

I have compiled a list of the top photogentic Front Range boulder problems. Of course these may not be the most classic boulder problems in the state, or nearly the hardest, but it isn't about that. For me, it is all about natural light, the angle of the shot, the postion of the boulder, and body position of the climber when it counts.

TOP 15:

1. *The Shark Arête* **V3** (Flagstaff)
2. *Mavericks* **V5** (Clear Creek Canyon)
3. *Right Eliminater* **V3** (Horsetooth Reservior)
4. *The Streaked Corner* **V5** (Eldorado Canyon)
5. *The Turning Point* **V8** (Flatirons)
6. *Kahuna Roof* **V6** (Carter Lake)
7. *The Sweet Arête* **V5** (Green Mountain)
8. *Eastern Preist* **V4** (Eldorado Canyon)
9. *Fleshfest* **V10** (Flatirons)
10. *Absolute Surrender* **V5** (Flatirons)
11. *Black Ice* **V10** (Flatirons)
12. *Tower of Power* **V10** (Flatirons)
13. *PB Arête project* **V?** (Flatirons)
14. *Burguny Boulder Direct Face* **V4** (Flatirons)
15. *Merest Excrescences* **V5** (Flatirons)

Castlewood Canyon

Kristen Kirkland on the Nine Lives Arête V5   Photo: Justin Jaeger

CASTLEWOOD CANYON

Located east of the sprawling suburb of Castle Rock, Castlewood Canyon stands in sharp contrast to the slapstick homes being built in the surrounding hills. The conglomerate sandstone has an incredible variety of shapes, holds and texture. Hundreds of boulders line both hillsides down to the creek. With boulders oriented in every direction and plenty of shade in the summer, bouldering is a year round affair. Problems worth doing include the *Cave Route Direct* in the Fountainebleau Area, *Scary Monsters* on the Scary Monsters Boulder and any of the Warm-Up Wall's superb slab problems.

Note: The canyon has dense scrub oak stands and requires patience in locating many of the boulders due to the trail systems disappearing in thick brush. Also a fee is required to enter the State Park. Rattlesnakes abound in the summer. Be sure you take note of when the park closes upon entry, rangers can be ticket-happy.

Directions: From Interstate 25 exit onto Founders Parkway eastbound. Take Founders Parkway to Hwy 86, go east on Hwy 86 4.0 miles to Franktown. Turn South on Hwy 83 (S. Parker Rd) and head 5.0 miles south to the main park entrance. To reach the west entrance, turn on Castlewood Canyon Road before reaching Franktown.

The Streamside Area is the first bouldering spot when entering the canyon from the west entrance. Unlike many of the boulders well-hidden in the dense scrub oak of Castlewood, this cluster of water-polished blocks sits immediately adjacent to Cherry Creek and is actually visible from the parking lot. Park at the Lucas Homestead Historic Site parking lot, which is the first lot on your left when entering the north/west entry of the park from Highway 86. The stone remnants of the home are clearly visible when you pull in. Take the main Homestead Trail downhill. The Homestead Trail will eventually split into the Creekbottom Trail and the Rimrock Trail. For the Rimrock Trail approach: Cross the small wooden bridge over Cherry Creek. Thirty yards or so after crossing the small wooden bridge over Cherry Creek, catch a faint climber's trail to the right. This faint trail takes you across the sandy dry floodplain and creekbed. Work your way south along the side of the stream until you run into the very obvious cluster of boulders after about 200 yards or so. Try to follow the single track. While this 'trail' is on gravel, it would be best not to disturb the little vegetation that is growing. For the Creekbottom Trail approach: Continue on the Creekbottom trail, which counterintuitively stays a level above the creek. After about 250 yards, keep a keen eye looking towards the actual creek bottom to the left to judge the location of the cluster of large blocks below. Eventually there will be an extremely faint climber's trail that drops off to the left in a wooded section directly above one of the largest blocks which might be faintly visible. This approach is somewhat more direct, but harder to identify. It may be good to leave your first session this way to better identify the turn-off on return visits.

Five and Dime Area is located 0.1 mile up the road. Park in the Homestead Trail parking area on the left. Walk further up the road for approximately 100 yards (southeast) and look up the hill on the right. The Slab is a massive gray boulder 50 yards due west up the hill and The Pyramid (a good landmark—not a perfect pyramid with a hueco-covered east face) is due west from The Slab and easily seen below the cliff. Walk up the steep hill to reach the boulders in this area.

Fountainebleau Area is located 0.7 mile past the kiosk. Park on the right for the Climber's Trail. Walk up the Climber's Trail until it splits (just before reaching the cliff). Go right and walk under the cliff (a few bolted routes can be seen) for approximately 120 yards until the trail squeezes between the cliff and an adjacent boulder. On the right (north) are the Fountainebleau Boulders, which lie on the hillside below the trail.

Central City Area is located at 0.9 mile past the kiosk. Park at the Falls Trailhead parking area on the left. Walk the Falls Trail to the Creekside Trail headed right (south) until walking past a long wooden fence. A waterfall is just past in the creek—cross above the waterfall down a steep slope and scramble up the loose gully. A trail on the west side of the creek goes north and south above the creek. Go north for a few hundred yards to reach 9 Lives Area (the trail becomes intermittent through the thick scrub oak stands). The boulder sits 25 yards from the mud cliff above the creek.

For the Big Blocks Area, Warm-Up Wall and Scary Monsters, head straight up the hillside on a distinct trail. All the boulders near the Buoux Block (the huge square boulder with a shorter boulder below with a crack on its south face) are south and east in the scrub oaks. For The Warm-Up Wall walk up to the cliff and skirt it going north for approximately 150 yards on a good trail (passing a few huge roofs). The Warm-Up Wall is defined by a perfectly flat landing along the base of a vertical wall stretching 40-odd yards and shaded by trees. The Scary Monsters and Pebble Roof Rock are down the hillside from The Warm-Up Wall. Inner Canyon Area is located by continuing on State Route 86 to Franktown. Turn right on State Route 83 going south 4.7 miles to the Main Park Entry. Turn right and park at the large west parking area and walk down (north) on a cement sidewalk to the creekbed below the ridge. Cross the creek on the bridge and go left (west) for approximately 60 yards to The Phallic Boulder.

The Turd Ball Boulders are further west down the creek approximately 120 yards. Cross two wooden bridges; do not go past the huge dead tree on the right side of the trail. Head straight uphill (north) through the scrub oaks just after the second bridge until reaching the ridge (a few large blocks are on the hillside below the tiered ridge).

The Creek Boulders, Trailside Boulders and Buddha and Berthoud Caves are reached by continuing west on the trail past the dead tree for a few minutes. The Creek Boulders are on the left side of the creek while the Trailside Boulders are on the right. Just past Trailside Boulder One look up and right (north) to the ridge. A large dead tree spans the entire height of the cliff. The Caves are below and left from the tree (in-depth directions are included with the Cave's description).

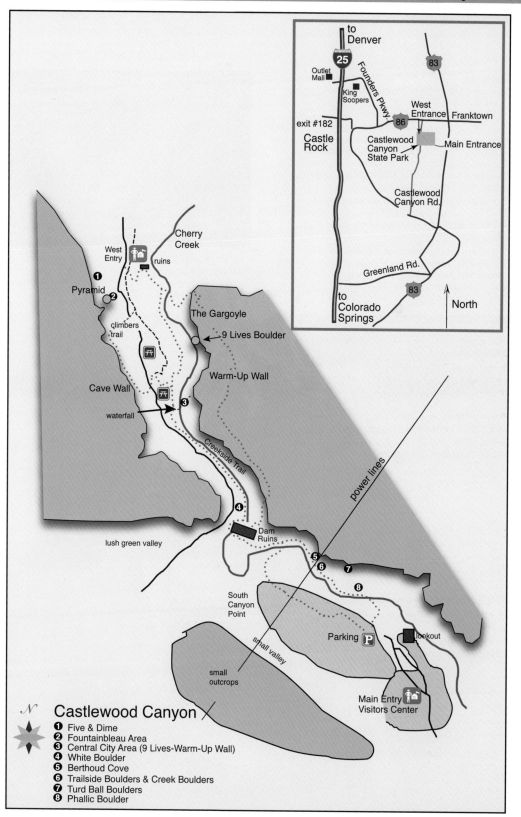

to Denver
Outlet Mall
King Soopers
exit #182
Castle Rock
Founders Pkwy.
West Entrance Franktown
Castlewood Canyon State Park
Main Entrance
Castlewood Canyon Rd.
Greenland Rd.
to Colorado Springs
North

Cherry Creek
West Entry
ruins
Pyramid
climbers trail
Cave Wall
waterfall
The Gargoyle
9 Lives Boulder
Warm-Up Wall
Creekside Trail
power lines
lush green valley
Dam Ruins
South Canyon Point
small valley
small outcrops
Parking
lookout
Main Entry Visitors Center

N

Castlewood Canyon

❶ Five & Dime
❷ Fountainbleau Area
❸ Central City Area (9 Lives–Warm-Up Wall)
❹ White Boulder
❺ Berthoud Cove
❻ Trailside Boulders & Creek Boulders
❼ Turd Ball Boulders
❽ Phallic Boulder

STREAMSIDE AREA

A recently developed bouldering area and home to the uber-classic *Punani*, these boulders are absolutely worth a visit. Climbers should take note that this sandy, grassy creekbed area harbors Castlewood bouldering's highest concentration of ticks starting in mid-April and continuing through July when the heat of the summer really sets in. Also, watch for rattlesnakes in the warm months.

PUNANI

The large boulder with an obvious dihedral holds several excellent problems.

☐ 1. Punani V7 ★★★★

Some of the better stone at Castlewood. Start with an obvious left-hand sidepull and right hand on the arête. Climb the arête with a crux move to gain the lip before a reasonable top-out that keeps your attention. A few low starts have been done, The original low start begins matched at the bottom lip of the boulder on a horizontal rail feature (V9).

☐ 2. Gerbil in a Chute V3 ★★★

Climb the dihedral. Start by reaching to a decent sidepull with your left hand, with the right hand on a cobble. Move up the dihedral with a lunge at the top.

☐ 3. Pleasure by Ambush V6 ★

Start right of *Gerbil in a Chute*, under the small roof on two crimpy edges about three feet from the ground. Either lunge to an obvious jug or use a sloping crimp to aid with the big move. Top out the backside slab on fragile rock.

☐ 4. Dry Spell V7 ★

Start as for *Pleasure by Ambush*. From the jug, traverse left using jugs at first until the holds force you downward. A difficult drop-down move leads into the low start of *Punani*.

Sarah Marvez on Punani V7   Photo: Justin Jaeger

FIVE AND DIME AREA

These boulders line the hillside to the north and south for over a 100 yards. The Pyramid serves as the main southern landmark. There are three main areas: The Slab (below The Pyramid and close to the road); The Traverse Cave Rock Area (southwest on the cliff above The Pyramid) and the Electric Kite Wall Area (to the north from The Pyramid). Expect serious bushwhacking, blood letting, and cussing to reach these boulders.

THE SLAB

A massive gray boulder, with a tall north face, located down the hillside (east) from The Pyramid. Walk along the road for approximately 50 yards, then travel about 100 yards (a No Parking sign is directly below The Slab next to the road) from the Homestead parking area.

❒ **1. V3** ★

The Slab

Climb up the left side of the north face on the arête/dihedral.

❒ **2. V2** ★

Climb straight above the small ledge and through the black lichen.

Note: A huge jumble of blocks is located to the south and west of The Slab with problems ranging from V0 to V6. Many have terrible landings and the problems see very little traffic in comparison to the other areas.

THE TRAVERSE CAVE ROCK AREA

Directly uphill (west approximately 120 yards) from The Slab and along the cliff are a number of fine problems. The Pyramid sits just east from the Traverse Cave Rock. Problems can be done on small blocks adjacent to the cliff as well as on the cliff (Traverse Cave Rock).

TRAVERSE CAVE ROCK AKA TED'S HOLE

One of the few true roofs at Castlewood with exceptional holds and a bad landing.

Ted's Hole

Ted's Hole

❒ **1. Ted's Hole V6** ★★

Traverse the long horizontal roof starting at the dingy crack and coming out and around on to the east face.

PUZZLE BLOCK

This small block is located north 10 yards from Traverse Cave Rock and has a number of good face problems on the east face. The top-outs are covered in pine needles and mowable lichen.

Puzzle Block

❒ **1. Ledge Reach V0**

Climb the left side of the east face on pockets. One move. A crap problem.

❒ **2. Corner Pockets V1** ★

Climb the pockets a few feet right of #1.

❒ **3. The Face V1**

Climb the face a couple of feet right of #2.

SQUARE AWAY BLOCK

Just north from Puzzle Block a few yards. Not pictured.

❒ **The Point V0**

On the left arête of the east face is a problem on big pockets and jugs. The top is the hard part.

❒ **Undercling Reach V2**

Immediately right of *The Point* is an undercling eight feet off the dirt. Climb straight up using the arête for the left hand.

THE ELECTRIC KITE WALL AREA

This area of boulders is located by walking north from The Pyramid approximately 100 yards along the base of the cliff. The first boulder encountered from The Pyramid is Bright Brilliant, then Book Block and The Gap Block (a tight gap between two boulders).

BRIGHT BRILLIANT WALL

This attractive tall wall is on the ridgeline before reaching The Gap Block. The wall is approximately 30 feet from The Gap Block and has an open alcove with a colorful left wall. A V1 highball climbs the left wall. A V3 climbs the right wall from underclings to bad edges.

BOOK BLOCK

A mere 15 feet south of The Gap Block is a yellow and green lichen-covered corner and tight alcove. Problems climb both sides of the alcove as well as the overhanging arête.

❒ **V5** ★★
Climb the overhanging north arête from a sds.

❒ **V0** ★★
Climb the left side of the tight gap.

❒ **V1** ★★
Climb the right side of the gap.

Book Block

THE GAP BLOCK

The east block that makes up the gap. The trail from The Pyramid squeezes through this gap. The opposite boulder making up the gap has two problems.

❒ **1. V6** ★
The left problem straight up on the left (east) block making up the gap.

❒ **2. V6**
Start from a sds a few feet to the right of #1.

❒ **3. Gap Block Traverse V6** ★★
A great problem. Start sitting as for #2 and traverse right through pockets and dishes to a sloping crimp before a deadpoint to a sloping shelf. Top out right through the tunnel. The stone and moves on this climb more than make up for the grovel at the exit. One may start sitting further left on the wall to add moves and difficulty.

❒ **4. V1** ★
Traverse the right block from the dark recesses to the big pockets near the exit.

❒ **5. V0**
Climbs the big pockets straight up.

The Gap Block

BEAUTY POCKET BOULDER

Located just outside the gap of Gap Block to the north 10 yards. Not pictured.

❒ **1. V2** ★★
A traverse of the east face from right to left across the excellent pockets.

ELECTRIC KITE WALL

Continue north from Beauty Pocket Boulder through dense scrub oaks for approximately 40 yards. Electric Kite is defined by a white overhanging wall with many pockets and an open break halfway up the face on the right.

❒ **1. Center Pocket V6** ★★ 🌐
Start on a lone pocket and jump up to the sloping shelf. A big pull then reaches the high set of holds. Traversing in right from the right-hand pocket and left-hand pod down and left is *Hoagie Heaven* V9.

❒ **2. Kite Arête V7**
The right arête on the east face. Too dirty and licheny to earn more description. Not recommended.

Electric Kite Wall

❒ **3. The Leaker V6** ★★
A right to left traverse approximately 25 yards above the Electric Kite boulder on a tan east-facing boulder.

❒ **4. Electric Lunge V7** ★
On the right side of the wall, climb through pockets high on the face to gain a poor crimp on the lip and make a blind lunge to a hold on the slab before a mantle exit.

SALAMANDER BOULDERS

Two blocks just 10 yards northeast from Electric Kite Wall. The slab problems on the northeast face tend to be lichen-covered and low quality. The Salamander Boulders are not pictured.

❒ **1. V0**
Climb the pockets in the southeast dihedral.

❏ 2. **V1**
Climb the pockets and pebbles on the east face, starting off the adjacent block.

❏ 3. **Corners V2**
The left side of the left boulder. Filthy!

❏ 4. **Right Face V0 - V2**
The slab problems right of the gap between the two blocks. Lichen-covered, but solid, holds up high.

FOUNTAINBLEAU AREA

This area has very different rock than the rest of the canyon. It's smooth surface bears enough resemblance to the rock of Fountainebleau, France to warrant this name. Many fine problems can be done in this shaded area, from the superb *Cave Route Direct* to *Up Staged* on The Stage Boulder.

THE STAGE BOULDER

This is the first boulder seen to the right after passing through the gap between the cliff and the small adjacent block. It has a slightly overhanging east face. Direct starts can be done to all these problems.

❏ 1. **The Hold Up Traverse V4** ★★
Traverse the east face from left to right starting on the two big pockets low and left.

❏ 2. **V2** ★
On the far left side of the east face, climb straight up and right.

❏ 3. **Up Staged V2** ★★
Climb the middle of the face just right of the seam with a pocket. The seam with the pocket is V1.

❏ 4. **Center Stage V5**
Up the thin face right of #3. Fragile stone and not recommended.

❏ 5. **Back Stage V0**
Climb the end of the traverse on big pockets.

FOUNTAIN LIP BOULDER (LEFT BOULDER)

This boulder is situated 10 yards to the northeast from The Stage Boulder. It has a severely overhanging wall within a small gap.

❏ 1. **Fountain Lip Traverse V3** ★
Climb the overhanging arête on the west face using good edges and pockets.

❏ 2. **Cave Route Direct V6** ★★★
Climb the overhang within the gap starting off the low horizontal rail. Feet often hit the adjacent block on the high dyno.

❏ 3. **V0** ★
Climb the north face on the block that Fountain Lip rests on.

❏ 4. **V1** ★
Climb the northwest arête using the seam for the right hand.

❏ 5. **V1**
A tall slab with a disconcerting top-out faces *Cave Route Direct*.

DISTANCE BOULDER

Located approximately 60 yards across the wooded meadow to the northwest from Fountain Lip.

❏ 1. **V0** ★★
Climb the big, sharp pockets on the left side of the southeast face.

❏ 2. **V2** ★★
Climb the left-diagonaling seam using the good pebbles. Start low on sloping edges in the seam.

❏ 3. **V3** ★★
The right problem through the overhang that starts on a sharp pebble and a good edge. A sds goes at V7.

Stage Boulder

Fountain Lip Boulder

Cave Route Direct

Distance Boulder

South Block

This block is found to the southeast from Fountain Lip Boulder approximately 10 yards.

☐ 1. V0
On the left (northeast) face is a problem on pockets and edges. Dirty top-out.

☐ 2. V1 ★★
Climb up the north face on positive crimps.

Super Mario

☐ 1. Super Mario V7 ★★
Start on break under roof and make a long pull to gain the lip. Much harder if you are short.

☐ 2. Power Up V3 ★
A mantel trainer.

Hobble Cobble

One of the better blocks in the canyon for movement. A hundred yards or so past the trailhead for the "font area" is a trail on the right side of the road marked "Cave Trail." Park on the opposite side of the road, but take this trail uphill toward the cliff line. Whenever the trail forks, take the path that goes directly uphill. Once you reach the cliff line, walk left along it for about 70 yards, passing under a cubed block that rests against the cliff forming a cave (which has some devious problems on its slabby face) until seeing an obvious cube with a severe overhang facing towards the cliff.

☐ 1. Hobble Direct V6 ★★★
Climb straight up the vertical face from the sit start on sloping holds.

☐ 2. Hobble Cobble V7 ★★★
Start sitting under the roof on hueco-esque holds, gain the arête with a long reach, and trend right along the steep arête before an awkward but fun mantle.

☐ 3. Early and Often V9 ★★
From the sit of *Hobble Cobble*, make powerful moves to climb through the roof of the boulder and gain the right arête, then slap back left on the lip to top out the slab.

South Block

Super Mario

Hobble Cobble

Matt Miller on Hobble Cobble V7   photo: Justin Jaeger

CENTRAL CITY AREA / 9 LIVES AREA

The boulders on the west side of Cherry Creek stretch from the north and south from Buoux Block for over 500 yards. The 9 Lives Boulder is the northern-most boulder and the White Boulder is the southern-most boulder. The Warm-Up Wall and the main Central City boulders are within 200 yards from Buoux Block to the north and southwest.

9 LIVES BOULDER

To locate this huge block walk north for 300-plus yards once crossing Cherry Creek, staying within sight of the mud cliff above the creek. The boulder appears approximately 20 yards from the mud cliff and has three problems on its tall, west face. Expect to bushwhack with gusto to reach this boulder.

☐ **1. Cam's Arête V7** ★★
The man in black leaves his mark.

☐ **2. The Custodian V9** ★★
Climb through pods to a difficult exit via a vertical crack. Unrepeated to date.

☐ **3. Double Dick Dyno V6** ★★★
Climb up the middle of the west face starting matched on a cobble and going to an undercling hueco, to a right-facing dihedral near the top.

☐ **4. Nine Lives Arête V5** ★★★
Climb the overhanging southwest arête starting low.

☐ **5. South Face Problems V1 - V2** ★
Four excellent problems climb the south face.

☐ **6. The Pillar V5** ★
A lone pillar approximately 30 yards southeast has an overhanging north side on pebbles and edge/pods.

THE WORLD'S SLOPIEST BOULDER

An eroded, short block approximately 45 yards south of 9 Lives with odd shapes along its west face. A few contrived problems can be done utilizing the sloping holds.

☐ **1. V4** ★★
Traverse the boulder from left to right.

☐ **2. V3** ★★
Climb the right side of the boulder past the deep scoop. Use the lefthand arête and large brown crystal for the feet.

THE WARM-UP WALL AREA

Short walks on fairly good trails separate the boulders in this area. The best starting point to locate the boulders is to start at the Warm-Up Wall, then walk down the hillside to the other blocks.

WARM-UP WALL

This wall is a superb spot to get the juices flowing for the multitude of problems down the hillside. It is easily distinguishable as it is vertical, covered in pockets, sports a couple of cracks, is shaded by trees, and has a flat landing. Problems are listed from left to right.

☐ **1. V0** ★
The huecos just right of the wide crack on the left side of the wall.

☐ **2. V0** ★
The next set of huecos in a black streak.

☐ **3. V3** ★★
Climb the pebbles through the thick black streak 15 feet right of #2.

9 Lives

World's Slopiest Boulder

Warm-Up Wall

☐ **4. V6** ★★
Just right of #3 are small pockets at arms reach. Climb straight up past the two small overlaps.

☐ **5. V4** ★★★
Right of #4 before the tree is a dynamic problem that reaches the protruding pebble halfway up the face.

☐ **6. V4** ★★★
Right of the tree and before the crack is a committing problem on sloping holds that starts in big pockets.

☐ **7. V1** ★★★
The crack before the wall becomes covered in lichen.

☐ **8. V3**
At the far right end of the wall is a white pebble. Climb straight up using monos.

Pebbled Roof Rock aka Dr. Love's Rock

This fine boulder is located down the hillside from Warm-Up Wall approximately 80 yards to the southeast (headed back toward the Buoux Block slightly). A faint trail below Warm-Up Wall leads to the boulder, which is defined by a small roof about eight feet off the deck.

☐ **1. V3** ★★

Climb up through the overhang, starting left, to a long reach for a pebble on the vertical upper part of the wall.

☐ **2. V2** ★

Climb just right of the right pod/groove and over the roof. Licheny!

Locals Boulder

A small block with a nice overhanging southeast face. Many contrived problems can be done to get the most out of the boulder. It is located approximately 30 yards to the southwest from Pebble Roof.

☐ **1. Locals Only V5** ★★★

Climb through the overhang from a low start to a long reach for a pebble on the vertical upper wall.

☐ **2. V4** ★

Climb the east arête from a low start.

Scary Monsters

A nice boulder with committing problems on its gray north face and golden east face. It is located by bushwhacking a little to the northwest approximately 90 yards from Locals Boulder. A faint trail can be picked up through the scrub oak. The north face problems from left to right (1-4).

☐ **1. V4** ★★

The problem on the left beginning off the flat block then through the crystal hole. Be ever mindful of exploding pebbles. Sds on the rock for *Explodopop* V6.

☐ **2. V8** ★★

Start left of the graffiti on terrible holds, then straight up to slopers and good pebbles.

☐ **3. Splatt V7** ★★★

Start right of the graffiti and climb directly left to the finishing holds on the V8.

☐ **4. V3** ★★

The rightmost problem on the north face, up big pebbles and pockets.

☐ **5. V2** ★

From the large, low pod on the west face climb straight up using sidepulls. Many contrived problems can be done using the monos or dynoing to the lip. Sds on #5 and traverse into #6 for a V8. A difficult sequence on poor holds.

☐ **6. V7** ★★

Start the same as #7, but deadpoint with the right hand to the shallow pocket right of the seam, then finish to the left.

☐ **7. Scary Monsters V5** ★★★

Begin in the seam on laybacks and climb up and right to the hole and pebbles. A killer jug is at the lip.

Dr. Love's

Locals

Scary Monsters

Scary Monsters

Slab Master Boulder

Walk uphill approximately 50 yards to the north from Scary Monsters. The boulder is defined by having a tall, pebble-strewn slab on its south face with a large pine on the right. The Slab Master Boulder is not pictured.

☐ **1. V2** ★

The left side of the west face. Climb from a bomber pocket to a pod then up.

☐ **2. V4** ★★

Just right on the tan face is a pebble and pocket problem with long reaches.

☐ **3. V3** ★

The right arête of the west face.

☐ **4. V3** ★★

The left arête of the south face.

☐ **5. V4** ★

Up the middle of the south face above the large crystal.

15 Paces Boulder

A short long block approximately 30 yards uphill from Slab Master Boulder. The 15 Paces Boulder is not pictured.

❏ 1. **15 Paces V4** ⋆

A long traverse from left to right on the west face.

Central City Area

The giant boulderfield first encountered after crossing Cherry Creek. The Buoux Boulder (directly above the boulder with the perfect crack on its south face) is the defining landmark to find the other boulders.

Hank's Block

A tilted rectangular block approximately 40 yards to the south from Buoux Boulder and less than 10 yards from the cliff. Hank's Block is not pictured.

❏ 1. **V5** ⋆

On the west face a problem starts off the adjacent block and moves right on extremely sharp pockets to the arête.

❏ 2. **V2** ⋆

Just below Hank's Block are a couple of problems on the north face of a separate boulder.

Orange Boulder

Downhill to the southeast from Buoux Boulder (approximately 50 yards) is a big block with a tall south face. The Orange Boulder is not pictured.

❏ 1. **V1** ⋆⋆⋆

Climb the middle of the south face up huge incuts. A superb problem!

❏ 2. **V2**

Start the same as #1 but move right into the lichen.

Plate Rock

The next block south of Orange Boulder. A low roof faces Orange Boulder. Plate Rock is not pictured.

❏ 1. **V2** ⋆⋆⋆

A classic highball problem on the west face that climbs the lichen slab on many vertical pods and plate-like holds.

❏ 2. **V1**

Just to the right of the open slot. Climb the pockets to a dirty finish.

❏ 3. **V4** ⋆⋆

Climb the big pebbles right of the arête on the south face to a long reach which gains the lip.

❏ 4. **V3**

Right of #3 off the block on the ground, climb straight up.

❏ 5. **V2**

Just right of #4 are bomber flakes.

❏ 6. **V4** ⋆

On the north face climb through the roof and finish out left.

❏ 7. **V3**

A right to left traverse below the north face roof.

Despicable Boulder

Straight downhill from Plate Rock follow a trail for approximately 40 yards to a boulder with a tall southwest face. The Despicable Boulder is not pictured.

❏ 1. **Despicable Man V4** ⋆

Climbs the left wall above the horizontal crack. Mandatory long reaches.

❏ 2. **V2** ⋆

A dynamic problem off the horizontal white flake on the right side of the wall.

White Boulder

This lone boulder is found on the Creek Bottom Trail a few hundred yards south from the waterfall and before reaching the dam. A few problems climb up and are rated V1 to V3. The White Boulder is not pictured.

Todd Breitzke on Cave Route Direct V6   Photo: Kyler Deutmeyer

INNER CANYON AREA

The boulders and cliffs in this area are reached by walking the Inner Canyon Trail along the creek from the parking at the Main Park Entry. Boulders are located on the trail or can be easily spotted across the creek, as well as on the cliffs to the north.

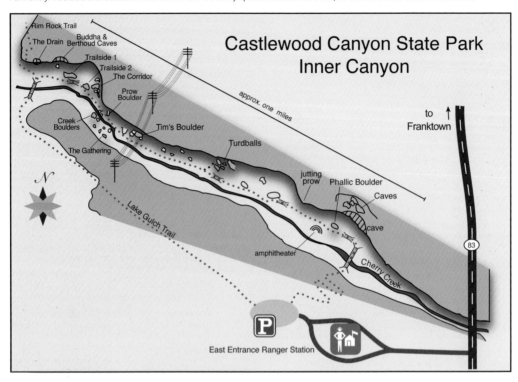

Castlewood Canyon State Park
Inner Canyon

Rim Rock Trail
The Drain   Buddha & Berthoud Caves
Trailside 1
Trailside 2
The Corridor
Prow Boulder
Creek Boulders
Tim's Boulder
The Gathering
Turdballs
approx. one miles
jutting prow   Phallic Boulder
Caves
cave
amphitheater
Lake Gulch Trail
Cherry Creek
to ↑ Franktown
83
P
East Entrance Ranger Station

PHALLIC BOULDER

A large separate block sitting in the middle of the Inner Canyon Trail just west from the bridge that crosses the creek. A superb block to warm up on if the height does not bother you. Be mindful of explosive pebbles and leaf-filled cracks.

❏ 1. **V2** 🔵
Climb the southeast blunt arête. Watch for loose pebbles.

❏ 2. **V1** ★ 🔵
Climb up the middle of the east face on small pebbles and pockets.

❏ 3. **V0** ★ 🔵
The crack on the right side of the north face. Also the downclimb.

❏ 4. **V1** 🔵
Climb up the west face on large pebbles.

❏ 5. **V1** 🔵
Climb the crack on the left side of the south face, starting on thin jams before the upper wide crack.

Phallic

Phallic

❏ 6. **V2** ★★ 🔵
Just right of the crack up good pebbles. A long reach or dynamic move gets you going.

❏ 7. **V1** ★ 🔵
The right side of the south face on pockets and large holes.

Pete Zoller on the Phallic Boulder   Photo: Pete Takeda

The Tombstone

TURD BALL BOULDERS

An area of large boulders below a tiered cliff with all but a couple of the problems on the tiers above the boulders. One of the best moderate bouldering areas in Castlewood. These problems are fresh and are not completely clean. The tiers vary in size from 10 to 30 feet to test one's comfort and commitment level.

❒ **The Tombstone V7** ★★★
One of only a few problems done in the boulderfield below the tiers. It is located on a north-facing pocketed wall down (southwest) about 10 yards from Turd Ball Un. A compelling line! Another V5 is on the south face.

TURD BALL BOULDER UN

❒ **1. V1** ★★★ 🌀
Climbs straight up a west-facing black face, starting with two large pebbles at chest height.

TURD BALL DEUX

A wall similar in size to Turd Ball Un and directly above and left. It is west-facing and has a small gap from which the problems begin.

Turd Ball Un

❒ **1. V2** ★★★ 🌀
Start low and left above a jumble of blocks. Climb straight up off a pebble and edge to better holds. A super jug is over the top.

❒ **2. V3** ★★ 🌀
The middle line on the wall starting at the base of the black streaks on flat, sloping edges. Exit right.

❒ **3. V2** ★★★ 🌀
Just left of the right, blunt southwest arête is a straight-up problem that climbs through a big flat pocket.

TURD BALL TROIS

Directly east from Turd Ball Deux, approximately 25 feet, is a long west-facing wall with two distinct crack systems. An extension of this wall is immediately right and has three additional problems. The Turd Ball Trios are not pictured.

❒ **V4** ★★ 🌀
This problem is on a separate block that sits directly in front of Turd Ball Trois. This sds on the overhanging west arête starts by pinching the holds on both sides of the arête. Problems listed left to right:

Turd Ball Deux

LEFT WALL

❒ **1. V2** ★★ 🌀
Start in the middle of the wall left of the left (north) crack. Straight up to edges and a sloping pocket.

❒ **2. V3** ★★★ 🌀
Start in a low letter box just left of the left crack. Climb up the perfect pockets.

❒ **3. V2** ★★
Just right of the crack through a horizontal break eight feet up. Climb straight up to a bad edge.

MIDDLE WALL

❒ **4. V3** ★★★ 🌀
On the wall right of the right (south) crack is a straight-up problem 10 feet left of the far right arête. Begin with a long reach, then move left to big pebbles up high.

❒ **5. V2** ★★ 🌀
Just left of the right arête is a straight up problem with a long reach to start.

RIGHT WALL

❒ **6. Small Wall Tim V3** ★★
On the next west-facing wall to the right of #5 is a thin problem on the left side.

❒ **7. Trixie's Wall V2** ★★
Climb the middle of the wall on thin pebbles and pockets.

❒ **8. V1** ★
Climb the right side on pebbles.

❒ **9. V1**
On another west-facing wall approximately 30 feet right of #8 is a 25-plus foot problem that climbs up and through the big holes on the left side of the wall. A dirty problem for the demented boulderer.

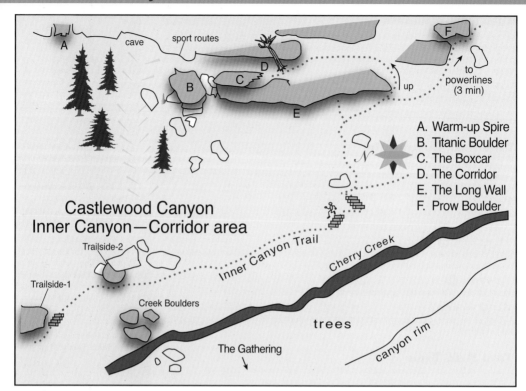

Castlewood Canyon
Inner Canyon—Corridor area

A. Warm-up Spire
B. Titanic Boulder
C. The Boxcar
D. The Corridor
E. The Long Wall
F. Prow Boulder

TIM'S BOULDER (POWERLINES)

This excellent, overhanging wall sits directly below the high-tension power lines that cross the canyon, offering some of the smoothest and steepest rock at Castlewood.

Directions: Head up the hill from the trail once you reach the power lines. The boulder is just below the cliff line in a cluster of blocks. It is a very overhanging, southwest-facing white wall.

☐ 1. Tiger Woods V7 ★★★
The leftmost line out the cave. Start on double underclings and bust past the huge, sloping hole to a good flake, then chossy lip.

☐ 2. Pain V5 ★
From a painful, incut undercling hole, six feet right of #1, move up to a bad sloper in the horizontal crack, then throw for a bucket.

☐ 3. Flakes of Wrath V3 ★★
Begin on #2 but move right into a good pocket, then follow the flake system diagonally up and left to finish. Thuggy.

THE CORRIDOR AREA

This curiously neglected zone didn't see much action until the late 90s, despite its obvious array of large, clean blocks perched above a scenic bend in the canyon. The Corridor itself provides superb V1-V3 vertical face climbs on smooth, tan-and-green stone with surprisingly difficult top-outs. The long, vertical wall one tier down from The Corridor offers a myriad of decent face problems in the V1-V4 range, while a taller set of walls on the benches to the south and east of The Corridor offers highball versions of the same. The Corridor Area is not pictured.

Directions: After the power lines, just before the trail descends via stairs to the creek, cut up and right around a boulder and head directly uphill to Long Wall. Head right (south) around Long Wall, then back north to reach the upper bench where The Corridor sits.

A. WARM-UP SPIRE

Just left of a rotten cave, 50 feet up the hill from the enormous ponderosa pine is this tall, slabby, spire-like feature on the canyon rim. Though the problems aren't exceptionally hard (V0-V2), they do provide good warm-ups on nice stone. The aesthetic black wall to the right has toprope bolts on top but can be bouldered out, sort of. The Warm-up Spire is not pictured.

B. THE TITANIC

Easily visible from the canyon floor, this enormous block can be recognized by its black, overhanging west face high up in a jumble of rocks. Many steep, hard problems are found in the network of caves under and around this block.

Titanic

Titanic

□ 1. Soice in a Blender V7 ★★ 🔵🔵

This long problem is in a grotto/pit just below and north of The Titanic. Start with your right hand in a mouth-pocket up and left around the corner in the cave. Drop down on cobbles, trend right around the corner, then punch straight up the white face. V2 from the stand-up.

□ 2. Kate Winslet V5 ★★ 🔵

Chubby yet appealing! This technical problem climbs the scooped face on the south side of the grotto. Start on rough slopers and traverse left to the arête, then out the arête on cobbles. V7 and crimpy if you start all the way right.

□ 3. King of the World V6 ★★★ 🔵🔵

Sds in the horizontal crack and head for the obvious hueco. Spectacular position.

□ 4. Pit Monkey V6 ★★ 🔵

Start on a good hueco in the pit below #3. Move right to the arête, traverse around the corner on pockets, and finish out on the orange face over the bad landing.

□ 5. Grease Monkey V9 ★★

Powerful stuff. Sds at the base of a triangular, four-foot long depression in the east cave, bust into bad underclings and power up.

□ 6. Ass Monkey V3 ★★ 🔵

Just across the cave from the finish of #4. Start on the jug horn, head left to the arête, and make a long pull to the lip.

Titanic

CREEK BOULDERS

This conglomeration of blocks can be seen from Trailside Two. Walk 20 yards east past Trailside Two and cross the creek to some white boulders.

SOUTH BOULDER

A seperate small boulder in the meadow furthest from the creek.

□ 1. V2 ★

A low start on the blunt southwest arête.

□ 2. V3

Start off the low ledge and climb through the high crack.

Creek Boulders

Creek - South Boulder

MIDDLE BOULDER

The boulder 15 yards north of South Boulder. On its west face is an overhanging gap between an adjacent block.

□ 3. V4 ★★

Start on a left-angling crack on the north face and finish in the low-angle right-facing dihedral.

NORTH BOULDER

The boulder just north of Middle Boulder.

□ 4. V0

Climb the huge flake on the left of the east face.

□ 5. V4 ★

Begin straight up from the jug at the base of the east face and finish up a small right-facing corner.

THE BUDDHA AND BERTHOUD CAVES

Though a bit of a trudge (20 minutes), these caves offer Castlewood's highest concentration of steep problems in a stealthy hang well out of sight of the trail. This is not a very good place to warm up. The roofy nature and southern exposure of these walls guarantees their climbability even in the worst of conditions, though the top may drip with run-off.

Directions: 120 yards down from Trailside Boulder One (an enormous block on the trail just above a red footbridge and just downcanyon from the stairs), after the meadow, you'll see a slab on the right. Climb along this slab, head uphill another 50 feet then diagonal right towards the caves through scrub oak.

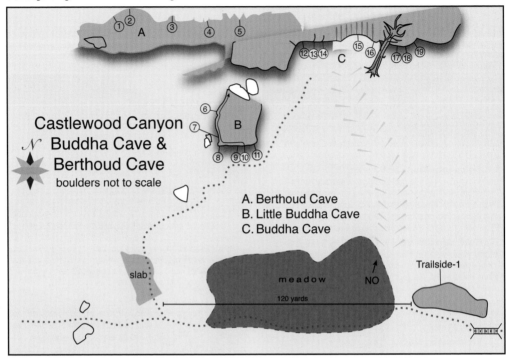

Castlewood Canyon
Buddha Cave &
Berthoud Cave
boulders not to scale

A. Berthoud Cave
B. Little Buddha Cave
C. Buddha Cave

A. THE BERTHOUD CAVE

Named after one of Colorado's finer hamlets, this grainy yet sunny attraction offers one of the largest horizontal roofs in the Front Range (and a bellyful of bad puns). Come early in the day with fresh skin and some snap in your arms, otherwise you'll hate the place. Although the problems can be finished at the lip of the cave (subtract a V-grade), real climbers will ante up for the headwall above.

❏ 1. After Berthoud V6 ★

Match hands in a perfectly round three-foot diameter hueco in the left side of the cave, sitting down with your head pointed east. Work past underclings and knee bars into the huge bowl. Climb out the left side of the bowl to a big cobble at the lip, then head straight over the tan-colored bulge to a highball finish. Off-routing the jugs in the back of the bowl and crossing the bowl through its middle to join the sloping rail on the cave finish of #2 is a great V8.

❏ 2. Giving Berthoud V8 ★★

Start 20 feet back in the cave, with your hands on the lip of a huge (body-sized) hole, and your head oriented south. Punch out to the huge bowl, then make a big move out with your right hand to a sloping, crystalline rail. Work right on the rail to the lip, then realm up the black streak past the football to finish. Finishing straight out the bowl into #1 is *The Placenta* V5.

❏ 3. Berthoud Canal V5 ★

Ohh, is it ever! This dynamic line out the obvious scoop on the right side of the cave offers fun, contorted moves on solid holds. Sds low at the bottom of the scoop, then out past holes to the lip. Reel left over the lip to top out, then jump to the pads. A super-low, butt-dragging start seems quite hard.

❏ 4. Berthoud Hips V7 ★★

Just right of the cave proper is a small brown buttress with a flared, black crack on its left side. Sds by underclinging an enormous, oblong bowl. Crank up, then move right onto crystals embedded in the buttress to finish. Sustained and powerful.

❏ 5. J.T's Prow V4

This is the middle one of three arêtes/fins to the right of the cave. Fall off high and you might find yourself 20 feet lower, back down at the Buddha Cave.

Berthoud Cave

Berthoud Cave

Buddha Cave

Little Buddha Boulder

B. LITTLE BUDDHA BOULDER

Not so little at all, this attractive cube with a very overhanging south face sits just 40 feet downhill and southwest of the Buddha Cave. Like all the best stuff at Castlewood, the rock on the south wall is blessed with an iron-hard white veneer, the result of calcification. The plumb line up the middle of the face has yielded a very difficult boulder problem.

❑ 6. West Face V1-V2
A host of short but interesting problems up pebbles and pockets on the solid west face.

❑ 7. Deuto's Face V2 ★
Start four feet left of the southwest arête with your left hand on top of a huge embedded plaque/cobble, stretch high and right for a jug pocket, then up the face.

❑ 8. Monkey Shots V7 ★★
The southwest corner of the block, working holds on both sides of the arête to a grueling top-out.

❑ 9. The Crystal Method V9 ★★★
The very steep central line up the wall, moving right from the sharp, jutting cobble to a sinker three-finger pocket in the white streak.

❑ 10. J.T.'s Arête V4 ★
This line would be perfect if not for the grainy bulge top-out. With your right hand in a good hole around the southeast arête, bust up to a licheny horizontal then master the terrifying bulge maneuver.

❑ 11. Deuto's Traverse V6 ★★
This 35-foot long gem is a blast! Start on the rightmost pocket on the south face, move left around the arête on good holds, punch up to the good right-hand pocket on #2 and head left again to the northwest arête (V0).

C. THE BUDDHA CAVE

Endowed with flat, piney landings and a warm southern aspect, this mini-amphitheater of solid rock also offers a short ice pillar in colder weather. The problems are powerful with long moves to good cobbles and crimpers. Finish the majority of the problems by dropping back to the pads from the dirt-covered ledge.

❑ 12. The Buddha V4 ★★★
Sds on an oval-shaped hueco under the prow, then bust past good holds into the overhanging corner. Beware the loose flake high and right!

❑ 13. Ned's Corner V5 ★
Sds six feet right over a flat block, your hands low in a hole. Hit cobbles over the lip, then crimp your way up the vertical corner above. Devious.

❑ 14. Rounded Prow V3 ★
Start with your right hand in a good, waist-high, three-finger pocket then amble up the rounded buttress on slopers and pebbles. Descend the dirty V0 corner just right.

❑ 15. Sometimes Wet V2 ★★
Just under the right side of the drainage, this little unit climbs the black streak from its lowest point on the wall. Sds and crank past good holes, then drop from the sandy lip.

❑ 16. Phillip's Problem V5 ★★★
Just what is his problem anyway? Sds directly under the rightmost portion of the streak in the bowl/cave, then make a big move to a flat incut cobble. V6 if you reel right and top out on #17.

❑ 17. Butt Crystal V3 ★
Start low in a good two-hand mouth, hit a horn and go left to a cobble then up. Bizarre and trickier than it looks.

❑ 18. Swirly Face V3 ★
Start on the guano-stained pillar/heap, shoulder roll to a super-incut pocket, then pimp up the swirls above.

❑ 19. Slime Pile V1
The rightmost problem on the wall climbs past holes to a choss-filth top-out. Horrible.

TRAILSIDE BOULDERS

TRAILSIDE BOULDER ONE
Located on the Inner Canyon Trail above the red bridge, this boulder offers good face problems on plate-like rock on the south face.

❑ 1. V1-V2 ★★
On the left side of the block facing the trail. Pick a line.

TRAILSIDE BOULDER TWO
This tall boulder is on the left side of the trail about 50 yards east of its sister.

❑ 1. V3 ★
The problem on the far left of the west face.

❑ 2. V3 ★
Just left of the crack.

❑ 3. V0
Climb the face right of the crack on good holds.

Lauren Lee on The Nose Lunge Block V0   Photo: Andy Mann

GARDEN OF THE GODS

Colorado Springs is graced with a myriad of boulderfields. What truly affects the city as a great bouldering destination is private property/access issues at areas like Ute Pass and Newlin Creek.

The Garden is a city owned park with unbelievable views of statuesque red sandstone towers with a backdrop of crystal blue skies. The bouldering found in the park consists of three main areas with long traverses and the small boulderfield of the Snake Pit. The soft sandstone found in The Corridor is replaced by harder rock at The Blowouts and Snake Pit. With bouldering on the west face of North Gateway Rock and in The Corridor, good temperatures can be found throughout the hot months, while wintertime sessions never cease in The Snake Pit.

Directions: From Interstate 70 in Colorado Springs take Exit #146 (Garden of the Gods Road) west. The road ends at a T intersection (30th Street). Go left until reaching the park's entrance. Mileage is given for each area from the stone Garden of the Gods sign.

The Corridor/The Blowouts Areas are located by parking at the main parking area 0.7 mile from the entrance sign on the left. Walk the Gateway Trail south to the gap between North and South Gateway Rocks. The Corridor is found by taking a dirt trail south at the intersection of the cement paths between the Gateway Rocks. Follow the trail approximately 65 yards through the bushes to a visible chasm on the east side of South Gateway Rock.

The Blowouts and Intermediate Area are found by continuing around the southwest side of North Gateway Rock (past the huge metal plaque). Just past a trail map on the left are a number of trails on the right heading to the southwest (hueco-covered) face of North Gateway Rock. The Intermediate Area is the first traverse seen from the trail (approximately 35 yards). To reach The Blowouts continue along the base of the southwest face for approximately 100 yards until below a huge overhang. The Blowouts is the obvious chalked traverse at the bottom.

The Snake Pit is located by continuing around the Juniper Way Loop (stay left on the road past Garden Drive and Ridge Road). At 2.2 miles park in a large paved parking area on the right. Walk north from the parking area down the Ute Trail for approximately 350 yards to a small boulderfield on the left (The Snake Pit).

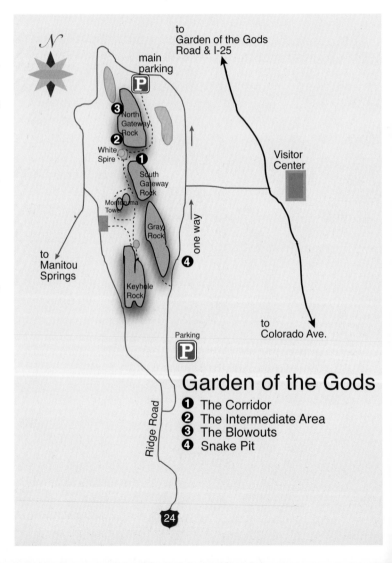

to
Garden of the Gods
Road & I-25

main
parking

❸ North
Gateway
Rock
❷
White
Spire   ❶
South
Gateway
Rock
Montezuma
Tower
Gray
Rock
❹

Visitor
Center

one way

to
Manitou
Springs

Keyhole
Rock

to
Colorado Ave.

Parking

Ridge Road

24

Garden of the Gods
❶ The Corridor
❷ The Intermediate Area
❸ The Blowouts
❹ Snake Pit

THE CORRIDOR

A hidden chasm on the east side of South Gateway Rock with a long traverse on the right side of the corridor. This is a great area to gain endurance and contrive problems ranging from V0 to V5.

THE INTERMEDIATE AREA

A short V0 to V1 traverse on the far right side of the southwest face of North Gateway Rock.

THE BLOWOUTS

The best area in the Garden to contrive problems. Many long traverses can be done as well as short power problems ranging from V0 to V11.

☐ **1. Mr. Bodangles V10** ★★
Climbs the arête proper from a low start dropping off at the jug.

The Blowouts

The Blowouts Right

Garden of the Gods at sunrise
Andy Mann Collection

Megan Mascarenas at The Blowouts

THE SNAKE PIT

On the opposite side of Juniper Way Loop below Gray Rock and adjacent to the Ute Trail. Four boulders make up this unique sandstone area.

THE NOSE LUNGE BLOCK

The first boulder off Ute Trail in The Snake Pit. It is defined by two overhanging arêtes surrounding a tall, vertical southwest face.

❑ 1. **V0** ★★
Start on the southwest arête just left of the flake system on a left-hand jug. Climb straight up without using the flake to the right. A V7 sds can be done in to this problem.

❑ 2. **V0** ★★
The flake on the far left side of the south face.

❑ 3. **V0** ★★
Start on the flat jugs left of the black rock and climb straight up. A low start makes it V2.

❑ 4. **V1** ★★
The straight-up problem in the black rock. Good crimps to a seam.

❑ 5. **V1** ★★
Directly before the arête, climb straight up.

❑ 6. **V2** ★
The southeast overhanging arête. *The Nose Lunge* (V4) does a dynamic move off the arête to the high sloping jug.

❑ 7. **V6 - V7** ★★ ⬤
The east face overhang has a few contrived problems.

❑ 8. **V0's**
The north face problems. Also the best downclimb.

❑ 9. **V2 - V7** ★★
In the northwest overhang many contrived problems can be done.

THE BOULDER

Just a few yards to the west from The Nose Lunge Block is this short block with problems on its east face.

❑ 1. **V2** ★★
Climb the southeast arête up positive flakes. A sds V6 starts off a terrible right-hand edge and left-hand undercling.

❑ 2. **V3** ★★★ ⬤
Climb the middle of the east face on sloping edges and laybacks.

❑ 3. **V1** ★
The right arête on the east face. A V2 is just left of the arête.

ARCH BOULDER

The westernmost block hidden by the bushes and to the left (south) of The Boulder. Every problem on this block is V0 and short.

TRAVERSE BOULDER

This huge boulder (except for the top) is hidden by thick bushes. Located to the northwest from The Nose Lunge Block.

❑ 1. **V1** ★
The left overhang on the southeast face on big, flat holds. A double-handed dyno is V5.

❑ 2. **V8** ★
A traverse from left to right across the southeast face to the east face. Ends on the right hand problem before the wall gets too short to climb on.

❑ 3. **V6** ★
A traverse from right to left. Start on the far right problem on the east face and end on #1.

❑ 4. **V6** ★
A huge one-move problem off the sloping edges on the east face all the way to the lip. The feet suck and the move is long.

Nose Lunge Block

The Boulder

Arch Boulder

Traverse Boulder

Phillip Benningfield has bouldered in Colorado for more than two decades. His first scrappy efforts at climbing were on a Colorado Outward Bound course in Elevenmile Canyon. His first real sojourns to boulders, without the need for knee pads, took place on the sandstone cliffs lining Dillon Reservoir during brief stints working at Keystone Ski Resort. After moving to Fort Collins in 1987 he bouldered at Horsetooth Reservoir and learned the finer points of the sport. This short-lived time in Fort Collins left an undeniable love for the ease and pleasure of bouldering. Upon leaving Fort Collins, Phillip moved to Boulder and discovered the wealth of bouldering from Flagstaff Mountain to Eldorado Canyon, spending years skipping classes at the university in an effort to master a few feet of unforgiving rock. During the 90s Morrison became a popular spot to thrutch and train, and the author took part in contriving new problems. As school left no time for the higher pursuits of climbing, he put classes on hold and concentrated on all aspects of climbing but the crazed (i.e. ice climbing). In the mid-90s Phillip worked at Climbing Magazine and moved back and forth from the Roaring Fork Valley. Those years were spent slaving away at Western Slope boulderfields including Unaweep Canyon and Independence Pass. Phillip again moved back to Boulder, repeating many more Front Range classics and exploring and developing in Castlewood Canyon, Estes Park, Eldorado Canyon, Gross Reservoir, Flagstaff and others. Phillip now lives in Salida, Colorado and owns a terrific coffeeshop and information hotspot for obscure bouldering areas...his latest work includes a new book on coffeeshop culture entitled *The Dark Roast*.

Matt Samet, a climber of 25+ years, has lived in Boulder, Colorado, for the last 20 of those. The former editor-in-chief of Climbing Magazine, he is currently a freelance writer and editor, and calls himself a "semi-retired boulderer," his old, aching knees having absorbed a few (thousand) too many ground falls—and his newborn son, Ivan, taking up his boulder-hunting time.

Index